Entrepreneurial Practice

Enterprise Skills for Lawyers Serving Emerging Client Populations

Entrepreneurial Practice

—

Enterprise Skills for Lawyers Serving Emerging Client Populations

Nelson P. Miller, Michael J. Dunn,
and John D. Crane

Entrepreneurial practice—enterprise skills for lawyers serving emerging client populations.

Miller, Nelson P., Dunn, Michael J. and Crane, John D.

Cover Design: Laura Fortin
Cover office photos courtesy of Smith Haughey Rice & Roegge

Published by:

Vandeplas Publishing LLC - July 2012

801 International Parkway
5th Floor
Lake Mary, FL. 32746
USA

www.vandeplaspublishing.com

ISBN: 978-1-60042-173-0

Thomas M. Cooley Law School
111 Commerce Avenue S.W.
Grand Rapids, MI 49503
(616) 301-6800 ext. 6963

To those having a hard time finding
or affording a good lawyer.

Table of Contents

Acknowledgments

The authors of this book see need to help lawyers find new tools to serve emerging client populations. Yet the direct inspiration for this book was the untimely passing of two outstanding law students. Carlos Carneiro was just 29 years old when he died suddenly earlier this year while a third-term evening student at Cooley Law School's Grand Rapids campus. Carlos, born in Brazil and a high school and college sports star, had looked forward to starting a new law practice in his nearby Kalamazoo community. Kelly Vitton was just 30 years old when she died suddenly earlier this year while in her first term at the Grand Rapids campus. Kelly was a road-patrol sheriff's deputy, former dispatcher, and university police officer, who, like Carlos, looked forward to serving her community as a lawyer. Carlos and Kelly would have made great lawyers. Their classmates will carry forward their mission of law service.

The authors also acknowledge the inspiration of recent graduates establishing innovative new law practices. After earning both a J.D. and LL.M. degree (the latter in taxation), Tamsen Horton established a mobile, virtual law practice serving business clients more ably at lower cost, garnering her well-deserved success and press even while balancing her rich family life. Right out of law school, Andrew Rodenhouse used his skill at discerning, reaching, and efficiently serving discrete client populations to build a five-person firm with his law partner Jessica Kuipers. Bobbi Barnes used her enterprise acumen and technology skills to establish a two-lawyer, two-location, virtual law practice serving three client populations across two metropolitan areas. Peter Kulas translated his passion for equal rights, advocacy skills, and enterprise talent into a practice serving an underserved population. Traci Schenkel used her project and pricing skills in a small-firm setting to build another thriving niche practice. Ben Symko used his firm's client-relationship-management system and strong interpersonal skills to substantially increase his small firm's clientele. Tamsen, Andrew, Jessica, Bobbi, Peter, Traci, Ben, and other new lawyers like them are a constant source of insight and inspiration in their new practice models. We have much to learn from them.

Introduction

Instruction in entrepreneurism is everywhere. College programs in entrepreneurship suddenly abound, as more college students realize that fewer employers may be handing out jobs after graduation. Community-development organizations target entrepreneurship activities for support, recognizing that communities depend on new small ventures for job regeneration and growth. Regional, state, and local government fund *economic gardening* initiatives that identify thriving small businesses to support with marketing and management services, and strategic visioning, for second-stage growth. You can hardly pick up a newspaper or magazine, or surf the internet, without seeing another celebration of entrepreneurism.

The current interest in entrepreneurship is certainly a sign of the times. If you have not noticed, things have been a little tough lately on the American pocketbook. Unemployment, underwater mortgages, bank failures, huge private- and public-pension liabilities, mammoth bankruptcies, and huge government debt weigh like stones on our outlooks and personal industry. Household wealth has fallen precipitously. Government seems to provide little hope of pulling us out of our economic malaise, looking instead more like it is doing everything it can simply to help us tread ever-more-perilous waters. Even dependable old mom and dad seem less able to throw us a financial lifeline from their nursing homes and assisted-living centers. Just the opposite—it takes enough to keep them from feeling as if they are one more burden.

This book, though, is a book of hope, not one of fear. We tend to have short memories of broader economic cycles. Things have been tough before, maybe a lot tougher. Each time, Americans have hitched up their pants, pulled their belts a little tighter, and leaned a little harder to the plow. And each time, that extra bit of personal industry that looked nearly impossible produced a rich harvest, one that grew well beyond our imagination. This book offers a sort of economic gardening for lawyers. Lawyers have always been entrepreneurs, whether in large or small firms, or as solo practitioners. We are natural second stagers. After all, we survived law school. We made our way into a profession rich with the possibility of serving others, demanding of us only that we apply ourselves to the best of our professional training and personal abilities.

Two circumstances make this book worth reading. First, few lawyers have substantial training or experience in business development, work processes, and organization management. Law schools do not generally train lawyers to be entrepreneurs, even though law practice is quite enterprising no matter how or where one practices it. Like other service professionals, lawyers depend for their practice primarily on providing individual service to individual clients, in what can look like self-employment even within a large firm. Lawyers must continue to find and create value for individual clients. Yet lawyers also increasingly depend on enterprise skills. They must form and institutionalize the practice-development activities, work processes, and organization systems to carry on, broaden, and share their individual work.

A second circumstance that makes this book worth reading is that many lawyers are naturally risk adverse, as befits their professional counsel. The profession is generally traditional and conservative in its norms, even though law practice today requires substantial innovation. This book helps the lawyer-reader recognize unproductive risk-avoiding behaviors and substitute productive, innovative, reasonable-risk initiatives that will help start a new law practice or grow an established practice. In today's particularly challenging, changing, and opportunistic global economic climate, the greatest thing that a lawyer has to fear is fear itself. Lawyers have the essential capacity that an information-soaked technology age demands. Lawyers turn information into useful knowledge. Lawyers who avoid new practice initiatives and ventures out of fear of failure or for lack of insight and direction are the lawyers who will fail.

Lawyers must embrace entrepreneurial practices and conduct their law practices as responsibly innovative enterprises if they are to survive and prosper, and bring prosperity to communities. The law profession and legal education face a divide. Many now argue that the nation needs fewer lawyers. They aim for lower law school enrollment and fewer bar admissions. Those actions—to reduce legal education and restrict access to the law profession—undermine central democratic commitments. Legal education and the law profession need instead to adopt and hone entrepreneurial skills that will enable lawyers to identify and serve traditionally underserved and emerging new client populations.

The nation needs a broad and diverse citizenry well educated in law, justice, and governance. History measures the quality of a society by the education of its citizenry, not the brilliance of its elite. Every epoch, every national event, makes it more apparent that the people, not its leaders, hold the future of the country. What its leaders cannot accomplish, too captured by their position and self-referential thought, its people can, having their own evidence on which to base more pragmatic thought. Broad education in the practice of law is precisely what gives our centuries-old national experiment the greatest hope for continued and even richer success. We need broader ability and greater individual will to think clearly, which is to think like lawyers. We need then to apply that thought, which is to practice law as lawyers.

Education in law's practice is education in the most valuable form of applied social science. Successful endeavor depends on deep, insightful, data-informed, consistent, accountable, and rational thought. In business, governance, finance, management, manufacturing, and other fields and industries, whoever thinks using the most data, wins. When we teach our people the practice of law, we teach them not just how to think logically but how to gather and evaluate evidence on which to base thought. We teach ourselves how to observe, apply logic to the observation, plan and implement action, and then assess and adjust. Always, the pragmatists and bottom-liners, lawyers think from the outside in rather than the inside out. We form premises not for the purpose of self-realization but to test and challenge them by hard evidence until we have the thinking right.

Then we act on it. Lawyers are cautious in a way, conservative in thought. We make great risk managers. Yet lawyers are also just the right kind of risk-takers. We calculate risk. Life and its ventures are fraught with risk. Risk management, though, is not some backward-looking rear-guard action. It is the essential creative process of any initiative. To manage risk is to move forward after effective evidence-gathering and productive thought. To manage risk is to create the conditions having the greatest productive capacity and the least capacity for loss.

The point is to use your intellect and expertise in this law-practice venture. We urge throughout that you actively identify and assess your practice development, client development, and professional activities, promoting new service offerings. Know the critical value to you of thoughtful reflection and action on these concepts. Lawyers, trained in issue identification, would recognize the reflection-and-action framework that we follow. First, identify your practice activities, relationships, and resources that give you new opportunities for service. Then, research the processes that will help you realize those opportunities. Develop a control system to monitor the progress of your work. Then pay attention to that progress. Assess your progress by gathering and evaluating data measuring progress toward your practice goals. Refine your activities until you discover what works. Then publish those results within your firm, confirming a culture of refinement and improvement.

Tools can help you evaluate and improve your law practice. Law firms can and do develop simple data systems to help them reform practice processes through process modeling, project management, self-assessment, and strategic planning. They can develop marketing information systems to discern practice opportunities, using focus groups, marketing research, inquiry approaches, and qualitative-versus-quantitative research. They can develop applications based on firm objectives. They can mine data using content analysis, decision-oriented analysis, client-centered analysis, causal-relationship research, conversation analysis, and cost-benefit analysis. Do not let practice conventions keep you from these and other thought tools by which other firms reform and improve their practices. Be an innovator. If your risk aversion refuses to allow you to innovate, then be an early adopter.

Lawyers must be enterprising if they are to reach the traditionally underserved and to serve emerging new client populations effectively. This book will help the lawyer-reader assess and improve the lawyer's practical entrepreneurship and practice readiness. Law practice is among the most exciting, meaningful, and satisfying of human endeavors. Its allure lies not only in creating value for individual clients but in replicating and broadening that value through institutionalized practices and organizational systems. Do more, and do it better.

Reach beyond professional survival to shared prosperity. This book's invitation is to more than simply what lawyers must do. Our invitation is to what makes any job or profession worthwhile. Study after study confirms that internal motivation is stronger than external motivation. Despite popular myth, not every lawyer is after money, power, and fame. Instead, we pursue what others pursue, primarily learning, challenge, responsibility, control, respect, passion, connection, and community. The activities that this book advocates serve those internal motivators. Enterprising law practice is meaningful and enjoyable practice. Too few know the powerful truth that economies reward the internally motivated.

Accept one caveat, then. The authors intend nothing in this book to advocate a shift in the profession's foundation from professional service to a purely business model. Law is a profession, not a business. Lawyers properly pursue their clients' interests through systems of law and justice to which they owe professional duties and fealty. When this book advocates practices to reach more clients with better service, it does so not for lawyers solely or primarily to increase revenues, maximize profits, and increase firm value. Businesses properly pursue value for their shareholder owners. By contrast, lawyers properly serve clients and justice.

Unlike some others, the authors do *not* advocate non-lawyer ownership of law-service firms. Some firms employ business managers, which is fine, as long as those non-lawyer managers do not supervise the law work of the firms' lawyers. Lawyers owe duties of independent professional judgment. Lawyers, not business managers, properly supervise other lawyers in those professional duties. We simply advocate that lawyers be wiser in the ways that entrepreneurial practices and inter-disciplinary fields can help lawyers serve more clients. We still have much to learn as a profession, to reach our greater potential. Greater prosperity for all is possible. Lawyers must design new products and services, and price and deliver those products and services in new ways, for all to achieve that greater prosperity—without distorting the profession's fundamentals in serving clients and justice.

The Framework

Law is at once increasingly broad and increasingly specialized. Law in our complex, technical, regulatory state affects more people more frequently and more deeply than ever before. More federal, state, and local laws, rules, and regulations cover more trades, professions, and industries, control more lands, premises, and activities, and create more liability and risk, than the nation has ever known. At the same time, and consequently, the middle class and poor have less access to reasonable-cost, high-quality, timely, and appropriate law services than ever before. Vast numbers of underserved individuals are losing their jobs, homes, health, finances, families, and futures because of their inability to locate, afford, and deploy timely, high-quality, and well-fitted law products.

These changes are global, national, and local. In the United Kingdom in 2007, Parliament's new Legal Services Act created an independent Legal Services Board explicitly to regulate law services from the consumer rather than the provider (the lawyers') standpoint. In a 2010 lecture *Training the Lawyer of the Future,* the new board's chair described the consumerism, technology change, and broader social change that augured the Legal Services Act. Worldwide law-firm consultant Richard Susskind wrote in the 2008 Oxford University Press book *The End of Lawyers?* (updated in 2010) about the enhanced lawyer-practitioners who will use standardized products to meet client demands to share and reduce the costs of law services. In the United States in 2009, national contract-services firm founder David Galbenski wrote in *Unbound: How Entrepreneurship Is Dramatically Transforming Legal Services Today* about the emerging new ways to buy, sell, organize, consolidate, publicize, perform, and train for providing law services.

At the local level, courts and communities are establishing dozens of new law self-help centers. One of the authors has been the board president of a courthouse-based center that serves 15,000 individuals each year. Lawyers have four ways to look at self-help centers. A first way for lawyers to regard self-help centers is to be proud that the centers promote access to justice for the poor and middle class. Lawyers help fund the author's center, as does the local government. A second way for lawyers to regard self-help centers is to be scared of the competition that the centers represent. If the clients can get free or cheap services at a self-help center, then why do they need lawyers? A third is to be concerned about the adequacy of the centers, which send their patrons into the courts unrepresented to receive what might be at times only a rough justice. The centers may be evidence of the profession's failure.

This book promotes a fourth way to look at such centers, as incubators for the law products and services, laboratories for the lawyers, and training grounds for the law students who will invent, package, price, and deliver the new law products and services to preserve, restore, and revitalize the American middle class. Stand in one of those centers watching the broken, scared, and confused people pour in and out. Their law needs identify responsible lawyers' public and private mission. The rudimentary forms, instructions, and services that the patrons receive identify needs that the products and services of responsible lawyers should be serving.

Effective lawyers will meet these new needs by packaging, pricing, and delivering law products and services in new ways. The shift, though, is broader than simply for consumer legal services. Enterprising lawyers will innovate in the packing, pricing, and delivery of law products and services in all fields and for all clients, in a shift called the *commoditization* of law. Lawyers must package products and services to meet new needs, whether for consumer or corporate services. They must efficiently fit those products for individual and corporate clients, price those products transparently, and deliver them timely by accessible means. Lawyers must disrupt the model that longer, slower, fancier, and more expensive is better, by bringing to market more-affordable law products that reach and serve more businesses, organizations, agencies, and individuals. They must do so by identifying and preserving core professional expertise while combining it with new managerial and entrepreneurial expertise.

Lawyers and law firms are highly conservative and risk averse, especially when considering changes to their practices. They have had good reason to be so risk averse. Law firms and lawyers have done well in recent decades. Because lawyers and law firms have done well, law schools, while reforming ethics, writing, and clinical programs, have not yet reformed instruction in law practice. Curricula are incorporating more practice skills and ethics, and shifting emphases among fields to include administrative, legislative, and international law. Instruction itself has improved vastly. Even so, law schools have not yet reformulated practice to meet emerging technical, global, interdisciplinary, and entrepreneurial demands on law practice. Many law firms still often organize practice groups around traditional fields, just as new practitioners still expect that their big question is the traditional focus of their practice area.

In the past few years, the law profession appears to have reached a consensus, imposed by clients and the markets for law services, that change is necessary but without discerning the necessary changes. We know that something must change in how we practice but have not developed confidence in new forms, fields, client populations, law products and services, and firm practices. The time is unusual in that senior lawyers following old practice conventions no longer necessarily hold sound views of productive practice. Management, economics, markets, systems, and populations have changed. Senior lawyers may be making more errors as managers and, beyond that, even in counseling clients.

Our knowledge of decision-making has itself changed, brought about by the insight and influence of new fields. A lawyer's stock in trade has been to strategize with judgment and advice grounded in game theory, decision trees, and subjective estimates of probabilities. Today, though, information asymmetry models, analytics, and behavioral economics teach us how powerfully inaccurate cognitive illusions can be. Our law practices deserve better-informed, more-deliberate decision-making, just as do our clients. For example, we should recognize the adverse selection and moral hazard that flow from information asymmetries, both for our clients and ourselves. We should know how to employ signaling and screening to ameliorate those decision-making hazards for our clients and ourselves.

This book models some of those new ways for thinking like a *practicing* lawyer, not merely thinking like a lawyer. We explain and provide examples of process models, project-management plans, project-improvement studies, network-activities assessments, and practice-readiness surveys. For example, see Appendix A for a sample process model for performing an examination under oath at the request of a client insurance company. Concepts and tools of this kind can make critical differences in creating and maintaining an effective law practice. The book also articulates a process for discerning new client populations. Publications continue to publicize hot practice areas, whether energy law, healthcare regulation, bankruptcy, or banking, and sub-specialties within those and other fields. How, though, do you discern those new fields for yourself and then (the bigger challenge) qualify yourself for them? Law schools are quite effective at training lawyers for inter-disciplinary study. Lawyers must recognize the process and then invest the time to engage those other fields that will help lawyers serve those new client populations.

Pay particular attention to the passages of this book that draw from other disciplines for insight into new managerial and entrepreneurial practices. Law professors have written many books on how to think like a lawyer. Lawyers have written more books on how to practice like lawyers. Lawyers have much to draw from and value in their traditional forms of reasoning and practicing. Yet lawyers also have much to learn from other disciplines. Indeed, that integrative skill drawing across disciplines to inform how individuals and organizations ought to conduct their affairs most profitably and beneficently is precisely the lost skill of lawyers that this book hopes in small respect to recover and burnish. We must get beyond thinking like lawyers in order to think like newly effective lawyers.

For example, notice passages in this book drawn from the fields of project management, process modeling, analytics, quality management, behavioral economics, pricing, cognitive psychology, and marketing. To one degree or another, at least some law firms and lawyers are using activities and methods drawn from these fields. Gradually, lawyers will adapt concepts and adopt practices from these and other fields to improve their law products and services, legal advice, and law practices. New lawyers, in particular, will learn the value of these new practice forms to package, price, and deliver law products and services more efficiently. They will do for traditional client populations while also identifying and serving new client populations.

Review the bibliography for texts in those and other fields. Consider for another example how cognitive psychologists would model problem solving. Cognitive psychology studies how mental processes affect thinking, emotion, and behavior. Its core research areas include knowledge representation, problem framing, and learning or altering behavior to improve function—all highly relevant subjects for lawyers. Lawyers need to reinvent law practice to serve new client populations. Cognitive psychology indicates that how lawyers represent or frame that problem will determine the solutions that they find. If lawyers continue to use reproductive thinking, applying well-worn paths, then they will produce well-worn solutions. Lawyers need productive rather than reproductive thinking. We need creative insight, produced by reflection that our current thought does not direct.

In cognitive terms, lawyers need to abandon well-established practice algorithms in favor of more productive heuristics just long enough to solve the problem of reaching emerging client populations. Well-established practice rules will not lead to practice reform. Lawyers should instead be employing problem-solving heuristics to identify and serve new client populations. Those heuristics may include working backward from the practice-growth goal. What are you practicing to achieve? What would be the last step before you get there, and then the step before that last step? Lawyers can also problem-solve using untested analogies drawn from research in other fields. What do emerging markets, growth solutions, and new delivery forms look like in other professions, industries, and fields? Lawyers can also use means-end analyses to discern new operators that may achieve the practice-growth goal. Who or what would bring a new dynamic to your practice's growth?

Employ these powerful meta-cognitive processes. Examine how you think about your practice growth, to employ new tools. Do not remain a simple generalist, drawing on general knowledge of client needs, decision-making, and market behavior. Instead, develop new domain-specific knowledge relating to practice growth. Cognitive psychology suggests that you stand a much greater probability of seeing new possibilities in your practice, when you learn better how to represent practice-growth opportunities within new domains. How do consumers make purchasing decisions? How does the way that you frame your law product and service offerings affect a client's willingness to engage your firm? How do you discern, produce, and prove client value? Lawyers who acquire knowledge in these other thought domains will find the answers to these questions.

Reinventing your practice or establishing a new practice will require these new skills and forms. Lawyers are project managers. They use complex processes. They are highly concerned with producing quality products and services, as are their clients in receiving that quality. Lawyers should know how economics affects individual behavior. They should know and avoid common fallacies of cognition in making critical judgments. Yet did you encounter any study of project management, process modeling, quality management, behavioral economics, or cognitive psychology in law school? Law schools teach research and reasoning skills, but lawyers bear the responsibility of expanding those skills to create vital new law practices using productive new insights drawn from inter-disciplinary study.

Success in law school does not necessarily translate into success in law practice. The entrepreneurial skills this book advocates are not necessarily the skills that academically successful law students and graduates have acquired. Success in the first years of practice at a firm large enough to generate substantial work for new associates does not necessarily translate into continued success in law practice. Hiring in as an academically accomplished associate is not the same as graduating to partner. Practice skills, particularly in building client value and relationships, are different from the academic skills that most law schools teach. The enterprise of law practice has more to do with serving people and their organizations in their needs than with classic legal reasoning.

Embrace the opportunity for meaningful practice that serving new client populations affords. Pick inter-disciplinary fields that fascinate and vitalize you. Do something that you enjoy, so that your clients can see your passion in it and so that you practice with energy and integrity. Most lawyers first do what is at hand. Over time, in the course of a law practice, most lawyers begin to do that which their character and commitments most suit them to do for themselves and others. Practices change one client at a time. Engage new subjects, studies, and fields that interest you so that you prepare to serve the one client who will begin to change your practice, adding to it a new field. The quality of your service will never be higher than when you transform your accumulated experience with new learning and skills, practicing in a field you chose.

Lawyers who learn these new law practice conventions will have more meaningful and rewarding careers that promote the order, openness, health, welfare, and economy of their communities. These lawyers will use more mobile and powerful technology in more clear, precise, and technical means to convey better-suited law products and services to better-served clients. They will go home more satisfied than lawyers who stick to old products and practices that fail to serve their clients so well. More significantly, the clients of the lawyers who pursue and develop new and regenerative law practices will go home well served.

This new work has an entrepreneurial spirit. An entrepreneur is one who initiates and pursues new enterprise using insight and skill to manage its risks for general gain. Entrepreneurs need not own or deploy substantial capital, as long as they can engineer and deliver products and services that produce gain in which they share. Entrepreneurs develop new work for old and new clients. They reorganize resources and redistribute work in newly efficient ways, using both old and new practices. They manage, assess, and improve established practices to produce new value for all concerned.

Entrepreneurs perceive where they and their clients want to be and then engineer how to reach that destination in new ways.

Law practice has an entrepreneurial quality to it, no matter whether the lawyer works within a large or small firm, or as a solo practitioner. Lawyers must account to their law partners and their clients for their relevancy, efficiency, and productivity, their mastery of law subjects, and their skill within law fields. Given the investment that a law degree represents and the capital that it takes to place a lawyer in the field, every action that a lawyer takes carries a measure of accountability, to be responsible to the financial and social well-being of the organizations and clients whom they serve. A lawyer becomes and remains accountable when drawing on the best entrepreneurial practices, adopting innovations in technology, marketing, and management, not randomly but within the context of a strategic practice plan.

Legal education can do a masterful job of preparing lawyers to serve corporate and business interests, to staff large and mid-sized firms. Legal education serves well the corporate and upper class. Legal education does not always do a masterful job of equipping individual lawyers to package, price, and deliver the reasonable-cost, reasonably appropriate law products that middle-income and low-income clients require. Much of legal education retains a 20th-century cast in a decidedly 21st-century economy and society.

Law products are increasingly available on the internet. For-profit, non-profit, and agency providers increasingly offer packaged, priced, and delivered law products. Yet many of those products are ill fit for their particular use by a particular client. Moreover, many clients have no sense of the poor fit or of their rights and responsibilities when purchasing and deploying those products. Product without fit and counsel does not solve, and rather often exacerbates, situations demanding law solutions. Many more clients have no access to those products, either lacking the technological means, the technical skill, or the education and general facility to purchase and deploy them.

What more clients need, and what more lawyers should be providing, is the packaged, priced, and delivered, reasonable-cost, high-quality law products and services. This book describes for the individual lawyer the approach to providing those products and services. It describes a set of attitudes and practices that will help the individual lawyer provide more law products and services at higher quality and lower cost to more clients than previously. It introduces real law practice for the 21st century, from which to build a meaningful and rewarding practice interacting with and supporting diverse middle- and lower-income clients.

Beyond indicating how lawyers can improve and innovate in packaging, pricing, and delivering law products and services, this book helps lawyers grasp for themselves and articulate to clients why they are packaging, pricing, and delivering law products and services in specific manners. The challenge for lawyers today is not simply to do an efficient job of serving clients but also to demonstrate and explain those efficiencies to clients, showing clients the value, fit, and personalization of the lawyer's products and services. Consumers generally need to understand the value of their purchases. That need to appreciate value is particularly acute when it comes to law products and services.

The point is that lawyers' ability to design, standardize, price, and fit law products and services for the middle class is not merely a matter of survival for lawyers. It is a matter of survival for the middle class. While a practical how-to guide, this book also makes the implicit argument that the commoditization of law has more to do with promoting the rise of a broad middle class than the commoditization of other goods like automobiles or services like haircuts. The stakes are no less than that. When lawyers do not provide affordable law services to the greatest number, we lose the middle class. Law services, properly done, have broadening, diversifying, enriching, and including effects. Law service done wrong has exclusive effects.

In that respect, this book is not about how to open a solo law practice or manage a small firm. Jay Foonberg and others have written sound and comprehensive resources for those purposes. Instead, this book is about how to serve clients better, build a stronger community, and preserve and broaden a middle class. It puts the focus on the clients, where lawyers should have their focus. Having a healthy law practice is fine. Yet having a healthy clientele is even better. No profession, trade, or industry has long survived serving itself. The professional who commits to saving the professional's clients will find new opportunity, riches, and life. You get not what you pursue for yourself but what you pursue for others. A lot is at stake, and not only for lawyers.

A commodity is a fungible good or service bearing a market price. Lawyers do not think of many law services, or even any law services, as commodities—and for good reason. Law practice entails a representation and relationship. Clients benefit from both representation and relationship, independent of the actual activities of the lawyer. Just having a lawyer makes a psychological, emotional, strategic, and reputational difference to a client, no matter what the lawyer does. Clients take solace in lawyers, learn from lawyers, and emulate lawyers, all of those gains independent of the law product or service that the lawyer provides.

Yet what the lawyer does for the client (meaning the service) or provides to the client (meaning the product) is also important. A lawyer's great reputation and relationship can mean nothing if the lawyer sits on the lawyer's hands, leaving the client without the needed product or service. Indeed, most clients would take the competent service and qualified product over the reputation and relationship. What good is it to have a big-shot lawyer who fails to deliver? Many clients are better off with the grunt lawyer who delivers the competent product on time at the right price than the fancy lawyer who cannot seem to get off the dime, then too late delivers an overwrought product that the client cannot afford.

Within this practice market, commoditization of many aspects of some law services is critical *to the client*, never mind to the lawyer. No matter the uniqueness of every client and situation, lawyers repeat aspects of what they do. The genius of efficient lawyers, as for other professions, trades, and industries, is to recognize what the lawyer can standardize to make law's production more efficient and therefore more affordable to more consumers. Think Henry Ford, not Rolls Royce or Bentley, but with aftermarket customization. To use another analogy, tailors made exquisite suits from scratch measurements for the wealthy. Clothiers gradually standardized suits into something that the middle class and even low-income could afford. With a little tailoring of the pant cuffs and sleeves, it was hard to distinguish the wealthy from the middle class and low-income, at least on Sunday morning when everyone got to wear their finest.

Likewise, enterprising lawyers find the right balance between standard product and custom service, between reasonable fees and affordable price, and between acceptable and exceptional quality. Every professional must strike these balances. Most do so only intuitively. Enterprising lawyers do so explicitly, strategically identifying the underserved client populations and their objectives, and then packaging, pricing, and delivering affordable law products and services to those clients. Enterprising lawyers optimize service by striking the right balances for new clients.

And isn't that America—that we all have reasonable access to what a broad middle class should be able to afford? The genius of the American experiment is not entitlements. Despite our personal and professional largesse, local bars and governments cannot afford enough self-help centers to serve all of the unrepresented middle class and poor. Commitments to philanthropy and pro bono service are powerful. Yet the power of profession lies only partly in its largesse. Its primary power will always be to package, price, and deliver law services that the middle class and low-income can locate, benefit from, and afford. Largesse is most necessary where professions fail. Precisely where we hear the greatest cry for pro bono and public funding of law services for unmet needs, lawyers should be examining their practices to provide reasonable-cost law products and services.

Enterprising lawyers will use disruptive new systems and technologies to do exactly that, identifying and effectively serving the unrepresented do-it-yourselfers before they go un-served or poorly served and suffer resultant loss and harm. The cycle of firms of all kinds, not just lawyers, has been that dominant players and practices emerge through competition. Yet then, the dominant providers sow the seeds of their own destruction by up-selling (gussying up) the product to beat the competition for the consumers whom the firms presently serve. At precisely that point, disruptive practitioners adopt develop new products that reach vast new consumer markets—in our case, the underserved middle class and low-income who flood the new self-help centers. The lawyers who prosper will be those who embrace new technologies and practices that disrupt old delivery systems that currently fail the middle class and poor.

Sound practice innovation, though, requires more than adopting new tools. Effective innovation begins with the fundamentals of any useful organization reform, whether the organization is a solo practice or small, medium, or large firm. Effective management systems that promote and support innovation have common features. Organization developers require innovators to ask four key questions: (1) who are we?; (2) in what do we believe?; (3) what do we do?; and (4) how well do we do it?

The first question, having to do with *organization* factors, requires you to define yourself, your firm, and the professional and competitive environment in which you practice. Be frank and authentic about the character, capabilities, and challenges of your practice. Are you, for instance, a deep-knowledge, boutique provider, or do you instead best serve all needs of a specific population with whom your firm has a special relationship? The second question, having to do with *design* principles, requires you to define your vision, values, and commitments. Are you, for instance, an agile, socially responsible, client-driven firm that values its employees?

The third question, having to do with *business processes*, requires you to evaluate your firm's systems. Do you do periodic strategic planning? Do you do market research? Do you survey client satisfaction? Do you document, evaluate, and improve firm processes? The last question has to do with the maturity and effectiveness of your practice. Do you benchmark your practice against reliable performance measures? Do you have clear data demonstrating how good you are at what you do? You cannot automate and improve processes until you elicit them. You must identify and document your processes and then study and benchmark them, to improve. When you elicit and document your firm's processes, they become your knowledge advantage and intellectual property. Your practice's processes are its value.

Your answers to these questions are what make your practice unique. No two practices are so alike that they fail to reflect the lawyers who lead them. The last question involving benchmarking, though, is one that permits uniform comparison and contrast. All firms can measure their maturity along a similar scale. If you have no systematic approach to managing your practice, then your practice has the lowest maturity. At the next level, your practice may react well to problems but do little to head them off before they occur. Better yet, your practice may have some basic management systems in place. At the next level, you may at least occasionally study and improve those management systems. Better yet, you may routinely study and integrate your practice's systems to optimize their effects in achieving your chosen practice goals.

At best, though, you would benchmark your firm against other firms employing the profession's best practices. Benchmarking is a practice-management tool and commitment. You first document your own processes, selecting critical processes to benchmark. You then discern data points that help you contrast the quality of your processes against the processes of top performers in the same or similar field. That analysis enables you to plan, implement, and measure process improvements to close quality gaps, while monitoring the success of your improvements.

For more than a decade since its entry onto the corporate scene, benchmarking was available only to sophisticated organizations having substantial capital and management expertise. Today, benchmarking services are becoming commonplace among small entrepreneurs. Web services now allow entrepreneurs to benchmark anonymously their organizations against hundreds of other organizations. The smallest of firms—including solo practitioners—can now use powerful online analytic systems to determine how their practices measure against the best organizations. Benchmarking results can help pace, shape, and guide the firm's development in critical areas including leadership, financing, revenue model, quality control, product and service development, innovation, branding, office design, and marketing. Quality-improvement programs also focus on personnel practices, work procedures, time management, facilities, information-technology systems, accounting, supplier relationships, and emergency management.

The study here is in part to improve case management and matter management, for which vendors already offer increasingly complex and useful software and software-service systems. The greater study is to improve practice management, for which vendors are also beginning to offer helpful systems. See, for example, the American Bar Association's book *The Lawyer's Guide to Practice Management Systems Software*, now in its second edition. Practice-management software can help integrate case or matter management with document management and production, financial management, and communications. Yet this study's primary purpose is that you grasp and employ the entrepreneurial practices and enterprise principles that make software and systems of that kind, useful tools in achieving broader purposes. If you do not grasp their rationale within a much broader set of principled commitments, tools of that kind can become expensive distractions.

We hope to give you the understanding and inspiration to systematize, improve, and benchmark your practice. To that end, this book has three parts, packaging, pricing, and delivery. The three parts outline approaches for lawyers preparing to serve more effectively a broader poor and middle class. Each of the three parts has five sections articulating what it takes to deliver more law services to greater numbers at lower cost. Each section begins with two vignettes. The first vignette is of a lawyer failing a client or situation in the section's particular subject, by employing traditional practices. The second vignette is of a lawyer succeeding with a similar client or in a similar situation by employing the necessary new practices. Each section then includes a discussion of how lawyers can identify and acquire those essential new practices to create and sustain a law practice that enriches and uplifts a broader community. Co-author Mike Dunn enlivens these prosaic sections with Practice Tip practitioner lore echoing many of the concepts that the text draws from inter-disciplinary research. Co-author

John Crane enlivens the text with practical steps to take. Each section concludes with questions for reflection.

Reflection

1. Do you think of yourself as an entrepreneur in your work as a lawyer? Why or why not? What alternative self-conceptions do you have for your work as a lawyer, such as professional, humanitarian, or change agent? What difference do self-conceptions make to professional performance—any difference?

2. Identify three practices in which you regularly engage that have some aspect of enterprise about them. For instance, do you deliberately market law products or services? Do you account for your productivity whether by tracking your hours, billings, or revenue? Do you plan for your professional development?

3. Do you wish others to think of you as enterprising or entrepreneurial? What would an enterprising or entrepreneurial lawyer look like to you?

4. Review two or three recent ABA Journals or other lawyer journals depicting practitioners. What evidence do you see of enterprising lawyers? What impression do the journals convey about those lawyers? How profitable, productive, and engaged do those lawyers appear? Can you think of examples of enterprising lawyers whom you admire?

Part I

Packaging Services

The new associate had been at the firm full-time for just two months, but already his doubt about his choice—and the firm's decision to hire him—were crystallizing into something stronger than doubt and more like fear or conviction. At first, his academic success had seemed like a gift, elevating his employment prospects above many of his peers, who had joined small firms, begun solo practices, or taken contract or legal-services work. He had won the coveted large-firm job, riding his high grades through on-campus interviews into his associate position with a solid old-line firm serving a corporate clientele. His many hours on law review had honed his writing skills, impressing prospective large-firm employers.

The associate had wondered what he was missing in the competitions, clinics, pro bono service, and student-organization work that his less-academically successful peers had embraced and so seemed to enjoy. The associate-position offer had masked his unease for a time. Yet now, he could see it more clearly. He had no clue how to connect the projects that the lawyers in his firm were giving him to the law services he had hoped to provide. In two months at the firm full time, the associate had yet to meet a client. Worse, he had no clear sense of who the clients were, what were their needs, and how he was serving them.

The associate now envied his school peers, several of whom had already shared with him the satisfaction they were taking in making a difference in the lives of their clients. By contrast, he had no sense of his clients even having lives, no less what difference he was making to them. Worse yet, the associate was discovering that the partners who assigned him his work had a similar sense that their old conventions were no longer serving their clients as they once did. The associate had discovered an unsettling unease at the old-line firm, a bit like it might have been on the first sign of trouble on the Titanic. The partners seemed in some weird sense to be looking to him, their newest associate, to bring new forms. He had no idea how to respond to them. They were all, he now knew, looking for direction.

~

There were days that she just about had to pinch herself. Law school had seemed at first like a lost cause, especially after she received her first-term grades. She learned then that she would not be repeating her undergraduate academic success. Ouch. Yet in retrospect, that initial shock had turned out to be her first good moment when she had set aside competitive academics and begun to think about what would make her a good lawyer. Suddenly, the third-year students whom she wished to emulate were not the academic stars shooting for federal-court clerkships. Instead, she saw hope, faith, sensibility, and skill in the clinic students, the student-organization leaders, and the students sharing pro bono service with local lawyers. Without much other choice, she had followed that skills and engagement path.

Now, look where that path had taken her. Just six months after starting her solo practice, she had more work than she could handle. Of course, the work presented her with great challenges. She knew that it would take her years to develop and refine the many law products that would serve the clients who had begun to make her busy days stretch into late afternoon and early evening. She could not yet competently serve many of those clients. She spent a lot of her time referring her new clients to other lawyers and then following those clients to their first meeting with those new lawyers. Yet even there, she was seeing new opportunities. Some of those lawyers were sharing their products, forms, and systems with her, helping her to keep those clients she was still referring. In other instances, she was seeing things that the lawyers to whom she sent those clients were not doing but could be doing to serve those clients.

The difference was that she had the clients. She had discovered populations to serve while maintaining attitudes and developing practices that were going to serve those clients well for as long as she wished to practice. She had found the clients right where she had seen them in her law school volunteering and pro bono service. The clients whom she served were like her, and she was like them. She understood their problems, even if she was still learning how to provide them with the law products and services that provide them with solutions. While small frustrations arose frequently, every day was yet overall rewarding, and some days were exciting. Her network of lawyer friends was growing. She had no doubt that she was in the right place to make the difference that she had hoped a law career would enable. She just wanted to discover and develop more tools to make more of a difference to more people.

~

Marketing is certainly a legitimate concern of lawyers and law firms, even though appropriately colored by the profession's special commitment to law and justice through client service. Lawyers constantly think and talk about marketing, and adopt marketing practices, even while they also keep their figurative eye on the professional ball. Marketing is an important and legitimate concern simply because it addresses how lawyers create and deliver law products and services for specific client segments. Marketing principles can therefore legitimately guide lawyer practices. Marketing activities are legitimate means of increasing the positive professional influence and reach of a lawyer's services. An otherwise-fine lawyer with no sense of how to create and deliver law products and services is not an effective lawyer. Lawyers may legitimately plan, implement, and control marketing activities.

Practice Tip

The solo practitioner quickly learns that the most important adage is to focus on the quality of the work. The money will take care of itself. Of course, the adage may seem trite when you have to pay your first month's rent. Yet with diligent and dedicated attention to all aspects of your practice, months (not years) from now, you will wonder why you ever worried about finding enough work to pay the bills.

Marketers even have a term, *customer-objectives marketing*, for the kind of marketing that lawyers may do most consistent with their professional obligations to the client. Those who are unfamiliar with marketing lore may assume that marketing has only sales and profit objectives. Yet to the contrary, firms can and do plan marketing research and activities around client rather than firm objectives. Client-centered marketing objectives determine how a firm wants clients to regard the firm's products and services. What discernible attitudes and measurable behaviors should clients reflect toward the lawyer and law firm if the marketing succeeds? Lawyers and firms can legitimately institute and modify marketing plans that define, measure, and monitor client attitudes and behaviors toward the planned and provided law products and services.

Marketers even go beyond client-objective orientation in their marketing plans, to fashion plans around *societal marketing*. Societal marketing goes beyond considering immediate client interests to value clients' long-term interests. It also supports a firm's consideration of the effect of its product-and-service offerings on the community as a whole. Lawyers and firms can use marketing principles to ensure that their services have broad benefits consistent with the profession's full commitments, not just the immediate interests of individual clients.

These concepts are simply marketing basics. See the Haworth Press book *Marketing Planning Guide* as an example of the resources available to lawyers to learn more about planning marketing in ways responsible to the public and profession.

Yet this book is not simply about marketing basics. Experienced lawyers know that client decisions to purchase law services carry with them more than the usual amount of misinformation, mental obstacles, and emotional baggage. Clients are not perfectly rational economic optimizers when they consider buying law services. Standard economics assumes that enough consumers are sufficiently well-informed and rational that economists should model markets based on consumers optimizing gain in their buying decisions. Empirical study of consumer decision-making provides substantial contrary evidence that many consumers make what a perfect optimizer would call poor buying decisions. Standard economics has given ground to *behavioral* economics, using psychology, cognition, and other studies to understand consumer-buying decisions.

Studies in behavioral economics suggest that consumers generally operate within a sort of *bounded rationality* in which they have only incomplete information about the purchased product or service. Given their information constraints, consumers seek only to do a little better than before or a little better than their neighbors do rather than to maximize benefits fully. Behavioral economists label as *satisficing* the consumer's safe seeking of only marginal gain. Pursuing what behavioral economists label a *certainty effect,* consumers seek satisfaction from that which will suffice at no risk rather than accepting reasonable risk for greater gain. The sensitivity and complexity of law services tend to accentuate these bounded purchasing effects.

Social psychology's *prospect theory* (that consumers evaluate transaction prospects through cognitive lenses) can help lawyers understand some of the purchasing anomalies that these effects produce. Studies indicate that consumers generally over-emphasize certainty when seeking gains. They want the sure thing, passing up opportunities to make greater gains justified by small risks. Consumers are risk averse when seeking gains. They prefer the known status quo over the unknown associated with probable gainful change. On the other hand, consumers tend to accept greater-than-justified risk when incurring losses, in what behavioral economists call the *endowment effect.* Consumers hold onto things—assets, surely, but also positions, relationships, attitudes, or stances—longer than a frank assessment of the risk would warrant. Behavioral economists label as *hedonic editing* the consumer's peculiarly subjective process of evaluating gain or loss from purchase offers.

Practice Tip

A distraught man called a lawyer at home on Thanksgiving Day. The man told the lawyer that he had purposely set his house on fire. He assured the lawyer that he lived alone and that no one was hurt but admitted that he did not know what now to do. The lawyer asked him how long ago the fire had taken place. The man replied that the home was burning as they spoke and then asked again, what he should do. Call the fire department, the lawyer answered. Clients know that lawyers solve problems, even when the solution is as obvious as to call the fire department.

Prospect-theory studies indicate that consumers often correct their misjudgments over transaction gain or loss only when facing more immediately the calamity that earlier good judgments could have avoided. Think job loss, bankruptcy, divorce, or incarceration—the kinds of things that law services routinely address. Prospect theory also teaches that consumers decide from specific reference points rather than from wise overall assessments of gain and loss. How one puts the purchasing question to the consumer—the sellers *framing* of the purchase—may be more important to the consumer's decision than the seller presenting relevant information on which a wise consumer could evaluate gain. Consumers are not blank slates. They begin their purchase evaluation with simple heuristics through which they perceive the offer and that the seller must recognize and ameliorate if the seller is to help the consumer maximize gain. Clients can act even more bizarrely when purchasing law services because of the high cost of law services and the emotionally sensitive subjects that law services address.

To remove more of the connotation of profit-seeking behavior, we will use the concept of *packaging* law products and services rather than *marketing* them. Packaging law products and services means to discern the standard features of the services that clients need, so that then the lawyer can develop systems, forms, and routines that will facilitate their low-cost, reliable, and timely delivery. What, though, is the lawyer to package? How do lawyers know what law products and services to prepare for pricing and delivery? Who, in other words, are the clients, and what are their needs? Firm managers think of these product- and service-development questions as *differentiation* and *market-niche* strategies. The first step to packaging law products and services, to identify the client population with unmet needs, requires the lawyer's reflection leading to authentic commitment. Lawyers work most competently and diligently when they are passionate about serving their clients.

Practice Tip

Solo and small-firm practitioners find refuge in the seemingly small cases. Do not hesitate to work on small matters while charging accordingly. Providing a small product or service worth more than the client paid makes for happy clients. Happy clients are the best form of advertising. Clients form bonds with the practitioners who satisfy them, returning with additional and larger matters. Always remember that you are selling your time and education. Keep your door open. Keep selling. Keep serving.

Take a step back at this point. Pursuing new practice opportunities is a strategic activity. Strategic planners urge that before you identify specific opportunities, you first evaluate your firm's strengths, weaknesses, opportunities, and threats. Firm strengths may include finances, goodwill, reputation, competencies, cost advantages, management skills, technology, flexibility, and pure talent. Weaknesses may include the opposite along with lack of focus, identity, and commitment. Opportunities may cluster around under-served populations, latent skill at developing new competencies, engaged staff, other firms' failures, and new technology. Organizational threats may include lower-cost or higher-quality competitors, product and service obsolescence, regulation, supplier disruption, demographic shifts, and damage to reputation.

Effective firms develop strategic visions incorporating these considerations. A firm's client-service mission should reflect the firm's strategic vision. A useful mission statement reflects the organization's *who* (the clients), *what* (the service), and *where* (the direction). A firm should include in its strategic visioning a collection of guiding principles. Those principles should include the professional bedrock of high ethical standards, client satisfaction, and support of the profession. Yet they can also include such business-related concerns as workforce development, databased assessment, and continual improvement of work processes. Guiding principles can also include quality commitments, engagement of staff, and social and environmental sustainability. Engage others within the firm, particularly stakeholders over processes, in developing your firm's strategic vision, mission statement, and guiding principles.

After passionate commitment, packaging the right law products and services depends on four next steps, the first of which involves discerning those clients' objectives. What are those clients trying to achieve? The third step involves recognizing the law products and services as commodities. What are the standardized products and services that will meet those clients' needs? The fourth step involves determining what fit the products and services must have to individual clients. How do individual clients differ in their use of standardized products and services? The fifth and final step involves determining an appropriate level of product and service quality. What is the minimum—yes, the minimum—quality product and service that will serve the clients' needs?

This first part on packaging law products and services focuses on answering those five questions as to who are the clients, what are their needs, what products and services meet those needs, how the products and services must fit individual clients, and what minimum quality the products and services must have. Appreciate that the skills necessary to answer these packaging questions are different from the skills having to do with the next two parts on pricing and delivering the products and services. You will notice that this first part on packaging focuses more on law fields and less on law skills and delivery systems. The skill of some lawyers is to discern and develop the standardized products and services—to package law products and services—rather than to price or deliver them. Persist in this packaging work even if product or service development is not your skill, and pricing and delivery instead seem to be your things. Packaging is a core skill for effective lawyers, critical to their success.

Consider the following five sections on packaging law products and services, beginning with client populations, followed by client objectives, services that meet those objectives, and the fitness and quality of those services.

Reflection

1. Have you ever purchased a law product or service? If so, then what did you know about the product or service, and how did you learn about it, before you communicated with the lawyer who offered it to you? How did you first discern your need for the product or service?

2. In what ways are law products and services commodities (meaning standardized and fungible goods)? In what respects are law products and services not commodities?

3. What benefits do you see to conceiving of your law practice as including the offering of packaged products or services? Could you streamline processes, focus marketing, improve design, or create economies of scale by making a clearer effort to standardize certain products and services? Could you reach new clients? Could you serve more clients more effectively?

4. What drawbacks do you see to commoditizing law products and services? Can a law firm operate without any standard products or services?

5. What is your practice mission? Write it out, study it, and reform it until it sounds most appropriate—something you can speak in any setting.

PACKAGING SERVICES
Populations
Objectives
Services
Fitness
Quality

A. Populations

The new associate had no clue what the client wanted from him. That mystery was just the thing. The associate kept telling the client the law, but it seemed to make no difference to the client. The client just kept talking about the client's problem repeatedly, expecting the associate to do something about it, when it was obvious there was nothing that the associate could do. The associate felt that the client needed financial, employment, and probably a social worker's counsel, not legal counsel. The client was in the wrong place.

The consultation had not gone well from the start. The client had been ill at ease waiting in the firm's reception area for the associate. The receptionist had made faces at the associate to convey her own displeasure at the client's presence, when the associate finally got off the telephone and came out to meet the client. The client was standing at the big window looking down at the streets. The client had jumped when the associate called his name. The associate never was able to put him at ease.

The consultation also did not end well. The client grew frustrated with the associate. He finally said that he had better just leave. The associate had wanted to show him to the door, but the client had turned his back on the associate and literally waved him away. Five minutes after the client left, the managing partner had walked into the associate's office to tell the associate not to engage any further clients "of that kind," whatever that meant. So much for building his own client base, the associate thought. Evidently, the client had said something untoward to the receptionist on the way out, and the receptionist had promptly told the managing partner rather than the associate. Oh, great, the associate thought in defeat, no client, unhappy receptionist, and unhappy managing partner.

~

Meeting new clients was the new solo practitioner's favorite activity. You never know what a client will bring, she thought. Although on the other hand, she had a good sense now, just months into her new practice, of what problems many of those clients would bring. She knew these clients and their problems, often even before they told her what those problems were. Her clinic, volunteer, and pro bono work in school had taught her a lot about clients and their common problems, and she had learned even more in her networking and social research. At the same time, she had quickly learned to be careful not to prejudge any client. They each had their unique situation. It was just that she was finding helpful patterns to their lives and problems, that she could use both as a general guide and then also to distinguish one client from another.

The solo practitioner found it fascinating how the law issues that individual clients had reflected national and even global problems. Job migration, recession, housing bubbles, and other regional, national, and global trends all translated into local individual and family problems. The solo practitioner had a sense, too, of how her clients could deploy the law products and tools that she increasingly had at her disposal to weather the storms created by those uncontrollable events. Her network of more-experienced lawyers lent her their historical perspective, that these things too would pass, which helped her convey the same hope and faith to her more-bewildered clients.

Yet the new solo practitioner found the clients' self-created problems to be even more fascinating. Clients could convince themselves of just about anything, she had soon realized. She was not a psychologist, social worker, or spiritual counselor. She was not an accountant, financial manager, or even a decent bookkeeper. She did have some sense of all those fields, though, and with these clients, she found herself quite able to provide some basic financial, social, and other counsel to clients who seemed to ask for it. She recognized from her research and increasing experience with underserved populations that her clients' relationship to her could be as important as anything tangible that she provided them. One of the law products that she was packaging was herself—the sense of competence and confidence from which her clients were drawing hope when they had no other present source for it.

~

Lawyer marketing inevitably involves discerning client needs, interests, and ambitions. Lawyers can learn much about those important issues from marketing databases. Most obviously, data can help lawyers identify potential clients who already seek the law product or service the lawyer offers. Lawyers can also discern new populations to which offer new or old products or services. They can also investigate offering those populations services that complement services the population is already receiving. Lawyers can also use database research to fine-tune networking, advertising, and other service-related activities and communications, estimate market potential, and conduct additional surveys and research among the database populations. Market-research steps begin with the research objective, then the methodology, data collection, and data analysis. Market research can be highly sophisticated or merely basic. The point remains that effective lawyers see the opportunity to examine population information to discern new client populations.

Steps to Take

Some marketing databases are free. You can purchase others from commercial vendors. When using free resources, evaluate the data critically before relying on it. All other practitioners have access to the same material. Commercial databases can be significantly more sensitive and valuable. However, their options, fees, reliability, and data-collection methods vary greatly. Shop around before committing to a database, list, or online subscription.

Sensitive marketers (whether lawyers or others) see populations as segmented. Geographic market segmentation can be hugely important for lawyers. Where are the clients? Demographic segmentation can also be hugely important. Who are the clients? Lifestyles (distinct living patterns around interests, activities, and opinions) further segment geographic and demographic markets. For instance, defense lawyers market successfully to newly drinking-age, college-attending partygoers. The particular benefits that clients would draw from the law product or service also segment the market, as does the extent that clients would use the product or service. Life cycles, such as adult children of elderly parents, segment client populations in a different way for law products and services. Motivations such as security, fear, risk-avoidance, stewardship, generosity, ambition, challenge, and efficiency also segment client populations.

Steps to Take

Extensive dialogue with current clients, and study of them, can help you discover segmentation issues. Examine, analyze, and sort your client list. Note the similarities and differences between clients. Develop your own market database based on your past and present clients. Mine its data. Use its information to design and implement your firm's marketing plan. Fill the gaps in your own database, or augment your database, with public and commercial sources. Remember: the one who uses the most data wins.

Research into underserved groups is necessary because the populations lacking reasonable-cost law products and services are no longer only members of the traditional groups who qualify for federally funded legal services. There was a day in 1963 when the law profession's main concern for representing the unrepresented involved the indigent facing criminal charges likely to result in incarceration—the *Gideon* defendant. Then came a day in 1974 when Congress created the Legal Services Corporation to ensure equal access for the poor to the civil justice system. For decades, the profession and public have expected publicly and privately funded defenders and legal-aid organizations to provide law products and services to the poor and underserved. The law profession also maintains a laudable commitment to pro bono service. Yet public defenders and legal-aid services do not meet all or even a substantial majority of the legal needs of the underserved. Pro bono services alone cannot fill the gaps in legal aid.

Today, thousands of unrepresented litigants flood the trial courts seeking all kinds of civil relief from eviction, foreclosure, job loss, personal-property loss, account conversion, identity theft, consumer fraud, and a variety of similar problems. Thousands more unrepresented litigants struggle through guardianship, conservatorship, decedent-estate, and other probate proceedings, while others face paternity, custody, divorce, termination of parental rights, and other family law proceedings. Millions more lack the preventive law products and services that would avoid or limit the effects of disruptive disputes and ensuing litigation. New service populations are constantly emerging while old ones are constantly changing. Both new and old service populations are ripe for new law products and services.

> *Practice Tip*
>
> Lawyers commonly misconceive that they should start offering pro bono service only after they have been in practice for a few years, when they can afford to spare the time. Nothing could be further from the truth. Nothing more fulfils, educates, and informs than serving those who have the highest barriers to accessing law services.

For an example of a new service population, approximately 7 to 10 million individuals in the United States now live together in partnerships or unions outside of marriage, a number and percentage that has increased substantially in the past two decades. Households including a married couple now constitute only approximately one-half of U.S. households, a historic low resulting from a continuous and sharp decline over the past four decades. The vast numbers of new partnerships, whether or not intimate, whether involving related or unrelated parties, and no matter the gender makeup, are largely unregulated by law. They have few or none of the law rights and responsibilities of individuals within marriage. Law does not yet promote and protect those households, and promote and protect the interests of the individuals within those partnerships, in the way that law protects marriages. Lawyers are just now discovering that underserved population.

For an example of an old service population with new law-product and -service needs, large numbers of small-business and family-business owners holding vast wealth collectively and in some cases individually are reaching retirement age. The generation of entrepreneurs arising with the digital revolution and enormous economic revival of the 1980s is graying. Those small-business and family-business owners do not necessarily wish to sell or dissolve their businesses but are beginning to recognize that they must do something with respect to the ownership, control, and benefit from those businesses if the businesses are not to dissolve or risk dissolution with their owners' demise. Whatever their particular goals, that population of aging small-business owners and family-business owners may be significantly underserved in their complex needs for law products and services. Lawyers are just recognizing the existence, size, and wealth of that small-business owner and family-business owner population.

Steps to Take

Educating prospective clients should become your daily practice. One of the great obstacles to effective law practice is that prospective clients hesitate to seek advice on embarrassing and otherwise sensitive issues. Educating prospective clients about those issues, including what law product or service can help them, overcomes that resistance. Consider your prospective clients' backgrounds, including such things as country of origin, education level, cultural affinities, and gender. Then develop a well-designed educational tool.

The challenge that lawyers must undertake is to identify continually those old underserved populations and newly emerging un-served populations, and to discern their law needs. Lawyers face hidden demand for law products and services. Out of privacy and confidentiality concerns, clients tend not to advertise their need for law products and services. Whether the matter involves cohabitation, divorce, job loss, small-business ownership, family-business ownership, or business start-up or dissolution, clients often expect to locate lawyers discretely, to preserve those same privacy interests.

Traditional groups have traditional and relatively well-known law needs. Lawyers know who the traditional clients are. Lawyers represent juveniles in delinquency proceedings and adults charged with crime. Lawyers offer contingency-fee agreements to persons who have suffered serious injury in motor-vehicle accidents. Lawyers help injured workers who face worker's compensation disputes. Lawyers assist the permanently disabled with Social Security hearings and draft wills for the elderly. Yet those groups are constantly changing, just as the substantive law, forums, and procedures change. Also, new groups continue to emerge with new law needs, under circumstances where those needs are not immediately evident.

The recent mortgage foreclosure crisis, like the recent vast increase in cohabiting unmarried couples and retiring small-business owners, is yet another example. Until recently, foreclosure defense was a relative backwater for law services. Today, hundreds of thousands of middle-class homeowners face foreclosure in a confusing complex of federal programs and state laws. Enterprising lawyers are discerning and packaging the law products and services to serve hundreds of homeowners, while thousands of other homeowners go unrepresented or inadequately served. The possibility of serving those homeowners exists. Their economic interests in preserving or escaping a home are alone substantial, as are their family interests and their related employment interests.

> *Practice Tip*
>
> New associates have few clearer paths to professional development than through pro bono service. Pro bono service kills several birds with one stone. First, the associate chooses and satisfies personal commitments, gaining an important sense of control, direction, and purpose. Second, the associate meets the firm's community-involvement requirement. Third, the associate can plan, handle, and complete a whole matter rather than only working piecemeal on a project planned and controlled by senior lawyers. The associate has real responsibility as the master of the client's best resolution—a new weight but also a new honor.

Other populations present equally great numbers of persons facing complex law issues without ready access to the law products and services to manage those issues responsibly. Most of the following populations have recently expanded significantly or only newly emerged:

- Consumer debt remains a substantial issue. Millions of consumers unable to pay current obligations face a range of law issues including contesting the obligation, controlling collections, articulating exemptions, and discharging the debt through negotiation or bankruptcy.

- Immigration and the migration of labor remain substantial issues as workers and their families move across borders. Millions of immigrants face a range of law issues including legal status, documentation, employability, access to services, cross-border travel, temporary guardianship of minor children, and care for other family members.

- The crisis in families continues unabated. Millions of parents face divorce, paternity, custody, support, and other family court proceedings, while millions more are already under modifiable family court orders. Abuse and neglect proceedings, juvenile proceedings, and parental-rights terminations affect millions of children.

- The collateral consequences of criminal conviction continue to affect adversely millions of Americans. Thousands of prisoners claim civil rights violations. Hundreds of thousands of recently released prisoners require assistance obtaining identification and expunging convictions, while thousands more face registration, housing, and public-benefits issues.

- Millions of small-business owners require help with choice of organization, formation, governance, compliance, customs, tariffs, trade, human resources, benefits, intellectual-property identification and management, asset protection, asset harvest, transfer, sale, and dissolution.
- Hundreds of thousands of servicemembers deploy for and return from active duty, requiring a host of law products and services such as powers of attorney, wills, minor guardianships, and termination or suspension of leases and other revolving accounts.
- Millions of additional individuals are now living in two-family households due to home foreclosures, huge declines in family net worth, and long-term unemployment. Those households may require or benefit from household-expense agreements, real-property deeds and leases, and advice on joint and separate obligations to creditors.
- Millions of disabled individuals and family members caring for disabled individuals require help with Social Security hearings, educational-services rights, employment- and testing-accommodation rights, insurance benefits, Family and Medical Leave Act rights, and other public and private rights and benefits.
- Millions of elderly require assistance with wills, trusts, powers of attorney, guardianships, conservatorships, healthcare planning, and other estate planning.

Steps to Take

Face it: discerning an emerging market for law services is a scary proposition fraught with uncertainty. Who are these prospective clients? What are their needs? What law products and services will they purchase through what message? View answering these questions as fun and engaging rather than scary. Make it a point to talk to two strangers each day for a few minutes.

Learn their interests, hobbies, and goals, and the interests, hobbies, and goals of their family members. The amount of information you gain from talking to others for the sake of getting to know them will surprise you. Do not make these conversations sales calls. Simply try to get to know the identity and interests of persons whom you have never met before.

Lawyers should have the skill of identifying and locating these underserved and new client populations. Lawyers can identify these emerging populations strategically, efficiently, and effectively, through planned activities interacting with these populations to gain insight into their needs. Lawyers identify service populations and their needs in several intentional ways. Nonprofit tax-exempt charitable organizations and government agencies already serve many of these populations. Charitable social-service organizations are often on the front line of social and financial changes. Lawyers who attend those agencies' events, join those agencies' governance or advisory boards, or network with those agencies' staff, learn those populations' needs and the programs and resources that will respond to those needs. Attending agency trainings, seminars, and events brings lawyers into contact with skilled professionals from other fields who articulate the population's law needs.

Lawyers must get out among those whom they would serve, with the plan to survey systematically and learn about their needs. It is not enough simply to show up at networking and other practice-development events. Instead, develop a routine practice of searching for those opportunities. Begin by articulating your professional mission. Then state more-specific goals for networking, of which you may have several, that will help you accomplish that mission. Then, list the people who can most help you achieve each goal, together with where you are most likely to meet them when they have the time and inclination to engage you. Then, evaluate in advance what helpful contacts or information your meeting with each person may produce.

Practice Tip

Repeat clients and new clients referred from former clients are the lifeblood of many practices. Close behind are new clients whom other lawyers and friends refer. Referrals from other lawyers and friends may be far more likely than having a new client choose your name off a website or out of a phone book. Recognize and respect the possibility that other lawyers and friends would like to refer new clients to you.

Do not underestimate the power of the people whom you know or can get to know. Consider writing down a list of those people. Starting with family and friends is fine. Each of us has a natural circle of support. Draw on it. Write down the name of every family member and friend, and next to each, write down how they can help you and you can help them. Then make the same list for people whom your family and friends know. Do the same for neighbors, not just from your current neighborhood but also from neighborhoods in your recent and distant past. Do the same for your current and past places of employment. Then list the people whom you know in faith and social organizations to which you belong, and how you can help them and they can help you. List educators and school classmates. Finally, list suppliers from whom you purchase products and services. Harvard Business School alum Keith Ferrazi recommends these and other networking activities in *Never Eat Alone*.

Finally, get your elevator speech ready that in the first 10 seconds meeting each network contact, you can state succinctly and powerfully what help you need and why the contact should provide it to you. Just as important as determining what you need is to anticipate and articulate how your contact can benefit from engaging with you. When attending each event, work to obtain the expected contacts and information. Be intentional. Also, be prepared to gather other contacts and information. After each event, record and evaluate the time you invested in the event and the results that it produced. Rate your experience, and then use your evaluation whether to continue attending like events. Appendix B includes an activities-assessment worksheet to help you with these steps.

Practice Tip

Trial lawyers urge newly empanelled juries not to "leave your common sense at the courthouse steps." The admonition means that we should continue to use life experience as a source of understanding in unfamiliar places. Night is dark even when a witness testifies that night is light. Lawyers need to use similar common sense. The first thing a new lawyer may realize is family, friends, colleagues, and other relationships in the community can supply great practice-development tools. Clients want to work with a lawyer they know and like.

Lawyers who accept pro bono cases from those community partners develop the products and learn the technical services to meet those law needs. Pro bono service in general, whether through an agency, court program, bar association, or lawyer network, exposes lawyers to both new and old unmet needs. Judges, especially in certain courts, see many unrepresented parties. They and the court clerks will often know who goes unrepresented in what causes. Pro bono services exist because of needs that the market for law services has not met. Lawyers do a substantial professional and community service when they find ways to provide law products to satisfy clients who would otherwise require pro bono service.

Likewise, cultural, community, religious, recreational, and educational centers are networks for social change. Leaders in faith, the arts, education, recreation, culture, and other community interests and events know populations having law needs. Lawyers who spend two or three evenings a week and additional weekend time engaging in community activities of these types, and who seek out their leaders to learn from them and support them, gradually discern the populations and their hidden and emerging needs.

To discern broad needs from direct interaction with service populations and others who serve them, lawyers can benefit by knowing demographic and psychographic profiles and trends. It is one skill to discern a client need. It is another skill to connect the perceived need of one client with similar needs of other similarly situated clients representing particular portions or profiles of broad populations. Lawyers can develop demographic and psychographic insight by following news and data on broad trends, and connecting those trends to the needs of the clients whom they serve. Read and follow the daily financial and business news to gain a sense of corporate, consumer, banking, finance, and other economic trends, so that you can connect individual clients and their experiences with those broader trends. Demographic and psychographic insights are intuitive skills that effective lawyers acquire through deliberate cultivation.

Practice Tip

Learn to recognize, develop, and use the abilities you already possess. Your skill is the sum of all of your education and experience, not simply what you learned in law school or law practice. If you speak Spanish but do not serve Spanish-speaking clients, then you are missing a great service opportunity. If you love numbers but do not use quantitative reasoning in your practice, then you are missing a great skill opportunity. If you can read financial statements but give no attention to finance in your practice, then you are missing a great management opportunity. Success begins with quality work using all of your abilities. Success continues with professional presentation. Success ends with satisfied clients.

Lawyers can also review demographic and psychographic journals and surveys, or hire demographic consultants and experts to acquire their insight. Lawyer magazines including national and state bar journals often summarize or reference those trends, as do other professional journals. Lawyers do well to acquire a demographics curiosity, reserve some time to research demographic trends, and even budget some funds to invest in consulting services. Even rudimentary interviews and surveys performed among family, friends, and law firm staff can help a lawyer discern underserved client profiles. The lawyer's first challenge is to recognize these underserved populations. In surveying emerging needs, consider the following range of five broad potential client populations each with many general service needs:

- Private-sector business clients require formation, finance, securities, management, governance, contract, competition, employment, labor, intellectual-property, tax, acquisition, construction, lease, licensing, immigration, compliance, trade, lobbying and advocacy, litigation, dispute-resolution, risk-management, estate-planning, and business-succession law services;

- Public-sector government and nonprofit clients require formation, finance, governance, research, drafting, contract, employment, administrative, immigration, tax, lobbying and advocacy, construction, lease, planning, environmental, litigation, dispute-resolution, and risk-management law services;
- Professional clients require association, management, intellectual-property, estate-planning, business-succession, contract, competition, immigration, tax, acquisition, lease, finance, litigation, dispute-resolution, employment, compliance, and risk-management law services;
- Property-owning clients require formation, finance, contract, lease, employment, construction, management, planning, environmental, securities, litigation, dispute-resolution, compliance, risk-management, and negotiation law services; and
- Social-sector clients engaging in recreation, leisure, travel, cultural, artistic, and other personal pursuits require association, competition, employment, construction, planning, contract, lease, licensing, immigration, intellectual-property, and risk-management law services.

The next challenge involves deep reflection as to which populations the lawyer is passionate about serving. Effective law practice involves such intellectual and emotional energy that lawyers and clients both benefit from the lawyer's passion. Authentic commitment is critical to serving clients with appropriately packaged law products and services. A lawyer's reflection may involve scholarship, journaling, meditation, prayer, or conversation. A lawyer's leading may involve general familiarity, personal experience, specific relationships, or peculiar events. Do not underestimate the power of personal and professional commitment to shape an entrepreneurial practice. Practice is not simply a matter of serving whoever shows up at the office door. Know your personal commitments and interests, and unique professional abilities.

Assess, identify, and then develop your interests strategically. No lawyer is good at everything. The lawyer who tries to be everything risks doing clients injustice.

Practice Tip

A recent law school graduate was raised in Russia by her grandmother. The grandmother worked at an orphanage, where she would take her young granddaughter for schooling. The child soon learned how the orphanage worked including which children the orphanage placed within Russia and overseas. While studying law in the United States years later, the granddaughter had little clue in what field she wanted to practice. Her friends' questions left her puzzled and concerned, feeling without root, connection, or direction. Yet not long after graduation, the granddaughter realized the great connections and experience that she already had. She spoke Russian and had intimate knowledge of adoptions.

While every client is unique, one client's matter inevitably shares attributes of other client matters. You cannot develop a commoditized product or service without recognizing the clients whom the product serves. The lawyer who sees the connections among clients and the law issues that clients face acquires an advantage in formulating the law products to serve those clients at higher quality and lower cost. Lawyers must see in individual clients the possibility of serving large enough numbers of other similar clients to justify packaging the law product or service for those clients. Packaging, though, entails more than finding the underserved clients. One must next discern their achievable objectives. Consider that subject in the next section.

Reflection

1. How would you define the client populations that your law practice serves? How are your clients like one another? How are they unlike one another? What similarities do they share that make your law products and services appropriate for your clients? Do you fit your law products and services in some way to the demographics or psychographics of your client population? In what ways do you do so?

2. Are the client populations that your law practice serves under-served in their needs for law products and services? In other words,

does the population include individuals who are unable to obtain law products and services like those that you offer? If so, then why? How might you or other lawyers reach those under-served segments of your client population?

3. What populations in your community have the greatest unmet needs for law products and services? What evidence do you have for your conclusion? If you can think of no local populations having unmet needs for law products and services, then how would you find out? Whom could you ask to learn more about local populations in need?

4. Identify one new need for law products or services that you discern has arisen in the past 10 years, in addition to the several identified above in this section. Who is serving the client population having that new need?

5. Which of the new needs identified above in this section would you be most qualified to meet? Which of the new needs would you be most interested in meeting? How would your efforts impact your local community?

PACKAGING SERVICES
Populations
Objectives
Services
Fitness
Quality

B. Objectives

The new associate gradually came to realize one clear reason why he felt such a miasma about his law firm work: his assignments seldom seemed to have much point. To test his hypothesis, a couple of times the associate had tried to get the partners who assigned him research memoranda to tell him what the clients were trying to achieve. Maybe, he had said, he could do a better job if he knew why the clients needed the research. The first partner whom he had asked just looked back at him with a blank expression that the associate could not read—except that he knew the partner did not like the associate asking. The partner had turned and walked out without answering, making the associate try to be extra prompt and accommodating with the work to make up for his mysterious offense. The second partner whom he asked had exploded in profanity, stormed out, and returned a minute later apologizing to the associate but still without explaining.

The associate had several theories for why he could not grasp the purpose for his work and figured that a grain of truth was in each of them. His first theory was that the work he was doing was exceedingly complex, so much so that the partners who assigned him the work often did not seem to understand it. The associate wondered what good law was when even its purveyors could not grasp it. His second theory was that the work had no point, and the partners knew it. They were just trying to keep the associate busy. The associate suspected that he knew what that reason meant about the confidence (or lack thereof) that the partners had in him and his future (or lack thereof) with the firm.

The associate's third theory was that his work's purpose was so obvious to others even if not to himself that the partners could not believe that the associate was missing it. That reason would explain the partners' odd reactions of disbelief and anger. He had better get a clue quickly. The associate's last theory was that the partners knew that he was catching on to something that they, too, realized about all of their work. They were all having a harder and harder time justifying it to themselves and their clients. The associate felt that this last reason was probably the scariest of them all but also the most soluble and encouraging from his personal standpoint. Maybe he did know a bit about what he was doing. Maybe he did know that it had less purpose than it ought to have. Maybe he was right to have questioned the partners politely, no matter how they reacted.

~

The best part of her meetings with new clients was helping her clients to ascertain achievable goals. She enjoyed listening to the clients describe their problems. Few of them got right to the point. Most of them sort of circled around the issues as if confronting them directly would be too risky or dangerous. Maybe, they seemed to think, the lawyer would kick them out of the office immediately if they came right in and told the lawyer what a mess they were in, whether of their own making or the making of another. Better, they seemed to think, to talk around problems than to talk about them. Yet soon enough, the problems were usually evident enough to the new solo practitioner. It often took just a few guiding questions, some softly compassionate sounds, and a wise nod or two of the head. Yes, the problems, and the clients' attitudes toward them, fascinated her.

Yet again, the best part was usually when the solo practitioner announced to the new client what the practitioner discerned was the client's goal. Almost invariably, the client would look back at the lawyer in stunned silence for two to three seconds, blinking, as if the client had hardly realized it, before giving a nod of relieved assent. The practitioner had quickly intuited why the clients were routinely so astounded at her announcing their goals: they seldom if ever achieved them. To identify and even (shudder the thought) speak them was if to put them even further beyond reach. The reason that the practitioner so enjoyed announcing the client's goal was that she usually had a reasonable belief that the goal was achievable.

The fact that the practitioner could articulate for the client an achievable goal meant more to the client and thus more to her than anything else she would do for them. Oh, sure, the planning to achieve the goal, implementing the plan, and assessing plan progress were all important. Nonetheless, the sheer act of faith that the practitioner exhibited when stating the client's goal meant more to the client's forward progress than the rest of what would follow. The practitioner was already discovering that she could even be wrong about whether the goal was achievable. That the client had a worthwhile and arguably achievable goal meant more than its actual accomplishment. Without a goal, a client has no hope. Without hope, a client has no faith. Without faith, a client has no care or commitment. Belief always precedes accomplishment of the goal. A client must see it before achieving it. The practitioner was above all packaging and selling hope, which was why she so absolutely loved her law practice.

~

Clients determine the goals and objectives of law products and lawyer services. When lawyers choose objectives, they reduce or eliminate client autonomy, distort the professional relationship, and undermine the value of the law product. The choice of objectives carries with it any number of judgments as to the value that the client places on the client's own attributes, commitments, meanings, and relationships. When a client decides to do this instead of that, the client may do so to preserve or promote personal, social, professional, and cultural relationships and identities. The client may draw on knowledge of persons, situations, experiences, and relationships. Clients may be preserving, constructing, or reconstructing finances, futures, or families. The role of a lawyer in offering products and services is not to reduce but to increase client autonomy—perhaps to reveal to the client the client's naiveté and procrastination, and increase the client's sophistication, but overall to ensure that the client makes informed decisions optimizing the client's gain.

Practice Tip

The new practitioner learns quickly not to be too eager with the diagnosis. A prospective client tells the office staff that he has a personal-injury case from a motor-vehicle accident. The eager lawyer soon learns that the client did indeed break his arm in an accident but one that the client caused as a drunk driver. The case is not a personal-injury case but a criminal case of drunk driving. Patient listening is often the lawyer's trade.

Lawyers must package law products to serve clients, not themselves. One cannot design and package a law product or service without discerning the objectives for which the clients would use that product. Products and services have purposes. Clear articulation of client goals and objectives ensures that the lawyer is offering the right products within the lawyer's best judgment and that the client has the benefit of that judgment. Subtle differences in the articulation of objectives can make significant differences in the appropriateness of various legal options and law products. A first step in packaging law products is to gain a clear sense of what the client populations have as their authentic objectives.

Practice Tip

A helpful tactic for the practitioner is to verbalize back to the client the problem and goal, as the practitioner and client *both* see it after thorough discussion. Restate the client's goal until you both agree. Then memorialize it in the fee agreement and in detail in an intake memorandum copied to the client.

Client goals and objectives are not to obtain law products or services. Law products and services are not the clients' ends in seeking lawyer counsel and representation, although to lawyers the products and services can seem to be those ends. Law products are one of a range of possible means to client ends. For example, a client does not have obtaining a will as the client's goal or objective. A will is merely one potential means to the client's other end. The client's end in seeking a will or other estate-planning product may be to act responsibly relieving other family members from estate administration, or to pass certain property on to a next generation, or to avoid property falling into the hands of a family member, to bless a house of worship or a charity, and so on.

Practice Tip

An exasperated truck driver was in the practitioner's office. Police had just arrested the client for drunk driving in what looked like a career-ending event. The arrest took place off a highway in the early evening after the client had been drinking. Although the client's blood-alcohol level was very low, the level was still illegal. The practitioner listened as the client explained that the client was going to lose a promotion off the road and into the office if he could not complete the summer driving. The court scheduled the date for early summer. The client knew that he was sunk. The lawyer thought. The client's goal was not to keep on driving. The client's goal was the off-road office promotion. With the prosecutor's and court's cooperation, the lawyer just might be able to time the case to save the client's career even if it cost him any further truck-driving opportunity. A lawyer finds some tools outside the law books.

Determining client objectives accurately is a particularly significant challenge for new lawyers. New lawyers necessarily tend to focus on the law and the skills that they are still learning to exercise, more so than focusing on the client. New lawyers, or other lawyers uncertain of their skill and knowledge, may attempt to provide clients with immediate explanations of law issues instead of working with clients to discern their underlying goals before beginning to articulate interim objectives and overarching strategies to achieve them. Well-grounded strategies can then help client and lawyer determine which actions lawyer and client should take at decision points presenting specific information sets. Effective lawyers clarify the objectives that determine the strategies, by listening carefully and using discussion leading to pointed queries ending in specific confirmation of client objectives.

Steps to Take

Newer practitioners should not underestimate the benefit to their practice development of role-playing a client intake with senior lawyers who practice in different fields. Many senior lawyers, especially those in your own law firm but also bar leaders and mentors, care about your practice development. Role-play may seem awkward at first but can quickly reveal fundamentals missing from your initial client communications. Role-play allows for instant feedback from a seasoned professional. What more could one ask?

For the schooled lawyer, clarifying one or more client objectives immediately generates a list of possible law products and services to achieve those ends. The objectives stand apart from the potential means for achieving them. By standing apart from the products, objectives give the lawyer and client the opportunity to consider a range of law products and services. Objective also give the lawyer and client criteria for evaluating the product quality and fit. For example, if the lawyer incorrectly sees a will as the client's end, then the lawyer might mistake a longer will, a more expensive will, or some other added feature or collection of features of the will as better achieving the end. To the contrary, a simple will or other less-costly estate-planning product might have better achieved the client's true objective at a more-affordable price. Discerning objectives is critical to supplying the right law product.

Consider again the cohabiting partners who lack the protection of the laws of marriage. Those cohabiting partners, whether or not intimate, whether or not related, and no matter their gender and their sexual orientation, may hold as an objective the desire to promote the duration of their partnership and household. They may, on the other hand, wish to define and limit its duration (and any joint obligations that arise out of the partnership), perhaps until marriage to someone else, or until financial recovery, employment, deployment, illness, injury, or some other event. They may wish to preserve individual rights to assets that one or both brought to the partnership, including individual ownership of the household's residence, or they may wish to share ownership immediately or gradually as the partnership endures or as one or both contribute services or income to the partnership. They may wish to provide for rights and responsibilities on partnership termination or in the event of a partner's illness, injury, or death. Their objectives, both individually and together, may be multiple, substantial, and varying, served by a single law product or service, or a variety of law products and services.

Similarly, consider again the large numbers of small-business and family-business owners who hold vast wealth collectively and in some cases individually but who are aging. Individual representatives of that emerging and growing population may have as an objective to draw wealth from the business for retirement, gift, bequest, or philanthropy. Their objective may be to pass control of the business to responsible and creative family members, partners, or third parties, while passing the profit from the business to family members or charities, and while retaining ownership or passing ownership to family members or third parties. They may have other objectives such as to prevent control, ownership, or benefit by specific family members, competitors, or others. They may have legacy goals to preserve or enhance individual, family, or corporate identity.

Articulating ends is a core lawyer competence, closely connected to developing and offering effective law products. In any given situation, masterful lawyers can discern and articulate for clients a wide range of possible ends. Consider the following example objectives for the same expanded, emerging, or changing populations listed in the prior section. Distinguish these objectives from the law products and services that might help meet those objectives:

- Consumers unable to pay current credit obligations may have as objectives to retain the property purchased with the credit, relinquish the property, determine property exempt from execution, protect exempt property, determine the extent of exempt income, protect exempt income, shift the obligation to a responsible other, remove the obligation from a non-responsible other, determine the true extent of the obligation, minimize repayment, maximize repayment, minimize harassment, or protect reputation.

- Immigrants may have as objectives to determine legal status for self or family members, secure lawful status or citizenship for self or family members, secure services or benefits because of immigrant status, secure services or benefits despite immigrant status, secure services or benefits for family members, obtain or preserve job or other income, obtain or preserve assets, convey income or assets to family members, travel cross-border, assist family members with cross-border travel, provide guardianship for children, minimize harassment, or avoid persecution.
- Spouses may have as objectives to preserve or end a marriage, end or reduce the risk of spousal abuse, end or avoid spousal abuse proceedings, obtain support within a marriage, obtain support while ending a marriage, determine the level of available support, maintain use of the marital home or other marital asset during or after termination of a marriage, determine the extent of marital assets, preserve marital assets, avoid the other spouse's debt, assume the other spouse's debt, obtain services for the other spouse, and obtain services from the other spouse.
- Parents may have as objectives to establish or disestablish paternity, determine custody, obtain or relinquish custody, determine available child support, obtain or avoid child support, increase or reduce child support, end child abuse or neglect, reduce the risk of child abuse or neglect, end or avoid the risk of abuse or neglect proceedings, obtain parenting time, preserve parenting time, increase parenting time, avoid termination of parental rights, obtain termination of parental rights, and assist their children in juvenile proceedings.
- Persons with criminal arrests or convictions may have as objectives outside of their criminal proceedings to improve conditions of incarceration, obtain compensation for injury from incarceration conditions, obtain or restore driver's license, obtain photographic identification, expunge conviction, expunge arrest, obtain

employment, determine responsibility for registration, register, determine availability of lawful housing and obtain housing within conviction restrictions, and determine and obtain available public benefits.

- Small-business owners may have as objectives to identify ownership, acquire ownership, document ownership, acquire control, share ownership and control, deny others ownership and control, confirm and document control, obtain capital, supply capital to others, obtain credit, offer credit, secure obligations, determine obligations, meet obligations, avoid taxes, determine taxes, dispute taxes, pay taxes, access trade, create or alter labor incentives, protect workers, protect management, protect ownership, protect assets, acquire assets, harvest assets, transfer assets, perpetuate business, transfer business, and end business.
- Servicemembers may have as objectives to determine enforceability of obligations during active-duty service, stay enforcement of obligations during active-duty service, terminate leases and other obligations for active-duty service, grant authority to others to manage financial and legal affairs during active-duty service, terminate authority of others to manage financial and legal affairs, grant or terminate guardianship of minor children, and ensure orderly transfer of wealth on demise.
- Disabled individuals and their family members may have as objectives to determine availability of public and private benefits, secure public and private benefits, determine availability of education services, obtain education services and accommodations, determine availability of employment and accommodation, obtain employment and accommodation, determine availability of family and medical leave, and secure family or medical leave.

Few things frustrate enterprising lawyers more than to see clients receive the wrong law product or service, receive substandard service, or receive no service, because another lawyer had failed to articulate the client's objectives and communicated the value of the right product or service. Effective lawyers develop and continually update checklists for common client objectives in specific areas. In a method that professionals in several fields call a *structured interview*, the interviewer uses a comprehensive checklist during the initial client meeting and intake process, guiding and structuring the communication without making the interaction robotic. The checklist is thorough top to bottom but can also serve as a conversation starter, allowing clients to deviate to identify objectives that they choose. Experienced lawyers follow this objective-setting process intuitively and expertly. Enterprising lawyers make the objective-setting process explicit to ensure full and appropriate coverage, and documentation, in every case.

> *Practice Tip*
>
> A prospective client met a practitioner for a free consultation. The client unfolded a piece of paper and, with great flourish, read the nonsensical demand, "I need a unilateral judicial ruling establishing a division of my pension between my wife and myself." The practitioner gradually and skillfully drew out that the client's wife was a homemaker who could not get her own credit because her husband, the client, had the couple's only income. The client wanted to split his income with his wife so that she could get a credit card. The event confirmed for the practitioner the skill and diligence that lawyers must exercise, to discern client objectives and frame them in the right language. Lawyers need skill to help clients tell their stories and to decipher the goal.

Consider again as an example the bullet-pointed paragraph above on a parent's possible objectives in consulting a lawyer. The parent may present the matter as one for divorce, seeking a divorce lawyer because divorce is what family-law clients assume lawyers do. In most cases, though, divorce is just one possible means of a client achieving other underlying goals. Effective lawyers will immediately explore with the client why the client perceives divorce to be the means, so that lawyer and client can articulate together and agree on the client's underlying goal and the multiple objectives that may be necessary to meet in order for the client to achieve that goal.

Objectives associated with a divorce action may include personal safety from physical violence or sexual disease. They may include protection from psychological manipulation and abuse, and protecting children from neglect or abuse. They may include participating in decisions over the upbringing and welfare of children, and excluding an unfit parent's participation in decisions over the upbringing and welfare of children. They may include protecting assets from conversion or waste, securing financial support, avoiding debt, and gaining or preserving access to housing and vehicles. Notice that the objectives of a client seeking a "divorce" may or may not actually include terminating the marital relationship. Even when the client articulates that seemingly ultimate divorce goal, the client may actually have other associated objectives, such as to begin a new marital or intimate relationship, the choice of which the lawyer ought to know.

Enterprising lawyers develop and employ checklists to ensure that clients see and approve the objectives to meet the agreed-upon goal. The experienced family-law lawyer will have already noticed how each of the above possible divorce objectives would entail different law products and services. A client might well achieve many of those objectives without divorce. Similarly, a client might fail to achieve many of those objectives even with a divorce. The lawyer who fails to discern and confirm client objectives runs a great risk of failing to serve the client, indeed would only randomly succeed in serving the client. Effective lawyers also help clients prioritize those objectives, so that lawyer and client can devote the available resources to prime objectives.

The manner in which effective lawyers confirm client objectives is to speak those objectives back to the client orally, listening carefully for verbal responses and watching carefully for nonverbal reactions, and then confirm the objectives in writing. Articulating objectives gives the client the opportunity to confirm or modify the articulation. Clients do not always know their own ends. Consulting a lawyer is often the means by which a client discerns the client's own ends. Lawyers are not necessary evils for clients to avoid until required in crisis. Lawyers are clients' partners in prosperity and productivity. Lawyers can envision and articulate for clients obscured or unimagined prosperities and productivities that clients cannot see for themselves. Education in law and the practice of law teach lawyers the art of the possible and path to prosperity.

Underserved clients may for a variety of reasons lack the ability to articulate what they might achieve to accomplish dreams that they may barely recognize that they hold. Those reasons include lack of education, training, or experience, and limitations of language, history, and culture. In those situations, lawyers can do the articulating for them. To articulate a goal and then offer the law product or service that will help a client accomplish it can be a beneficent act, increasing a client's vision, ambition, influence, and prosperity. For a marketer to create a customer appetite for a previously unimagined need for a previously unimagined product may distort the customer's commitments. Lawyers who help clients envision lawful and achievable goals consistent with the clients' commitments do great service for the clients, their families, and their communities.

Steps to Take

Did you know that experts provide training in non-verbal communication? Training in body language and non-verbal communication can have great value for the practitioner. Clients face significant communication challenges when meeting with lawyers. Have you ever noticed how hard some clients find it to talk to knowledgeable and loquacious lawyers? Instead of verbalizing their interests and concerns, clients often give subtle unspoken clues, concealed in their body language. Understanding clients through their unspoken behavior can give you great advantage in perceiving client interests and needs.

Lawyers who understand common needs of client populations and who effectively articulate client objectives assist clients in selecting effective law products. Before offering a law product, an effective lawyer helps a client articulate ends so that the client can choose among ends. A client's ends can also change over time. By distinguishing the law product from the client objective, an effective lawyer helps a client continue to assess the choice and value of the articulated end.

Client goals and objectives should on the other hand be achievable. Selling a product or service into a lost cause wastes client and lawyer resources, while producing unhappy clients. Lawyers usually have a fine sense (much finer than clients do) of what is achievable by law procedures and lawful means. Law-product development depends on not only discerning client objectives but also discerning which objectives the client is reasonably likely to achieve. Effective lawyers learn outcomes. Waiting your turn on a cattle-call docket will teach you a lot about what is possible, from the array of other motion outcomes. Observation, experience, and research all inform a lawyer of outcomes. Effective lawyers develop and offer law products that achieve client ends.

Legitimate, achievable client goals and objectives can be broader and more sensitive than some lawyers might think. Time is an example. Some situations cannot be resolved perfectly. Their unfavorable resolution to the client may be inevitable. Yet the timing of that resolution or some other feature of it may make a substantial difference to the client in achieving other client ends. For example, the client may have at one level hoped to maintain legal title to and practical possession of a home. Yet the client may also have as a secondary objective to remain in the home through the end of a school year or for another convenient period, or to preserve the client's credit, despite the ultimate loss of the home. A lawyer may develop and offer legitimate law products that achieve interim or subordinate ends, for which clients offer a reasonable market.

To put the point another way, a client may have multiple objectives only some of which law products can achieve. Lawyers provide significant value to clients when helping clients articulate multiple objectives while also identifying the achievable objectives. When lawyers communicate early to clients, before the clients purchase the law products or services, the clients' articulated ends that the law products or services ought to achieve, clients are more likely to recognize value in achieving some but less than all ends. Clients can choose among products and services to match priority achievable ends. When lawyers help them do so, clients gain autonomy and value in the transaction and representation. Consider next some examples of packaged law products and services.

Reflection

1. What would you say (or what do you say) to a client to discern the client's objectives? Do you have a get-to-the-point query for a client whose story seems to ramble?

2. Is exploring the client's objectives a part of your usual consultation practice? Do you record the client's objectives in any of your intake procedures? Do you document the client's objectives in your client files and communications with clients? Can you perceive any advantages (for you or the client) in doing so?

3. Can you recall an instance in practice when you mistook the client's objectives? If so, then why were you mistaken? What assumptions did you or the client make that led to the misunderstanding?

4. Can you recall instances from practice in which the client's objectives changed over the course of the representation? If so, then what events or circumstances augured the change?

5. Articulate the full range of objectives that your clients achieve for your most common law product or service. Then, rank the objectives from the most common and valuable to the least common and valuable, as reflected among the preferences and commitments of your clients.

6. Do you communicate to your clients that they may achieve all or many of those objectives through your product or service? Do they, in other words, appreciate the value to them of your product or service?

7. Describe by geography, demographic, lifestyle, or other characteristic the market segment that your most common product or service serves. Do the same for three other products or services you currently provide or are considering providing. Give each segment a memorable name.

PACKAGING SERVICES
Populations
Objectives
Services
Fitness
Quality

C. Services

The new associate's work ground on, hour after hour, day after day. His only solid connection with the impact of his work was the billing that he did for it. The billable hours were the goal, he sensed from the start of his work. His product, as far as he could tell, was the billable hour. His service was the performing of an endless string of vague activities that provided justification for the billable-hour product. The associate had no other sense of the commodity that he was producing. The commodity was his time itself. As long as he was working, it did not matter much what the work entailed or produced, or what difference it made for the client.

Actually, the associate knew that his sense that his time, charges, and billing relationship with the client were the products was a distorted image. He knew that there must be more to law practice than the endless hours and hourly bills. At least, he suspected that if there was nothing more to law practice within the firm than the hours he produced, then there was something wrong with the firm or wrong with its practice. The associate's problem was that he had nothing to substitute for that image. His document review, file review, and research memoranda seemed so disconnected from their effects that he could not shape them into anything more meaningful. He wanted to do something authentic and consequential. The associate simply could not identify the consequence and so could not identify the action and commoditize it into something deliverable. He was gaining an increasing sense that his firm's services needed to be meaningful, affordable, and deliverable commodities but had no sense of how to accomplish it.

~

One of the things that the solo practitioner most enjoyed about law practice was the sense of developing products and services to offer to her clients. Like many of her high school and college classmates, she had worked some in retail sales. She enjoyed interacting with customers, drawing energy from the interaction while satisfying her natural curiosity about people and their needs and interests. Entering law school, she had no idea that product or service sales were any special part of law practice. She had assumed that law was highly technical and that its practice therefore focused on the work rather than the client. Practice was teaching her that her first assumption was correct. Law is highly technical. Yet her second assumption that the focus was on the work was in part incorrect. You needed to do all things right, but she had learned quickly that the central focus is on the client.

Her practice skill, she realized, was developing the products and services that served her clients. It was not simply that she knew who her clients were and what their needs were, and liked serving them. Rather, she was refining her surprising capacity to package various products and services into deliverable items, and then to help her clients choose among them. One day she even laughed to herself after a particularly effective client interaction, that she now had her own little retail outlet. The client had been surprised at how many different ways the solo practitioner could help the client with various products and services. The practitioner had an intuitive sense of discerning bite-sized actions that she could take for clients, each of which would make some positive difference. She knew how those discrete actions could fit together into one comprehensive product but also how to separate them out, leaving other objectives for the client to accomplish.

The practitioner also appreciated the constant innovation in product and service development. Just when she thought that she had perfected her law commodity, she would learn a new facet that would enable her to modify the product, separate it into two or more products, or eliminate it altogether by adopting other innovations. She saw that law products changed quickly. Just look at the forms and templates that the lawyers in her professional network were sharing with her. For her, those forms and templates were only starting points for an improved product or service. The practitioner was an inventor. She loved invention, particularly when what she invented quickly became products and services that she could price for and deliver to clients to make their lives more productive and better. Who would have thought that law practice could be so enterprising?

~

Lawyers must be able at some level to conceive of law practice as identifying, developing, and offering products and services that meet client objectives. A product or service implies common attributes with other products and services, whether offered by one lawyer or by another lawyer. Law products and services certainly exist. Any experienced practitioner knows so. Law products and services, like other products and services, also have natural life cycles as the needs of consumers and clients, and their habits, capacities, and resources, change. A product does not become a product until its purveyor recognizes that it has the attributes of a product and refines the product on that basis. The same is true with a service. Anyone who does much of anything for a living has that responsibility, to identify common performances and practices. What do lawyers do repeatedly that serves client needs? Knowing what one does enables one to study the practice to repeat and improve it.

Practice Tip

Law practice can become hugely time-consuming if you do not develop and maintain a comprehensive form bank. Lawyers accumulate their form banks from several sources. Law libraries and online commercial services can certainly help, but so can practice-management institutes, continuing-legal-education institutes, and national, state, and local bar associations. A simple web search can give you surprising results. Do not overlook reaching out to other lawyers. When all else fails, develop your own form. You may be the best resource to meet your own needs.

As the prior two sections indicate, effective lawyers connect the products and services that they develop and offer, to meet specific objectives of identified client populations. Lawyers do not create new products and services in order to generate client demand. Unlike some entertainment and recreation industries, law practice does not entail discovering a product around which to create demand. Law product and service development is instead a process that begins with the activities that the prior two sections on client populations and their objectives describe. Product and service development begins only when a lawyer discerns the population and its objectives.

Then, the enterprising lawyer researches, designs, tests, and improves the products and services that will meet those objectives. The enterprising lawyer must then market the product or service. The client population may not yet know that the lawyer's product or service will help meet client objectives. Consumer demand may go unmet until consumers learn of the products and services that will meet their needs. Enterprising lawyers identify the client populations, discern the population's objectives, and develop and market the products and services to meet that demand. Enterprising lawyers are in that respect both leaders and followers, letting client populations lead them to objectives but then leading client populations to the products and services that will accomplish those objectives.

Treating a product or service as a commodity need not imply anything particularly negative. Treating a product or service as a commodity means to recognize its place in a market for fungible goods, to improve and trade better on its qualities and delivery. Clients to some extent have always treated law products and services as commodities. Clients are doing much more so today with the vast increase in information about law and law products and services. Clients are simply much more able than ever before to learn about their law needs and to learn who can serve their needs at what price. Communications technologies including particularly the internet and its search engines have made law information and information about law products much more accessible. Clients will commoditize law products and services even when lawyers do not.

Lawyers should perform that commoditization for clients if lawyers are to provide the most effective products and services for the ends that the clients most want. Commoditizing law products and services is a core lawyer competency. Developing a new practice product or service nearly always initially seems like wading into a mystery. Yet the lawyer's enterprise skill turns the mystery into a defined route. Clients achieve a beneficial resolution by acquiring the lawyer's commoditized product or service. To package a law product or service means to turn the mysterious means into a defined entity, a product or service that the client can recognize, evaluate, and select over other products or services.

Practice Tip

Associates begin their careers in firms the operation of which many do not yet understand. Even with the best internship, new associates find holding that first file on their own quite different, knowing that their work quality and ability face their first significant test. Firms rightly supervise new lawyers. Yet supervision can also be more confining than it need be. Innovative managers give clear direction but use less control. The role of new associates can include expanding a firm's client base and practice areas.

For example, consider again the millions of new households formed around partnerships that do not involve marriage. Because common law and statutory rights and remedies do not serve those households, protect the partnerships, and protect the individual partners from one another in the way that common law and statutes certainly do serve, promote, and protect marriages and married individuals, lawyers have an opportunity to package products and services. Lawyers can offer highly useful packaged products and services to unmarried partners, again whether related or unrelated, intimate or not intimate, and oriented one way or another with respect to gender. Through research, design, assessment, and improvement, lawyers are learning to develop, offer, and deliver cohabitation agreements of varying length, complexity, and components. Those agreements, delivered in connection with a variety of simple or complex services, can to a significant extent protect the financial and law interests of the cohabiting partners, in common and individually. Cohabitation agreements can anticipate and protect against the consequences of illness, injury, death, and partnership dissolution, not to the full extent of marriage laws but yet to a significant extent.

Cohabiting partners will not necessarily know of the availability of a lawyer's cohabitation agreement and related services. Marrying partners generally know of the availability of prenuptial agreements, although even in the case of that product, it took the work of enterprising and discerning lawyers to develop and market the product for clients' greatest benefit. Responsible, discerning, and enterprising lawyers will also market cohabitation agreements, if the need indeed exists and the product adequately serves it. If the lawyer has designed the cohabitation product and service effectively, then the product and service will benefit clients, more clients will learn of product-and-service availability, and specific demand for cohabitation agreements will grow, with concomitant benefit to the cohabiting partners and their communities.

For another example, consider again the aging small-business owners and family-business owners whose primary objective may be to harvest retirement assets from the business without necessarily relinquishing or conveying ownership or control. Standard estate-planning and business-planning products like wills and buy/sell agreements would not serve those clients' asset-harvest objectives. Enterprising lawyers are instead combining their estate-planning and business-planning skills with the expertise of financial and investment professionals to package new asset-harvest law products and services. Using the new products and services, those clients will be able to achieve new objectives that match, preserve, and reward their commitments. The clients and their families and communities find new value and productivity due to the ingenuity and enterprise of lawyers.

The point is that the same client population can have somewhat different or markedly different objectives, to which an effective lawyer matches appropriately packaged products and services. A client's difference in objectives can make all of the difference in the appropriateness of the product or service. Olympic-quality runners benefit incrementally (when increments make all of the difference) from the most sophisticated running products and training services. Health joggers get no benefit from those same sophisticated products and services but may get substantial benefit from other basic running products and training services. In the same way, enterprising lawyers discern the breadth of client objectives in order to design and offer matching products and services.

Law products and services can vary widely in their basic forms, no matter the particular use to which the lawyer and client put them. Lawyers are familiar with the traditional transactional products including correspondence, memoranda, opinion letters, requests for proposal, proposals, letters of intent, letters of commitment, offer forms, acceptance forms, leases, purchase options, buy/sell agreements, notes, mortgages, deeds, bills of sale, wills, trusts, powers of attorney, and the varied forms of articles, bylaws, and operating agreements for different business forms. Lawyers also know the traditional dispute-resolution products like notices of claims, demands, summonses, complaints, answers, interrogatories, document requests, admission requests, subpoenas, motions, briefs, responses, replies, pretrial orders, jury instructions, verdict forms, judgments, satisfactions of judgment, settlement agreements, and releases.

These traditional products are just a few of the forms through which lawyers package services. They barely begin to touch the products that lawyers have developed for specialty fields and currently use in those fields. Some lawyers are less familiar with the product and service possibilities latent in new and different forms, especially those emerging through mobile technology. Those new and different products and services can include e-journals, special advisories, interactive websites, compliance notices, e-retainers for constant mobile access, shared-document-drafting services, private and restricted-access portals, mobile teleconferencing, mobile applications, compliance audits, risk audits, protocol development, disaster planning, and a range of instructional, educational, and training tools.

Practice Tip

A lawyer's best strategy to survive within a firm may be to become an expert in an area that in which the firm has no other experts. Being one of 35 litigators can be problematic, especially when the firm needs only 34. Yet if you are the only civil litigator in your firm who also handles criminal environmental work for your firms' corporate clients, then you substantially increase your chances of survival.

For a specific example of an unconventional law service serving an emerging market, corporate training around law-related issues is a field ripe for lawyers and law firms to develop as service providers. Changes in healthcare regulations, nonprofit regulations, and the regulation of other fields mean that organizations must train their management and personnel to comply with those new regulatory regimes. Sarbanes-Oxley requirements for charitable nonprofits and Affordable Care Act requirements for nonprofit hospitals are just two examples. Consider how you can fashion and offer these regulatory-training products and services. Consider how your field is changing and what the needs of local businesses and agencies are to respond to those changes.

With appropriate study and design, your regulatory-training services can be more than information sessions on the latest legislation or regulation. You need not stop at simply offering information and discussion. Consider developing a value-added and value-measured service integrating your regulatory expertise into the client's business systems. Use your research and analytical skills to build your professional expertise in organizational behavior and development. Then connect your regulatory-training services with the client's business goals through processes designed to effect positive change within the client's organization.

For example, Dave Basarab in *Predictive Evaluation: Ensuring Training Delivers Business and Organizational Results* writes of linking training to specific business outcomes in an assessed, validated, and predictive manner. Have participants articulate intentions matching your regulatory-training goals. Then assess for the organization client the relevance of participants' intentions. Then have the participants articulate their adoptions, meaning activities that they commit to doing to carry out their intentions. Then assess for the organization client the relevance of participants' adoptions. Then define the business-value impact measurements of participants' adoptions, so that the organization client can track the value-add from your regulatory training. This feedback loop ensures measurement, continuous improvement, and ultimate value in your training. Distinguish your regulatory-training work with these values.

Law-product development should not occur entirely on the fly. Lawyers can acquire product-development strategies through the kind of mock-client exercises that mimic product development in other trades, professions, industries, and fields. Again, even interviewing or surveying family members, friends, and law firm staff, and testing innovative products with them, can help lawyers package new law products and services. Lawyers must see their craft as involving continual creation and refinement of law products and services. Lawyers who do will remain current and engaged, while finding rich new possibilities to serve many more underserved clients in new fields. Consider next the fitness of those products and services.

Reflection

1. Do you offer anything to clients that you would consider a packaged law product or service? Do you, in other words, have a relatively uniform product or service that you offer to clients at an established price? If so, then how did you develop that product or service? Why did you choose to offer it rather than some other product or service?

2. How many different law products or services do you offer? How did you choose those products or services—using what criteria?

3. Do you provide to individual clients more than one different product or service? Could you offer other products or services to the same clients who purchase your current products or services?

3. How are your law products and services like the products and services offered by other lawyers? Do your clients know that your products and services are like other lawyers' products and services? What comparisons are your clients making of your products and services to other lawyers' products and services, that is, by what means or with what information sources?

4. How are your law products and services distinct from the products and services of other lawyers? Do your clients know that your products or services are distinct from the products and services of other lawyers? If so, then how do they know? What contrasts are your clients making with to the products and services offered by other lawyers? In what respects are their distinctions valuable to clients?

5. Return for a moment to the market segments you listed at the end of the prior section. What objectives do your law products and services satisfy for those market segments? How could you adjust your law products or services to serve better those market segments in their objectives?

D. Fitness

The associate knew that he was having a classically bad day, one in a growing string of bad days. Where, he thought, was the bottom? He still hoped that he was reaching a nadir in his adjustment to law practice and that he would be on the upswing soon. More than hoping, the associate knew that he needed to gain some momentum in the other direction. Two of the partners had frankly told him so. In those encounters, which had happened on the same day just a week ago, the associate once again had a vague sense that the partners were not so much criticizing him as speaking an anxiety that they had about their own work. Things were not measuring up at the firm, and the responsibility for that failing was not entirely or even primarily the associate's failing.

The associate's problem this particularly bad day had to do with something that he had begun to notice repeatedly about the work that he was doing and how the partners and their clients received it. Over and over again, the associate was producing work product that did not meet expectations, whether the expectations of the partners or those of the clients. The associate had initially thought that his work was itself deficient—that something was wrong with the associate's basic skills and that he alone was not competent. Those days had disturbed the associate, although at the same time he believed that he would soon learn the skills that would make him competent and his work sufficient.

Yet gradually, the associate had on substantial evidence come to believe that his work was itself good. He had reviewed it repeatedly after each rejection and even met with one of his particularly critical old law professors about it. His work product gave no indication that it was deficient. It was all solid, sometimes even outstanding. He had good law understanding and had even learned solid writing and researching skills in law school. The problem lay outside of his work product. The associate was not really the problem.

On this particularly bad day, when he received yet another rebuke even after the two critical evaluations a week ago, the associate realized instead that something was wrong in the way that the associate, the partners, or the firm matched what he was producing to the expectations of the partners and clients. His work, though fine, did not fit criteria that he could not discern. The partners and their clients had not made their expectations sufficiently clear. He was a good shot but was shooting in the dark where even a genius would rarely hit the target. The associate was not ready to challenge the partners or even silently to blame them. He knew that doing so would be, well, counter-productive—that he may as well start looking for a new job before doing so. Yet the associate was going to figure it out. He had to, or he was not long for his current position.

~

Because she knew her clients and their needs so well, and had such a wide range of products and services to offer them, the solo practitioner usually had satisfied clients. When she first started in practice, she had some of the expected hiccups. Here and there, a client whom she had served would return, usually with polite questions about her work for them. The practitioner knew what those polite questions meant, that the clients were not finding their objectives to have been met. Those communications usually went well, though. The practitioner would review with the client the objectives that they had discerned together and then listen carefully to the client's concerns with her work product and its results.

Sometimes, the practitioner had indeed misunderstood the client's objective, in which instance the practitioner would promptly offer a different product or service, sometimes at no cost to the client and then sometimes at discounted or full cost, each time depending on the circumstance. At other times, the practitioner and client realized together that the client had new needs, in which instance the practitioner would offer the appropriate product or service at its fair price. These occasions had grown fewer in number and frequency as the practitioner grew more skilled, although the practitioner still had them and expected that she always would have them.

Indeed, the practitioner had come to appreciate the opportunities these occasions gave her to offer wider and more effective service. No client had yet succeeded in ruffling her, even though a few had clearly tried. As those clients would complain about her product or service, she would simply listen carefully and patiently to their complaints for the objective that they were trying to achieve. As soon as she discerned their true objective, or maybe a new objective different from their former objective, she would articulate that objective back to them along with her proposal to modify the product or supply a new product. She knew that her clients were not criticizing her or her product, even though some of her clients knew no better than to complain that way. The practitioner had such apt skill at re-fitting her products and services even for her few unhappy and cantankerous clients that she almost drew more confidence from these rare episodes than from her steady stream of satisfied clients.

~

An underserved client deserves not just any law product or service but *fit* products and services. Just because a population is underserved, finding only difficulty access to justice, does not mean that lawyers serve justice by providing access through unfit products and services. The fitness of law products and services is a critical ingredient in any law practice. Lawyers can design excellent law products and deliver excellent law services, truly top-of-the-line in every respect, meaning current, sensitive, and responsive to needs. Yet if those products and services do not fit the client's needs, they are can be worse than useless. Unfit products and services can mislead clients into believing that they are served when they have not been and that they are prepared and protected when they are not.

Fitness is not a question of quality, treated in the next section. Rather, fitness implies that the client has adequately specified the client's needs and objectives, and that the lawyer has selected, modified, and adjusted the product or service to meet those needs and objectives. Fitness implies a process as much as a product. The fitness that a lawyer must satisfy is not the fitness of merchantability, meaning that the law product is merely suited for the law product's ordinary purpose—a will as a will, a lease as a lease. Clients do not merely walk unattended into a law shop to select off-the-shelf products and services. Rather, clients communicate their needs and objectives to lawyers, who then play a critical role selecting and supplying the right product or service—a will but with co-personal representatives, a lease but with a termination clause on sale. Lawyers supply law products and services to specific clients to meet specified needs.

The concept of fitness creates a useful tension with the concept of designing standardized law products and services, treated in the prior sections. A lawyer's ability to design standard products and services that serve a client population's objectives does not mean that the same lawyer must sacrifice fitting those products and services to individual clients. The two concepts—standard design and individual fitness—are not at odds with one another. All consumer products have standard platforms. Yet many consumer products permit an extraordinary degree of individual fit. Effective lawyers design, implement, and control efficient processes to fit their standard products and services to individual clients.

Consider smart phones as an example. Electronics manufacturers design, produce, and sell standardized smart phones. Millions of individual consumers purchase those smart phones and their accompanying software and services according to standard licensing and purchase agreements. Yet in the process, sales personnel and individual consumers work together to customize each smart phone to the consumer's individual preferences. Sales personnel and consumers customize cases, screens, services, applications, contact databases, and other content and functions, until each smart phone reflects the style, preferences, and needs of the individual consumer. The same customization goes on with cars, computers, coffees, and myriad other consumer products and services.

Steps to Take

When you analyze a fitness issue in your practice, consider your own experiences with other service providers outside the practice of law. How did an upscale hotel or restaurant modify their service to meet your preferences and special needs? How did the provider of a medical service subtly change their routine to personalize their service for you? You can analyze the skills and practices that other service professionals use to improve the fitness of your law products and services.

For law products and services, fitness does not alone mean inserting the correct names and addresses into a standard lease, contract, will, or other law document. *Completing* a law document or service correctly by, for instance, ensuring that the names and subjects are all correct is not the same as *fitting* it to meet the client's objectives. Fitting a product may instead entail adding or removing substantive terms to a document that affect or may affect the legal rights and obligations of the client and others. Fitting a service may entail the lawyer taking additional actions or refraining from additional actions, whether (for instance) giving noticing, making filings, or refraining from notice and filings. Fitting implies the lawyer's exercise of professional judgment, not merely the scrivener's act of correct data entry and adjustment.

Consider the example of providing a service to a divorcing client, whether that service is drafting an estate plan, filing a bankruptcy proceeding, or assisting with the closing on a home sold by the client owner. The fact of the impending, pending, or recent divorce likely has significant direct implications for your service in those other areas. You must account for those implications in your service. Yet even if the fact of the divorce has no direct implications to the service you are providing (which in itself is unlikely) then you may still find it appropriate to fit your service to the divorcing client. You may offer meetings with or communications to the other spouse or, the opposite, a particular degree of confidentiality regarding information (contact information, relationships, etc.) that one would ordinarily otherwise disclose.

Fitting also implies tailoring the service to the client, not just the product for the client. Some clients require in-person meetings because of reading, hearing, language, or other limitations. Other clients prefer in-person meetings to personalize the relationship, product, and service. Enterprising lawyers can package and price the product and service accordingly. Other clients eschew in-person meetings in favor of email or other convenient communications, either because their own time is more valuable to them than meeting in person or because they prefer not to incur that additional cost of tailored in-person service. Some clients prefer to deal with office staff, while others prefer to deal with the lawyer. Each choice is about fitting the service to the client. Enterprising lawyers would not overlook that underwriting (absorbing) the additional cost of face-to-face meetings with clients may return the investment in repeat work and referrals.

Effective lawyers recognize individual differences and preferences among clients. Theories of social cognition teach that individuals learn through observation of social behaviors, developing and adopting cognitive schema through which they process environmental stimuli toward rewarding behavior. Not all clients share the same social observations building the same cognitive schema. Attribution theory cautions professionals to be astute and observant in selecting and modifying services to account for individual client cognition, preference, and benefit. What attracts and works for one client may offend and fail for another. Cultural and demographic markers may give clues to client preferences but may just as well bias and prejudice the professional's advice and destroy the desired effect of the service. Consider taking the Implicit Association Test, maintained online by Harvard University's Project Implicit, to evaluate your own attribution bias.

Steps to Take

Be aware of consumer decision-making and consumer-socialization issues when fitting law products and services to specific individuals. Consumers are savvy, each in their own way. They learn purchasing behaviors within their own social and cultural contexts. They develop decision-making protocols that work for them, not necessarily for you. You might be surprised how your clients evaluate the fitness of your services. Do not be surprised. Find out from them. Ask them.

A lawyer's effective cross-cultural service depends on the lawyer's ability to discern and adjust to each client's unique combination of attitudes, outlooks, attributes, and preferences. The professional skills necessary to serve diverse clients effectively are more complex than commonly assumed. Effective lawyers are keenly aware of their own viewpoint bias and able to recognize and mediate the viewpoint bias of others. A common assumption is that all that effective service to diverse clients requires is an open attitude toward the client. Actually, though, the skills necessary for effective cross-cultural service are significantly more complex. Inference theory encourages us to attribute client behaviors and beliefs not to client attributes but to client experiences—to causes rather than capacities. Developing an acute sense of how cross-cultural interaction works can help you acquire the skills necessary for effective cross-cultural service.

Professionals practice using hidden frameworks, protocols, or heuristics. A framework for cross-cultural interaction is an excellent way for a lawyer to discern quickly and adjust effectively to each client's unique processing and preferences. You can use such a framework to create for yourself an interactive multi-dimensional professional personality fitting to more clients. Individual clients are in some respects like all others, like some others, and like no others. Effective lawyers see clients at three levels: the universal, the group, and the individual. We make (in the social-psychology lexicon) better idiographic assessment when we see how these three levels work together to form the unique dignity of each client.

One framework that professionals can employ involves five dimensions that lawyers experience with every client. Your sensitive treatment of those five dimensions should place you on a solid cross-cultural foundation with any client. The five dimensions consider the client's (1) communication, (2) cognition, (3) reference, (4) resources, and (5) relationship. Notice that the five dimensions are (1) linguistic, (2) logical, (3) narrative, (4) strategic, and (5) personal. Effective lawyers possess attributive competence in these five dimensions because every client speaks, thinks, refers to shared knowledge, strategizes from resources, and relates. These five dimensions identify multiple intelligences through which clients operate. Improved cross-cultural skill in one dimension works synergistically to improve skill in other dimensions. Your sensitive idiographic assessment of these five dimensions should improve your skill in cross-cultural service.

The skills necessary for effective cross-cultural service are keys to all effective practice, not just effective cross-cultural practice. Uou can improve your skills in any setting using robust attribution frameworks. Develop a meta-cultural stance, not just cross-cultural skills. Understanding better how culture influences thought, expression, and action can enable you not only to mediate culture but also to choose and create culture. You can vary culture and draw consciously on culture for the most effective service using a robust attribution framework.

Practice Tip

Never underestimate the power of a positive connection with a client, both in serving that client and in reaching others who share the client's needs and interests.

Lawyers must see a substantial part of their role and practice as including fitting standard products to specific client needs. Effective lawyers possess or quickly develop the analytical and systems expertise necessary to fit products and services for specific clients. The first part of that process is to learn and articulate client objectives, as already indicated in the sections and discussion above. The client's objectives supply the initial criteria for the lawyer's offer of standard products and services. Yet beyond that initial selection for fitness, the lawyer must by some means inform the client of the specific product or service's features in order that the lawyer can confirm the product or service's fitness as is or modify the product or service to suit the client's needs.

One size does not fit all. Lawyers who expect standard products and services to serve clients effectively without some test for fit run the risk of having served at least some clients (and maybe many clients) poorly. Effective representation includes an interaction between lawyer and client the purpose of which is to fit the product or service to the client. That interaction can come at different times. The interaction can occur at the outset of the professional relationship, where a lawyer might immediately show to a client the features of a product or service meeting the client's needs, giving the client the opportunity to confirm the fit. The interaction can occur in a deliberative process in the middle of the representation, as in the joint redrafting of a standard document that the lawyer then processes. Or the interaction can occur at the conclusion of the representation when the product or service is complete and the lawyer explains and demonstrates its fitness and value.

The means of interaction can also vary. Lawyer and client do not always have to meet in person. A well-developed interactive website may be sufficient, or electronic communications may be enough. A well-designed intake process using a legal assistant may serve. Alternatively, fitting the product or service to the client may require an initial meeting between lawyer and client. Fit may require a joint work session after initial intake and before final processing. It may require a series of meetings at various stages of the work, such as initial meeting, work session over drafting, deliberative review, revision meeting, and final meeting for execution. Or it may require only a final meeting between lawyer and client for product or service delivery.

Practice Tip

The old saying is "do few things and do them well." Yet solo practitioners may not have that luxury. Limited service niches may not be their social and professional role. Some solo practitioners do best as street lawyers, handling most matters that come in the door. Broad practice requires organization and discipline in managing resources. Solo practitioners and other lawyers may properly delegate to a paralegal or well-trained administrative assistant intake and other functions that do not involve giving law advice.

No matter the time and means of fitting, or how simple or elaborate the process, the process of fitting must still exist. Lawyers are constantly fitting, adjusting, and in some cases redesigning standard products and services to meet specific client needs. Provide for fit in your law-practice processes. Do not ignore fit. You will save time and trouble by reducing the incidence of poorly served clients. Identify your fitness processes so that you recognize the cost and value of the time you devote to those processes. Do you sense that you rush through those client interactions in which you and the client are confirming and adjusting fit? If so, then you may have failed to recognize and price for those processes. Evaluate those processes to ensure that you are choosing the right time, using the efficient means, and using the right personnel to ensure fitness.

Consider again the new-form cohabitation agreement for unmarried couples mentioned briefly in the prior sections. A lawyer could readily offer such an agreement as an online form with no personal interaction with the client. Doing so may serve some clients, in some cases and with appropriate instructions and information. The lawyer's judgment as to which clients to whom to offer such basic agreements in what situations and with what instructions is a fitness question. The effective lawyer would give due thought to that question. The lawyer might then discern that fitting a more complex cohabitation agreement to serve a client would require one, two, or more meetings including recommendations that the other party to the agreement retain independent counsel.

You should see from this example that these questions of who to offer what products and services under what processes are the very core of law practice. These questions entail critical law analysis and informed lawyer judgment. The complexity of these questions is ordinarily well beyond the client's understanding. Clients ordinarily have little clue about lawyer conflicts of interests, for instance. They do not ordinarily discern the contrasting benefits and risks of a simpler or more-complex document or service. An effective lawyer must consider carefully these questions of fitness, so that clients make informed judgments about the fitness of the lawyer's products and services. The efficiency of a lawyer's fitness process likely has as much or more to do with the internal success of the lawyer's enterprise than any other measure. This book will turn in the next part on pricing to the lawyer's efficiency. Consider the last packaging issue, quality, before turning to those pricing issues.

Reflection

To answer the following questions, consider again the most common product or service that you provide to clients:

1. What process do you follow to fit the product or service to the particular client? Where did you learn that process or how did you develop it? Have you studied the process at any time? Have you made any changes to it?

2. Who (lawyers, paralegals, secretaries, or other staff) is involved in that process at what stages? What training do they have in the process? What supervision do they have? How effectively do you feel each person in the process performs? What would help them be more effective?

3. How efficient is your process? Can you eliminate or condense any of the steps in the process? Are you leaving out steps that make your process less efficient?

4. Do you automate any of the process by electronic or similar means? If not, then could you do so? What programs are other lawyers using to automate their document-assembly processes?

PACKAGING SERVICES
Populations
Objectives
Services
Fitness
Quality

E. Quality

One of the things that had attracted the new associate to his firm was that everything that the firm did seemed to be first class. At first, the firm's always-the-best approach made perfect sense to the associate. As he began to notice the significant differences among how lawyers and firms presented themselves and the quality of their work to the public, he had even wondered why other lawyers and firms could be so blind as to not see these quality issues and do as his firm did. Why didn't the other firms all use the same watermarked bond paper for every final transactional document, embossed letterhead for every correspondence, messenger services, catered lunch meetings, and other quality signals? Of course, he thought he knew why, that they both did not get it and, if they did, could not afford it. His firm's top-of-the-line approach had been in that sense strongly reassuring.

Now, though, after many months of practice at the firm, the associate was not so sure that he was right about the quality thing. He was finding his firm's quality practices less and less reassuring. He had even heard the partners talking about proposals to reduce expenses that included cutting out the catering entirely. As a result, the associate now took no reassurance from the catering. Indeed, just the opposite was true. The catering now made him nervous, as a sign that the firm's management might not have been as wise as he had at first thought.

Then came the managing partner's expense memorandum. Every lawyer and staff member in the firm received a copy of it. It remained the big topic of discussion within the firm for weeks, which was an eternity within the usual life cycle of hot topics. The firm had to cut expenses, it said. Every employee was responsible. Every employee was to examine every practice to find ways to reduce expenses. The memorandum mentioned food, travel, and supplies specifically. The firm's secretaries found big new boxes of plain white office paper in the supply room. Although the memorandum had said nothing specific about any particular practice, the secretaries began to hoard the watermarked bond paper and embossed stationery. Everything that they now did for the associate was on plain white paper, whether correspondence, memoranda, or even final documents.

The change was an ominous daily reminder for the associate that things were amiss at the firm in a way that probably affected him as much or more than anyone. The associate was actually a little surprised at his reaction, though. While he felt more and more resigned that things had changed at the firm for him, likely forever, he was also beginning to feel a little relief. Either his days at the firm were numbered and with a low rather than high number, or something else was going to change for him and the firm soon. He actually began to cheer up each time he saw his final documents and correspondence going out on plain white paper, even if he somewhat rued the impression the change must have had on those outside the firm who, like he previously did, judged those quality impressions to be important.

~

The new solo practitioner had learned early that she needed to adjust how she presented herself and her work from population to population. She knew that the little things counted, and not always in the same way to every client. At first, she had not done much of anything to impress any client. She certainly had not ordered any of the fancy embossed letterhead and watermarked paper that she saw coming out of some of the big firms and even a few of the small firms in town. The practitioner took care to make her computer-generated letterhead look a little fancy like the big firms in town. And she did buy a laser printer rather than a cheap ink-jet printer. Other than those concessions, though, she had initially thought little of how her work appeared to those clients who read and paid for it. The contents were what counted to her and, she thought, to the clients.

Yet something had soon changed that made her go ahead and order some of that fancy embossed letterhead. She was not sure what had been the motivating factor. It might have been when she met an experienced solo practitioner to discuss client referrals. The experienced solo had said how impressed he had been with some documentation the new solo had prepared in a transaction that they two of them had worked on representing different parties. The experienced solo's comment had made the new solo go back and compare their work. To her surprise, the main difference that she had found was that the experienced solo's product just looked better. The contents were about the same, but the new solo recognized immediately that the experienced solo had marked, branded, or otherwise identified his work as distinctly his.

The new solo had never really thought that professional identity or distinction was that important, except that she already knew in her own mind that she regarded the experienced solo as distinctly professional. He was both masterful *and* known for it. She, by contrast, was competent, sometimes even masterful (as the experienced solo had commented), but had no clear sense that she showed it to others. Mastery was certainly not a matter of embossed letterhead. Yet she could see that in some circumstances, she *and her clients* might benefit from communicating among themselves and to others that her mastery existed. Some clients might want her to think enough of her own work to package it in a way that communicated to others that it was quality, even if they could not otherwise distinguish her work from lesser products.

The new solo's reflection made her begin to recognize opportunities that seemed to call for embossed letterhead and watermarked bond stationery. It took only a few more such instances when she found herself suddenly regretting that she could not convey a product in a finer package for her to decide to try it. The new solo had developed a varied clientele from the very poor to the relatively well heeled. She began to notice the quality of some of the notes, cards, and correspondence that she received from clients, and not always her wealthier clients. She knew that she could put off some of her clients by in any way standing on airs. She knew that she needed and wanted to make her law products and services more affordable, not less affordable.

Yet by modifying some of her practices and segmenting them for various clients and services, she found that she could reduce overall costs while increasing some costs and, with the increases, actually increase the appearance of her work as a quality product. The next time that she wrote the experienced solo who had complimented her work, she used her new embossed letterhead. Folding the finished letter into its embossed envelope gave her a satisfaction that she had never previously felt, that her work not only was good but looked as if it was good. Are appearances that important, she pondered silently to herself with a broad smile?

~

Just as an underserved client deserves a fit product, the underserved client also deserves a quality product. *Quality*, though, does not presume to mean complex, intricate, multifaceted, detailed, featured, fancy, or lengthy. Quality often means having high value and worth to the client, particularly excellent for the specific person for whom and purpose for which the lawyer supplies the product or service. The challenge is not to increase the product's complexity unduly in a way that makes the product unaffordable. Effective lawyers instead ensure that product and service development looks at both increasing the quality while decreasing the cost and complexity—the challenge of any good design.

Notice that quality has a client-centered aspect to it. In effective firms, clients define quality. Just because the lawyer judges the product to be of high quality does not mean that the client will, too. Quality is a client-centered, market-driven, results-oriented concept, in which the lawyer's goal is to satisfy client needs while exceeding client expectations. Lawyers achieve quality by constantly improving products and services through systematic assessment of client satisfaction. Client satisfaction requires lawyer leadership, research, training, and empowerment in product and service design, and integration of firm systems.

Practice Tip

The best client is the one whom a former client sent to you. Referrals from former clients are the most reliable way to build a practice. Potential clients whom former clients refer will nearly always retain you. They also begin the representation with a higher level of confidence and trust than clients do whom you won by advertising or other methods. How do you begin marketing through former clients? Start one client at a time, with masterful, high-value, reasonably priced service.

Among expert managers of firms, quality has a second dimension beyond client satisfaction, referring to the consistency of the processes that the firm uses to procure the client's satisfaction. A client may be perfectly satisfied with the law product or service. Yet if the lawyer bungled his or her way through producing that ultimately satisfying product or service, requiring the firm to incur substantial unnecessary costs, then the lawyer will not have exactly been a quality producer. In management terms, quality has evolved beyond the unpredictable if ultimately worthy work of the lone artisan. Quality has even evolved well beyond simply inspection, consistent quality control, or even statistical (measured and analyzed) quality control. Quality today also implies statistical process control (measured and analyzed prevention), continuous improvement, and benchmarking to standards so high that we would once have thought them unattainable.

Quality issues can have far greater impact than untrained firm managers appreciate. The untrained only see the tip of the poor-quality iceberg. You might imagine only that a lawyer need only rework a poor-quality law product or service, losing only the time and expense of doing the work again. Yet also count the additional resources the lawyer must devote to accomplish expedited repeat work. Consider the liability risks and costs from sub-standard work. Add the administrative cost of accepting and processing the client complaint, and adjusting billing. Count the loss of client goodwill, loss of professional reputation among former or prospective clients, burden or disruption of other professional relationships (judges, experts, opposing counsel), and discouragement of skilled and committed employees. Poor quality has other hidden costs involving prevention, appraisal, compensation, and intangibles.

Expert process managers use the term *total quality* to refer to business efficiency, workforce sustainability, and other excellence in the people and processes that produce the client-satisfying product or service. Effective managers examine quality measures using benchmarking. They monitor employee empowerment, expectations, and attitudes. And they ensure process efficiency. Productivity and quality do not conflict but instead support one another. Sound product and process design, not supervision and inspection, ensure quality. Quality defects are not employee faults but system failures. Firm managers, not individual staff, are foremost responsible for quality through system design. The quality goal is not to reduce product defects and service errors but to eliminate them.

Practice Tip

Many individual clients (common consumers) hesitate to retain lawyers from larger firms. They may believe that larger firms serve only corporate clients or are more expensive, or they may just have an affinity for solo and small-firm practitioners. Lawyers practicing solo or in small firms can accentuate these personal connections with simple gestures like a warm handshake or handwritten holiday card.

A firm's quality culture depends on several commitments. Those commitments certainly include the client-centered approach already mentioned. Yet the commitments also include defining process objectives and then managing and operating to achieve those objectives while continually improving processes. Quality commitments also include solving problems rather than blaming people, while developing and augmenting client, staff, and supplier relationships. Quality is a matter of firm culture and process. Quality leaders plan and assess for quality. They expect, model, and mentor for quality. They orient toward quality and train for quality. These practices help well-managed firms develop a quality culture.

Quality includes several measures. It is a collective rather than singular concept, one that professionals and other product suppliers and service providers deal in every product or service transaction. Quality first implies the lawyer's competence to evaluate and advise on the client's situation. It then implies the fitness of the document or action to the client's needs. Yet quality can also involve the service's sensitivity, its distinction (the lawyer's brand), and its consistency, particularly as it aligns with the client's expectations. The client's perception of quality is just as important as the product or service's objective character. The client who receives the lawyer's handwritten note that the lawyer prepared a document especially for the client, or the lawyer's handwritten note of appreciation along with the lawyer's bill, may well think more of the quality of the lawyer's work than the client would without those personal touches.

When quality implies fitness, it does so not quite in the way described in the prior section. The kind of fitness that the concept of quality invokes has almost as much to do with the preference of the specific client than with the function in achieving the particular purpose. Law products and services might be roughly equivalent in their function and yet be distinct in their quality, at least (again) in the eyes of the certain client. Quality within one client population can mean one thing, while quality within another client population can mean another. Different demographics and psychographics have different ways of valuing products and services. Those differences have a lot to do with the way in which the clients perceive the product or service's worth than the product or service's actual function.

Enterprising lawyers discern and supply those quality preferences. Those preferences may be in the tone, manner, and content of automated telephone messages or live greetings, and personal responses. They may particularly be, though, in the willingness of the lawyer and lawyer's staff to respond to questions, comments, or concerns. Clients, like other consumers dealing with the purveyors of other products and services, guide lawyers to quality preferences, but they often do so only indirectly, with hints and suggestions. The enterprising lawyer treats those hints as gifts.

Consider taking these steps to determine client satisfaction with the quality of your law product or service. List the attributes of your product or service that you believe your clients value. Determine from your clients the order in which they prioritize those values. Get your clients to help you assess their satisfaction with the quality of each of those values. Then link your firm's processes to those assessments. Find ways to measure and accomplish quality improvements especially in those areas that will make the greatest difference to your clients. Implement and track implementation of those improvements. Gather updated information on client satisfaction in those areas. Make this quality process a habit. Use it to integrate improvements across processes.

Practice Tip

Practitioners must know what their clients hope or expect the outcome to be and should share the client's understanding. Clients reasonably expect lawyers to treat them as partners in pursuing winning outcomes. A judge had the reputation as the smartest in the county. The judge was so smart that he consistently fashioned resolutions that neither side wanted. His resolutions were so creative that lawyers having cases on his docket settled out of court. The judge's philosophy was that good results leave both sides unhappy. A lawyer's job is different. It is not to clear the docket. A lawyer's job is to fashion winning outcomes.

Quality can also mean distinction. A quality is an attribute or feature that distinguishes the product or service from other products or services. Handbags, luggage, jewelry, wristwatches, and other items made by recognized suppliers of luxury goods may have no additional value other than their distinction, and yet consumers value that distinction. Consumer service can also have its quality identity whether in hair styling, restaurant service, or coffee barista. Professionals face the same opportunities for distinctive products and services. Doctors, dentists, accountants, tax preparers, veterinarians, and other professionals study and implement service distinction, with deliberate effort and professional design and assistance. Consumers value and consume transcendent quality, meaning distinction.

Effective lawyers can also find ways to distinguish their products and services. Identity on business cards, document folders, educational brochures, websites, and applications can all be helpful. Optimizing your website for search engines to land potential clients on your website's specific page is just one example of the power of identity. Being distinct from others can be good, and not merely for one's own benefit but for the benefit of clients. Clients draw reassurance and increased value from connection with a lawyer whom others know to have specific knowledge and skills. Distinction alone is an attribute, when the value of the product or service lies in part on the client's trust in it. Other similar products and services supplied by other lawyers may often have similar value, and still, clients draw value from knowing that their particular product or service came from their own reliable lawyer supplier.

Practice Tip

Look the part in all essential functions and details, from the appearance of your website and letterhead, to the quality of the paper that you use, to the distinction of your business card. Appearances matter. Consider carefully the costs associated with appearances. Then allocate your resources to the appearances that make the most difference. Everyone sees the appearance. Fewer know the costs.

In that respect, clients can value the most unusual forms and methods of lawyer distinction. One lawyer, who happens to be the best trial lawyer in town, eschews expensive leather briefcases in favor of old shopping bags when he goes to trial. His individual clients, often down-and-outers whom expensive accoutrements would put off or intimidate, love it, as do jurors. Another lawyer wears bright sport coats and bowties, so distinctly that he also sports bowties on his business cards, office sign, and license plates. Another lawyer, whose practice is in divorce work, wears bright red lipstick and has a bright red kiss image on her business cards and billboards. Connection through identity, maybe with a double entendre or twist, distinguishes lawyers just as it distinguishes other goods and service providers.

Yet more than seeking mere distinction, effective product-and-service suppliers distinguish their products and services in large and small ways that also add product-and-service function. Any provider can put swoosh or apple on a product, but not everyone can distinguish a product or service in a way that also makes it easier to use and more functional. Effective lawyers find ways to package products and services using distinctions that make those products and services more functional. Many of those distinctions can be in the content and some of them in the form. Both form and content can add function.

For examples as to distinct *content* quality affecting function, one lawyer might routinely provide notarized signatures in documents that do not require them, in the off chance that the notarization would make a difference to someone somewhere in the use of the document. Another lawyer might commonly enhance products, services, or deliveries of products and services by using limited powers of attorney. Depending on the complexity of the work and sophistication of the client, another lawyer might include severability, arbitration, choice-of-law, or other special clauses in every document, in ways that clients notice and value, despite having only limited or rare function. Some clients would appreciate each of these content distinctions, while others might not. The key is not to enhance the content in all ways for every client but instead to know what quality one's clients value.

Practice Tip

Judges, judicial staff, court clerks, other lawyers, and their staffs all compare the work of the solo practitioner to the work of the largest law firm. If you are that solo practitioner, then do so likewise. Measure the content and appearance of your work against the content and appearance of the greatest, not the least, practitioners. Remember the adage of "form over substance" but make it "quality form and substance."

For examples as to distinct *form* quality affecting function, one lawyer might make three sets of original documents in every transaction that appears to require only one set, in the off chance that clients might benefit by having the extra sets. Another lawyer might enclose every document in a convenient folder that bears the lawyer's name and contact information, so that the client can not only keep the documents handy and confidential but also locate the lawyer quickly whenever using the documents. Another lawyer might include convenient links in every electronic signature of every email message. Another lawyer might supply helpful compliance guides to every new client and regulatory bulletins to every current or past client. Again, the key is not to enhance the form in all ways for every client but instead to know what quality one's clients value.

Lawyers have available to them intentional means to learn about actual and perceived quality. As the second of the vignettes at the beginning of this section suggests, those means include peer review and assessment. Look at what other lawyers do, ask them what they do, and show them what you do. Effective lawyers make constant adjustments to their product and service quality both to ensure relative uniformity with the market for those products and services and to ensure relative distinction from other similar products and services. Lawyers can also survey and interview current and former clients for their quality expectations and preferences. Making a practice of asking simple questions like "How am I doing?" "Where can I improve my service?" "What would you prefer?" Asking those questions is itself a distinguishing practice, even as it also generates information on improving quality.

Product-and-service quality is also an internal attribute, meaning a reflection of the lawyer's commitment. Quality is not fundamentally about product and service features. Quality is instead about the overall impression or spirit that products and services convey. Clients will forgive a lack of quality or function in a particular product or service on a particular occasion, if they already associate quality with the lawyer and lawyer's products and services. Written products that are clear, concise, and crafted, and services that are consistent, considerate, and caring, convey lasting impressions. Given their relative lack of sophistication about complex law products and services, impressions are often all that clients have to judge the quality of a lawyer's products and services.

Practice Tip

Too many new lawyers ignore the best professional-development resources. Those resources include seasoned lawyers who will gladly act as mentor on request but also spending time in court and other places observing skilled lawyers. Ask a new lawyer who wants to be a litigator how much time they have spent just observing court. The answer may surprise you. New lawyers should not overlook the court clerk's office. Wise lawyers know that one does just as well to know the clerk as the judge. Practice begins at the clerk's office and judicial secretary's desk. Court staff will know everything from the judge's mood to the judge's preference regarding type size. They may also influence the docket, which can be your greatest enemy or friend.

Write down how you would like clients to think of you, especially as it conveys a sense of your value to them. When a potential client reads or hears your name, what would you like them to think? Articulate it in writing, and then improve upon it until it represents you in the way you think best. Then study your presentations and practices. How well or poorly do you represent how you wish others to perceive you? Practice saying your personal statement of quality until it sounds natural. Then find places to use that statement, among potential clients but especially among people who influence potential clients, whether those persons are media representatives, tax preparers, accountants, pastors, hairstylists, tradespersons, educators, stockbrokers, bankers, public officials, agency officials, social workers, or other information, product, and service providers.

A lawyer's challenge is to package affordable law products and services in ways that communicate quality, not communicate cheapness. Underserved clients deserve quality law products and services, not cheap law products. Every product and service provider faces the same challenge. The lawyer's image, reputation, professional dress, and professional demeanor should communicate value. Lawyers should not add big-law costs but should signal and build-in authentic value. With due attention to expectations, lawyers can look and act enterprising in the way that big-law so often appears so, no matter their firm size, practice field, or resources. Word processing, electronic communication, and other new technologies have been great levelers in equipping all lawyers to offer quality products and services.

Practice Tip

The next time you are at court, take a moment to watch the lawyers as they walk in and out of the courthouse. Ask yourself which ones you would hire. Practicing law, though a noble service, can also be challenging, frustrating, draining, and otherwise hard. Clients do not always see the time and effort that lawyers put into achieving results. Clients do, on the other hand, see a lawyer's outward appearance. They notice when you look and act the part of a lawyer. As you watch the lawyers around your local courthouse, are some dressed casually or slovenly, while others dress professionally—even to perfection? Whom would you hire? Would you be willing to pay more for the lawyer who treated the work with the greater respect?

Lawyers do well to give due attention to product and service quality as a significant part of a product or service's overall packaging, just as they give attention to the client populations, their objectives, the product or service meeting those objectives, and the fitness of the product or service. Having reflected on product and service packaging, consider next several issues having to do with appropriate product and service pricing.

Reflection

1. Do you see law products and services offered by non-lawyers from time to time? If so, then what do you think of the quality of those offerings? Have you observed clearly substandard law products and services offered by non-lawyers? What negative consequences, if any, have you seen from substandard law products and services offered by non-lawyers?

2. Do you see evidence of other lawyers' work from time to time? If so, then what do you think of the quality of those other lawyers' work? Do you observe a range in quality of other lawyers' products and services? Have you observed clearly substandard law products and services offered by other lawyers? If so, then do you think that the lawyer knew that the products and services were substandard?

3. Think again of your most common product or service. What is its quality?

4. Could you make your most commonly provided product or service a higher-quality product or service? If so, then what would you do to make it a higher-quality product or service? How if at all would those changes serve your clients better? How would those changes increase the cost of the product or service? Would your clients understand the increase in value? Would they pay the increase in costs?

5. Could you make your most commonly provided product or service a lower-quality product or service *without making the product or service substandard* and while decreasing the cost of the product or service? If so, then what would you do to make it a lower-quality, lower-cost product or service? Would clients still pay for the product or service?

Part II

Pricing Services

The associate had originally treated the pricing of his services as solely a matter of keeping accurate track of his hours including the detail that the firm required. That responsibility meant ensuring that by the end of each day, he had completed and submitted his electronic record of the work that he had done that day with the time that the work required, recorded down to the tenth of an hour. For his first few weeks at the firm, the quantity of his hours, accuracy of his time entries, and description of his work were his only considerations.

Gradually, though, the associate had come to learn that pricing his services entailed more than accurate recordkeeping of hours. His first lesson was that the quantity of his hours needed to be large relative to the total number of waking hours in a week. The associate could not now even remember how he had first learned that the firm expected him to record so many hours. No one had told him, at least whom he could recall. The expectation was simply everywhere, woven into the culture of the firm. The associate found himself getting to work a little earlier each day, leaving a little later, and keeping his lunch and break times a little shorter.

The associate's second lesson was that his hours need to approximate or (better yet) surpass the hours of the firm's other associates. The associate had realized this fact of life at the firm at the beginning of his second month on the job, when he received an email that disclosed the number of hours each associate had billed the prior month. He was disappointed to see that his name was at the bottom of the list, by a good measure. The associate was also disappointed because he thought that he had been in the office about as much as the other associates. Again, no one said anything about it to him. Yet the associate promptly increased his hours. He began taking work home, working several evenings and much of the weekend each week. In subsequent months, his name barely moved up from the bottom of the list.

It took a few months for the associate's other lesson to sink in. In the middle of the associate's third month on the job, the managing partner had brought a client's bill into the associate's office, asking the associate to explain why two of his projects reflected on the bill had taken so long. The associate had explained the projects calmly as he tried to discern the managing partner's concern. The managing partner had seemed satisfied with the associate's explanation.

Yet off and on for several months thereafter, the managing partner had called the associate into the partner's office to explain why other projects had taken so long. On each of these occasions, the managing partner had shaken his head slightly, after the associate's explanation, and marked on the bill. On the last such occasion, the managing partner, shaking his head more clearly this time, had said that he was going to have to reduce the associate's billed hours in half. Caught off guard, the associate had asked the managing partner what was wrong with the hours. The managing partner had answered only, "Too many." The associate could tell that the managing partner had not liked the associate's question.

The associate's lessons in pricing his services, like so much else he was learning at the firm, seemed more painful and unsettling than they should have been. No one had explained the firm's pricing model. The associate had no clear idea of the cost of his work or how it compared to the firm's pricing criteria. He suspected from his encounters with the managing partner that the firm had no objective pricing criteria, only the subjective judgment of the managing partner, the basis for which the managing partner was unwilling or unable to disclose.

~

When she started, the solo practitioner had been uneasy about billing her clients. The practitioner soon realized that her uneasiness was in part from her ill-considered attitude toward billing. She had no conceptual basis for billing. The practitioner took a while to discern and then improve her billing approach. She knew that her law services had value to her clients. She wanted to be able to convey that same impression to her clients. She could not live with herself or satisfy her clients unless she did so. The question was what criteria she and her clients would use to judge how soundly she priced her law products and services.

The practitioner did not take long to discern the criteria on which her clients should take confidence in her billing practices. Her services first of all had to be affordable to her clients or they would not pay for them. That much was obvious to her. She knew her clients well enough to know their income levels and how they spent their money. She would have to give more thought to what impact the cost of her law services would have on their monthly budgets. The practitioner took longer to discern that she had to price each law service *relative to its value* to her clients. She had to price according to how her clients would use her law services to preserve or improve their situation. The practitioner had no illusion. Her clients were highly price conscious. Although they were not sophisticated in the law or even in personal finance, they knew the value of value. She had to show them that her law services justified their price.

The practitioner also knew that the price of her law services had to be apparent. Her clients were shoppers. They bought groceries, clothing, cars, haircuts, insurance, and other goods and services knowing their price before they committed to them. They would not buy her law services unless they knew in advance what they were paying for them. The practitioner also felt that her clients need to have choices in what they paid for her law services. They had choices and compared prices for just about everything else. She felt that they should have choices and be able to compare prices for her law services.

The practitioner knew the last piece of her pricing puzzle innately. She had entered law school valuing her integrity. She valued it even more by the time that she graduated. She liked to be liked. She wanted every client satisfied and happy with her. Unfortunately, as a practitioner she had quickly learned that she could not please every client. Client issues were too challenging, complex, and uncertain for her to guarantee their outcomes. Yet she could still price and perform in ways that made the clients respect her, even with the worst of outcomes. She realized that respect depended on price accountability. When she had provided the law product or service, and the client had paid the price for it, she needed to remain accountable for the product or service's performance and value.

~

Packaging a product or service useful to an underserved client population is only a first step in a lawyer's overall enterprise. Packaging invokes one set of skills, outlined above. Pricing invokes a different set of considerations, especially as to emerging client populations. To price a law product or service effectively involves knowledge, investigation, and activities unlike those that will serve to discern and package a useful law service or product. Product and service pricing is a subject that lawyers seldom discuss and law schools do not necessarily address. Yet every lawyer, whether in a large or small firm or as a solo practitioner, must be responsible to the product or service's price if the lawyer is to remain effective. Some associates in some firms can get away for a while without addressing pricing considerations. That honeymoon will not last long.

Practice Tip

New associates need to limit the number of questions they ask of managing partners. This hard lesson seems counterintuitive. Supervision is important.

Mentors are important. Avoiding mistakes is important. Yet managing partners set directions, establish systems, and design and assess processes. They have less interest in directing and controlling individual lawyers. In fact, they employ those lawyers to exercise their creative judgment in pursuit of the firm's service mission and within its practice guidelines. Firms evaluate lawyers on their ability to solve problems on their own within those guidelines. Use your judgment. Take strategic, not tactical, questions to your managing partner.

Pricing is ultimately an essential consideration for all lawyers in private practice. Pricing is particularly significant when reaching emerging service populations. Before considering five specific aspects related to pricing practices for lawyers, consider some basic pricing theory. We do not expect many lawyers or firms to perform or retain others to perform the complex pricing analyses that major organizations use. That expertise is well beyond the means and needs of most solo practitioners and small-firm lawyers. Yet a practitioner's rudimentary knowledge of pricing theory can aid the practitioner's insight into pricing's effects on practice. Within their law fields, lawyers have great skill in substituting simple heuristics for complex knowledge. Lawyers can exercise the same skill using inter-disciplinary knowledge to improve their practices.

Steps to Take

Try learning two or three of the pricing theories you read about in this section. Once you grasp those theories, use each theory to develop a different pricing option or approach for each product or service you offer. When a client rejects a pricing option, you will then have additional options to offer. Over time, you will develop the skill of easily identifying which clients will respond best to which pricing option. This skill optimizes your time, productivity, and bottom line. You base your skill not on blind guess but by knowing how pricing influences client choices.

Anyone familiar with basic pricing theory, including most practicing lawyers, knows the principle of what pricing experts call *price optimization.* Products and services tend to have elastic demand, meaning that the lower the price, the greater the willingness of the customers and clients to purchase. High prices discourage purchases.

Most law products and services have elastic demand, although a few (think of homicide defense) have inelastic or less elastic demand. Product-and-service producers, like lawyers and firms, tend also to have a mix of fixed costs, incurred whether or not clients purchase, and variable costs, incurred only when clients purchase. In the case of elastic demand and mixed fixed-and-variable costs, an optimum price exists that will give the lawyer or firm maximum return for the offering.

Although most lawyers know these basics of pricing, as in the case of marketing, pricing is a subject that lawyers can research. Pricing involves both internal considerations of the firm's costs and revenues, and external considerations of client demand and market competition. Internal and external considerations are both important. Lawyers must price products and services in a manner that enable them to continue to practice. Yet lawyers must also price products and services at levels that clients will afford, and that bears appropriate relationship to (higher, lower, or the same as) what other lawyers are charging. Pricing above the market requires additional value. Pricing at the market requires differentiation of products and services. Pricing below the market will likely require elastic demand increasing the number of clients enough to justify the lower price per client.

Lawyers and firms can and do price by cost. They determine the product or service cost, estimate or test the market at that cost, and then offer the product or service only if it produces enough revenue to pay the service's cost. As you can see, a problem with cost pricing is that demand will then determine whether the firm can continue to offer the service. If clients have no demand for the product priced relative to its cost, then the firm will not be able to offer it for long without underwriting it through other services.

Practice Tip

Associates practicing at medium and large firms carry a different mindset than the solo practitioner does. Associates work on projects that partners generate. Partners handle most client contact, which can make associates little more than profit-center labor. Associates please partners more so than they please clients, and associates do so by working more hours rather than fewer hours to produce the same-quality law product or service. In every role, lawyers should be making of themselves capital, rather than labor. Make yourself a repository and generator of value.

Lawyers and firms can also price by demand rather than by cost. Demand pricing enables the lawyer or firm to change the product or service features to adjust the product price to that level that generates optimum total return. The lawyer or firm can then offer any featured product or service that generates sufficient total return to pay the service's cost. Indeed, either the firm can set the price where it knows clients will pay and then adjust the product or service features to the allowable cost, or it can test various features at different prices to find a product or service the demand for which justifies its cost. Demand pricing is more flexible than cost pricing.

Demand pricing intimates what pricing experts call an *exchange-value model.* New law products and services will have no demand data from which to establish initial prices. In the offer of a new product or service, a lawyer or firm can estimate the value of the product or service to the client, and then price the product or service in proportion to that value. Using an exchange-value model for pricing also enables the lawyer or firm to develop marketing that communicates those values to clients. Exchange-value models help set prices while simultaneously communicating product or service value.

Whenever you can, adopt exchange-value models for your practice's pricing. Demonstrate to clients that you price according to their value. The Uniform Task-Based Management System developed by the American Corporate Counsel Association, American Bar Association Section on Litigation, and major corporate clients and law firms, has exchange-value pricing theory as its basis. The System classifies, standardizes, and codes litigation activities in order to provide corporate clients with more-meaningful information about the performance and value of corporate-law services. Corporate clients needed to know what their retained lawyers were doing relating to the clients' needs, not just that those lawyers were skilled—and expensive.

Standardized billing codes allow corporate clients to analyze product and service value across cases, matters, and firms. Standard codes also enable the firms to demonstrate greater value and improved efficiencies for the clients. You do not have to bill by narrative description of traditional law tasks. By adopting billing codes that reflect clients' business-value judgments, firms are able to show specifically how each billed task within their products and services support any number of client objectives. Coding schemes can link to client business values like budgeting, planning, preparation, management, monitoring, strategizing, risk evaluation, option generating, training, marketing, product development, identifying and preserving intellectual property, financing, and profitability.

Practice Tip

Managing fees can be as complex as much of the law work itself. Time spent developing and refining your pricing structure is well worth it. Your fees must bear the right relationship to the market. They must equate with value. They must show the client that you are frugal with their money. Yet they also have to keep you gainfully employed. Charging fixed fees can be an excellent idea. You still need to account for every second of the effort so that you can review your fixed fee to ensure you are meeting your hourly cost and income target.

Pricing experts recognize yet another helpful pricing theory known as *perception pricing.* In perception pricing, lawyers and firms price according to market surveys of what clients will pay for products and services having various features. Perception pricing offers two advantages over exchange-value pricing. The first advantage is that perception pricing can accurately determine the actual market for products and services at specific prices, not just the predicted value about which clients may not be aware. The second advantage to perception pricing is that market research can determine feature packages that optimize offerings. Perception pricing answers the important question for what features clients will pay at what price.

Pricing researchers call this latter process of optimizing features with price *conjoint analysis.* Conjoint analysis, in which clients share their preferences among products, services, and features, can help firms match prices to the maturity of product and service markets. Markets for products and services can be new, evolving, or mature. Firms can use exchange-value and perception pricing to help clients value and purchase new products and services. They can also use conjoint analysis to help price differently featured products and services into an evolving market for not-so-new products and services. In mature markets, firms tend to use price optimization to set prices.

Steps to Take

Lawyers perform what could pass for a quasi-conjoint analysis, when they appreciate how clients experience lawyers and the market for law products and services. When engaging clients in conversational tone during intake, skilled lawyers are evaluating their clients' experiences to discern the optimum pricing model to offer. You need not necessarily question the client explicitly. For example, simply learning the other firms that a client has approached or engaged can tell you much about the client's pricing perception. Your pricing information and approach should differ when a client's only experience has been with the rock-bottom flat-fee pricing of Jones & Jones or, by contrast, the perceptual pricing of Highwater Associates.

Conjoint analysis pushes the lawyer offering the product or service to identify the specific attributes of the product or service that clients will value. Sensitive pricing research can help the lawyer or firm develop a price-to-benefits map. Clients want to pay prices that leave them value. Price-to-benefits maps help lawyers and firms judge where in the pricing range of specific products clients will perceive sufficient value to make more purchases of the product or service. Every price has a zone of indifference where small price changes make little or no difference in the number of purchases. Changes beyond that indifference zone may make the product value-advantaged or value-disadvantaged, increasing or decreasing client demand.

Practice Tip

Some new practitioners believe that you get new clients by under-pricing all other local lawyers, perhaps charging one-half the going rate. Nothing is further from the truth. Clients value services not based on rock-bottom pricing but on quality results coupled with positive effort. Rock-bottom pricing may simply communicate low value and skill. Clients are often reasonable. They know when they present you with a difficult task. You can satisfy clients with less-successful results when the client sees your loyalty, skill, and tenacity.

Clients will pay just to have someone in their corner fighting for them, which in otherwise hopeless situations can create great value.

Of course, clients' value determinations remain largely subjective. The subjectivity of value determinations is what makes important various psychological and socio-cultural factors. Knowing those factors and their effects can help lawyers and firms overcome subjective price resistance for the client to recognize and embrace product-and-service value. Interestingly, pricing experts find that strong branding tends to blunt those subjective factors.

For our purposes, we will treat pricing like packaging as raising five concerns, although the pricing concerns are different from the packaging concerns already stated. The first concern is affordability, that the product or service must be something that the underserved clients can reach financially and afford within their means. The second concern has to do with value. Simply because a product or service is affordable does not mean that it carries the value justifying its purchase. The third concern is transparency. Products and services can be affordable and valuable but have their costs hidden from the consumer in a way that removes the client's autonomy. Transparency is a particularly acute issue when lawyers attempt to reach emerging client populations.

Steps to Take

When a client reflects raises (or you perceive) an affordability issue, do not overlook the possibility of limited-scope services. Evaluate the client's competence to manage responsibly some of the steps that will accomplish the client's objectives. Limited-scope representation may meet satisfy pricing issues while enabling the client to achieve objectives. The client lowers the bill while receiving some professional assistance. You have an additional satisfied client who may return with other matters.

Transparency relates to the next concern, which is choice. Choice, like transparency, is a particularly acute concern when an enterprising lawyer seeks to serve an emerging client population. Clients should get to choose what law products and services they want rather than have lawyers or others tell them that for which they must pay. Consumers have choice elsewhere and expect it with law products and services. The final concern is accountability, that the enterprising lawyer must remain responsible to the client for each of the above concerns including affordability, value, transparency, and choice. Just as with transparency and choice, accountability in pricing is critical to reaching emerging populations. Traditional markets for law products and services grant lawyers some room as to transparency, choice, and accountability. Emerging markets do not. Clients (and lawyers) tend to know the pricing conventions for traditional products and services. Clients will not have those expectations for new products and services.

Practice Tip

Flat-fee service can be a hugely valuable addition to a practice. The simplicity of flat fees provides the client with certainty. Many potential clients fear the unknown fees associated with lawyers. Those persons will attempt to do complicated legal work on their own rather than risk incurring an unaffordable fee. Charging a flat fee for a divorce without children or a bankruptcy eliminates the fear. Flat fees can also improve the representation and relationship. The client feels more comfortable asking questions without fearing additional cost. The lawyer also benefits from a flat fee's certainty. Even with flat fees, though, be sure to track hours to analyze the cost of the service and adjust the flat fee in future cases.

Lawyers of any experience will immediately recognize some of the issues surrounding each of these five pricing concerns, affordability, value, transparency, choice, and accountability. The following five sections do not necessarily propose revolutionary new ways of addressing each of those five concerns. The main point of this part on pricing is that you see the relationship of each of these five concerns to the other concerns and then accept that an effective lawyer must address all of them, particularly when for new products and services. Practices already common among lawyers may be sufficient to address all five pricing concerns, although innovation in one or more of those concerns may also be helpful. Yet satisfying one or two of the five concerns is not sufficient. Effective lawyers examine and improve their pricing practices in all five areas. Consider the following five sections on affordability, value, transparency, choice, and accountability.

Reflection

1. How do lawyers establish the prices for their products and services? How could lawyers establish the prices for their products and services? How should lawyers establish the prices for their products and services?

2. How do lawyers communicate to clients the price of their products and services? How could lawyers communicate to clients the price of their products and services? How should lawyers communicate to clients the price of their products and services.

3. Can you recall an instance when a client or prospective client declined your offer of a product or service because of its high cost? Can you recall an instance when a client or prospective client was surprised at the price of your products or services? How do your clients regard (high, reasonable, low, etc.) the price of your products or services?

4. Do clients attempt to negotiate price with you? Do you negotiate price with clients?

5. Which of the fee methods listed in this section do you use, and with which products and services? Have you abandoned a fee method? If so, then why? How did your change in fee methods affect the quantity and quality of the services you were able to provide? How did it affect your professional relationship with clients?

6. Which of the fee methods listed in this section have you not yet used but you anticipate that you may someday use in the future? What advantage would that fee method give you and what advantage would it give your client?

A. Affordability

The associate had never met with a client over a bill before when the managing partner called him into the office. The associate did not recognize the silver-haired gentleman sitting across the desk from the managing partner. The managing partner just motioned to the associate to sit down next to the gentleman. The managing partner explained briefly to the associate that the gentleman was the estate-planning client for whom the associate had done some research last month. The managing partner then turned again to the client who resumed a complaint the gentleman appeared to have already begun before the partner had called the associate into the office. The client was explaining, in so many words, that he had not authorized the associate's research, did not need it, did not understand it, could not afford it, and was not going to pay for it.

The associate felt himself blushing, partly in anger, partly in embarrassment, and partly in frustration. The managing partner did not look at the associate but instead just looked at the client, nodding now and then while listening to the client complain. The associate soon noticed how upset and vulnerable the client looked. When the client had finished, the managing partner apologized and told the client that he was withdrawing the bill. The partner then turned to the associate and said simply that the associate may return to work. Dumfounded, the associate stood up, turned, and left the managing partner's office. The associate did not return to his own office, though. Instead, he walked out of the firm's office suite, down through the lobby, and out to his car, where he sat in silence, composing his thoughts while recollecting the work he had done for the estate-planning client.

One of the firm's other partners had told the associate to research the estate-planning issue. The associate felt that he had actually produced some of his best work yet in completing the research memorandum for the partner. He could not recall the partner having given him any estimate of the time that the associate should take on the project. The associate had no idea of how large or small was the client's estate, or how much was at stake relating to the research issue. The associate seldom if ever received any such guidance. So the associate had taken what to him seemed to be about the standard amount of time that a quality research memorandum required, which was (if the associate recalled the work correctly) about a day and a half, or around 15 hours. He made a note to check his time records.

Just then, the associate saw the client leaving the building. As soon as the coast was clear, the associate got out of his car, returned to his office, and resumed working. He had cooled off and composed himself. His check of his time records indeed indicated 15 hours, for which the firm would have billed the client around $3,000, the amount that the managing partner had now withdrawn from the billing. The associate half expected to hear again from the managing partner. Yet later that day when they passed in the hallway, the managing partner had just smiled weakly and nodded to the associate as he usually did, as if nothing had happened. The associate felt relieved. At the same time, the associate resolved to ask the partners who assigned him work what expectations the clients would have about his hours.

~

The solo practitioner saw her clients frequently outside of her office. She would bump into them at the post office, grocery store, dry cleaner, and dentist's office. She saw some of them at her children's school and others at the gym or dog park. The practitioner knew what vehicles they drove, what restaurants at which they ate, and at what shops they bought their clothes. These encounters and other information that she gleaned from representing them kept the practitioner well informed about her clients' available finances. She felt that she could guess pretty well at what they could pay and what they would pay for her law products and services. She also watched and listened closely to how they reacted to the quotes that she gave them for her services.

It took one event, though, for the practitioner to decide to do more than just guess, watch, and listen regarding how she priced her law products and services. She had put a fair amount of time into developing a range of low-cost, simple estate-planning products and services, promoting those products and services in the same manner that she promoted her other products and services. Yet after a few months, the practitioner noticed that she had not succeeded in providing to clients just about any of those estate-planning products and services that she had so meticulously packaged. Her frustration was that she knew that clients needed those products and services, and that she had enough respect around town to be supplying them.

Then it dawned on her. The practitioner gathered a diverse group of individuals in her office one Saturday morning, offering them coffee and baked goods as an inducement. She spread her estate-planning products (wills, durable powers of attorney, healthcare advocate designations, deeds in joint tenancy, funeral plans, etc.) on her conference table, encouraging her friends to comment on them and ask her questions about related services. Their comments and questions confirmed for the practitioner that they needed and desired the products and services that she was offering.

The practitioner then handed each individual a list of the products and services, each with a brief description. She asked them to write down the price that they would pay for each product or service, assuming that they had the need for it. She assured them that she would treat their answers as confidential, using their answers only for her own survey purposes in setting fair and affordable prices. Finally, when they had all written down their prices, the practitioner handed out her brochures and business cards, and told them about her education, experience, family, and community commitments. She then asked them to write down any prices that they would change based on this last information that she had just shared.

The practitioner had guessed that her prices on the products and services had been too high, explaining her lack of success in supplying them. When she examined the confidential responses, though, to her surprise, the practitioner discovered that most of the prices that the individuals gave for most of the products and services were higher than the prices at which she had been offering them. They priced only one of her products consistently below where she had priced that product. Several individuals had also increased prices based on her personal and professional information.

The practitioner drew four lessons from the brief exercise. First, she needed to make her prices apparent because clients might be assuming that her products and services were more expensive than their actual costs. Second, some of her prices may be misleading her clients into thinking that they were not quality products and services. Her prices needed to reflect their value. Third, she needed to differentiate her prices lower and higher to fit her clients' particular expectations as to the cost and value of each product or service. And fourth, the practitioner needed to share information about her professional qualifications and personal commitments when sharing price information.

~

As the above vignettes and common sense suggest, clients must be able to afford law products and services if they are to purchase them. Never mind the market for law products and services. When a lawyer prices products and services beyond what a client can absolutely bear, the lawyer has little or no chance of supplying the product or service while getting paid for it. Prices must be within clients' reach. Many persons may desire a Rolls Royce or Bentley, but few persons can afford one. Rolls Royce and Bentley accordingly sell relatively few products.

Enterprising lawyers know what their clients can afford and will pay for products and services. They price those products and services accordingly.

Enterprising lawyers use various methods to determine what their clients will pay for products and services. One method is to offer price options to new clients. Clients will choose affordable options. Yet behavioral economics teaches that many individuals make buying decisions less rationally than once supposed. Individuals instead often choose by rough approximations or heuristics. Some heuristics perform powerfully, approximating optimal decisions based on very little information. Yet other heuristics bias clients into making poor decisions. Enterprising lawyers know clients' anecdotes of lawyers overcharging based on excessive hours or hidden costs. They know clients' bias against seeking professional help built by stereotypes of greedy, overpriced lawyers.

Enterprising lawyers also know what price information to share and the way to share it to overcome the market anomalies created by price obstacles that other lawyers build or that clients place in front of themselves. Behavioral economics studies the irrationality of client purchase decisions. A simple, accessible text like Hugh Schwartz's *A Guide to Behavioral Economics* or a richer text like Edward Cartwright's *Behavioral Economics* (both cited in the Bibliography), can help a lawyer discern and overcome some of the irrational ways in which clients make purchasing decisions.

Steps to Take

Do not overlook the *behavioral* aspect of behavioral economics. Many law-practice features can affect client purchase decisions. Those features include practice location, office size, design layout, available materials, and staff assistance. Recognize that all of these and other elements work together to affect how clients make purchase decisions. Insightful lawyers discern the features most likely to affect a client during intake. They then modify their procedures accordingly to ensure that their total presentation reassures and supports the client most positively in the client's purchase decision.

Consider some of the following behavioral-economics theories as they might influence pricing communications:

- availability bias refers to the over-emphasis that clients may place on information that is readily available to them, when more significant information affecting their purchase of a law product or service may not be so readily available. Astute lawyers recognize when clients unwisely seize on available feature, cost, price, or risk information to make a decision without considering other discoverable information;

- anchoring and adjustment bias occurs when clients settle quickly on a known value while only reluctantly adjusting subsequent considerations against that beginning value. The client's over-emphasis on the anchored value distorts the client's subsequent decision-making. Astute lawyers help the client balance all purchase considerations without over-emphasizing initial data;

- prospect theory teaches that individuals assign values to outcomes of economic decisions, in our case, whether to purchase a law product or service. Yet when they do so, they tend to overvalue small-probability outcomes and undervalue high-probability outcomes. Enterprising lawyers help clients properly assign and consider outcome probabilities;

- loss-aversion theory teaches that individuals overvalue holdings, undervalue investment, and over-avoid appropriate levels of risk. Enterprising lawyers communicate risk information to help clients avoid unwise loss aversion;

- disappointment theory teaches that individuals will be disappointed even with a good outcome if it fails to exceed expectations. Enterprising lawyers avoid exaggerating probable outcomes (over-selling products and services) to help clients appreciate real value in outcomes;

- status quo bias causes individuals to prefer unduly the status quo (prefer not to decide) over choosing achievable gains. Enterprising lawyers help clients see non-action as disruption of the status quo, thereby reversing the status-quo default to achieve optimal choice;

- gambler's fallacy theory teaches that individuals will believe that a series of anomalous occurrences will make the opposite occurrence more likely, like coming up heads when flipping a coin makes the next flip tails more likely. Enterprising lawyers help clients see the independence of probabilities, that lightning striking once says nothing about whether lightning will strike twice;
- self-serving bias causes individuals to attribute success to their own actions but failure to the actions of others. Enterprising lawyers help clients recognize events that their own actions do and do not control to help clients make sound decisions;
- herd-behavior or group-think theory teaches that individuals often make decisions based on how others in their group are acting rather than after informed thought about outcomes. Enterprising lawyers help clients identify and avoid harmful herd behaviors.

Practice Tip

Above all, lawyers are counselors, which is why many firms still use "Attorney and Counselor" on their letterhead. Clients come to lawyers for many reasons but often for the lawyer to take charge in advocating for the client's position. Yet advocacy does little or no good if the client has no prospect for gaining the desired outcome. As a result, practitioners must help clients evaluate how their expectations align with probable outcomes. Communicate thoroughly and sensitively about realistic outcomes. Help clients develop reasonable expectations.

Clients may also frame price decisions within emotional contexts, creating other selection biases. Behavioral economists have helped businesses look beyond emotion as an *interference* with purchase decisions to emotion as a *legitimate component* of those decisions. Social and emotional factors based on peer pressure, the desire to emulate others, the perception of how others will regard one, and the perception of inertia or momentum, can all affect how a potential client responds to a product or service offering. You can help potential clients evaluate a product or service offering by identifying these factors to the client and discussing them, or at least recognizing how they may be affecting purchase decisions. Precisely designed affective presentations emphasizing the health-and-welfare enhancing qualities of a law product or service, and accurately presenting real risks in an emotive manner, can aid clients who will decide based on social and emotional factors over analytic value factors.

Of course, lawyers do not determine prices in the abstract. From the lawyer's standpoint, price, as the key to affordability, depends on four factors. Price is first a function of the scope of any project. The broader is the scope, the higher must be the price to accommodate the greater amount of work that the project will entail. Price is next a function of the resources such as lawyer skill and time, assistant skill and time, administrative skill and time, travel, expert consultants or witnesses, etc., necessary to devote to accomplishing the matter's objective. The more resources are necessary, the higher the price. Price is next a function of the risk of the work, whether the lawyers can discern and quantify all potential costs in advance of the price agreement. The more risk that a law matter carries, the higher the price must be to accommodate the risk. Finally, price depends on a project's timing. The shorter the period within which the client requires the lawyer to complete the project, the higher the price may have to be because the lawyer must devote premium time rather than down time to the project.

Practice Tip

Poor communication about the scope of work can be a big source of practice problems. Define your work clearly in a writing to which the client commits. Defining the work lets you both know when you have started and finished your work. When you are done with the work, say so in writing. Consider including phrases like "entry of this divorce judgment ends the representation of the attorneys." Make it your option whether you want to take new assignments from the same client later. Communicate in writing at the beginning and the end.

Markets also tell lawyers how to price law products and services. The lawyer who prices a product or service well above what other lawyers charge for it may find few clients for it. Markets depend on price information. Price information as to law products and services was once less available than it is today. Before the advent of mass advertising and, especially, the internet, fewer clients knew what law products and services cost. Today, price information for law products and services is more available, although not comprehensively available. Effective lawyers usually have a good sense of the market price for their services. They know what clients must pay to get similar law products and services elsewhere.

Yet affordability is more complex than one might initially think as a pricing consideration. Just because a client can get a law product or service from one lawyer for one price does not mean that the client cannot or will not purchase a similar law product or service from another lawyer. Law products and services have intangible values associated with the unique attributes of each lawyer and unique aspects of each lawyer-client relationship. When in the second illustration above the practitioner had individuals estimate prices for the lawyer's products and services, they were estimating the values that they put on her providing those services, not some other lawyer providing those services. Law products and services are only in part commodities and in part fungible. A client may only be able to afford one price for one lawyer but a higher price for another lawyer when the second lawyer provides values beyond the first lawyer's services. Enterprising lawyers build their practices around these added values.

Steps to Take

Control and communication of intangible values are how law firms help clients construct a comprehensive image for the firm. Try this exercise. Visit a few local service businesses such as spas, restaurants, hotels, or conference centers. Ask what they offer in terms of overall client experience. Explain that you are looking for a place to hold meetings, bring in speakers, and give promotional gifts (an excellent idea, by the way), for clients of your law firm. The premier location should clearly emerge after you visit a few establishments. How did that location make you feel welcome? What services did they offer in addition to the space, set-up, sound system, and food the other locations offered? The difference was likely the intangible nature of the overall experience.

The foregoing discussion suggests that affordability does not depend simply on a client's discretionary income. Assume a client has none. A client may have to spend non-discretionary income on law services simply to preserve or obtain income, food, housing, and other essentials. A client may be willing to spend non-discretionary income to preserve marital, child-custody, or business relationships, or to terminate marital or business relationships. Affordability relates to the value of the lawyer's service, not solely to a client's available or discretionary income. Pricing information should therefore include information on product or service value. Clients may not pay for a law product or service unless its apparent value compels its affordability.

Most significantly, affordability also relates to the pricing and payment mechanisms. The foregoing discussion assumes a fixed fee for law product or service, paid in a single payment. In actuality, though, lawyers have several more pricing and payment mechanisms other than fixed fees, each of which may be the clue to the affordability of any particular product or service. Certainly, lawyers can and do charge hourly fees. They do so with and without retainer fees. Some lawyers simply start billing, usually monthly. Other lawyers require a retainer and then bill against the retainer. When the billing exhausts the retainer, some lawyers require additional retainers, while other lawyers simply keep billing without additional retainer. Some lawyers will mix a fixed fee with hourly billing. Other lawyers will permit payments on a fixed fee in an account receivable with or without interest. Some lawyers will require security from the client to carry an unpaid fee. Other lawyers use value billing, setting the fee based not on a fixed amount or hourly charges but on a mechanism determining the work's value.

Practice Tip

Associates join law firms with high hopes and expectations. An associate who discerns that the firm's immediate goal is to bill the most hours need not relinquish those high hopes and expectations. Careful observation teaches associates many valuable lessons. Using hours to determine a reasonable cost for services is an art that associates can learn from more experienced lawyers.

Contingency fees are one value-billing method. Contingency agreements base the lawyer's fee on a percentage of the client's recovery. Contingency fees are no revelation for lawyers. They are instead common, even ubiquitous, in certain fields like personal injury.

Yet it may surprise some lawyers just where contingency fees may be appropriate. Client disputes with health and no-fault insurers, to pay third parties such as healthcare providers, are examples. At first blush, the situation may not look to be appropriate for a contingency fee because a prevailing client would make no personal recovery out of which to pay a fee. The recovery in healthcare insurance-coverage disputes goes to the providers. Those providers, though, ordinarily share in the cost of recovery, meaning that an effective lawyer can receive a contingency fee.

Practice Tip

Practitioners learn quickly that an ethics-based practice can be worth its weight in gold. Fair fees can be clients' greatest ethics concern about lawyers and law services. Lawyers have many ways to charge clients. Each way, though, must be ethical. When improperly applied without informed client agreement, value billing and results billing can look to the client and grievance officials much more like greed than good client service.

So far, the discussion in this section has been in the abstract, as if pricing was solely a matter of choosing what clients can and should afford relative to the law product or service's value. Lawyers and other producers of goods and services do not have that luxury. Pricing is only in part dependent on the consumer's ability to afford purchasing the commodity. Pricing also depends on the producer's ability to afford creating the commodity. Lawyers incur costs in offering products and services. The revenue that their pricing and sales of products and services produces must be able to cover costs of production. Efficient production is critical to pricing flexibility. The more effective that a lawyer is in designing commoditized products and services, and implementing the systems to produce and deliver them, the more flexibility the lawyer has in pricing. Every gain in efficiency opens a door to a new pricing opportunity to reach more clients and provide broader service.

Cost reductions also create new pricing opportunities. Consider the following few examples of how effective lawyers can reduce the costs of producing products and services:

- locate offices in districts where rents, parking, staffing, and other costs are lower;
- reduce the size of fixed office space by using smaller offices, sharing offices and conference space, and eliminating libraries and other unused or non-productive space;
- reduce the cost of office furniture, limit expensive artwork, and avoid other non-productive but expensive appointments and trappings;
- maintain a mobile office reducing the necessity for travel to and use of fixed office space;
- outsource information-technology services including treating software as a service (SaaS), platforms as a service (PaaS), and infrastructure as a service (IaaS), and using cloud-based storage, products, and services; and
- meet and work by videoconference rather than traveling to distant worksites.

The point in this section on affordability is not to teach lawyers how to manage a law office efficiently, how to bill, or how to list all of the pricing and payment mechanisms. Other resources offer detailed explanations of fee practices including form agreements. The point here is to connect the fee method to the important question of the product or service's affordability, as one component of several other pricing issues. To be effective, lawyers must not only price the law product or service within the general reach of clients. Lawyers must also design and offer pricing methods that make the law product or service affordable, and then innovate in practice to be able to deliver reasonably priced products and services. Pay attention to affordability. Learn the optimum price by surveying family, friends, neighbors, and clients. Test the pricing of your products and services, and examine pricing results. Connect affordability to value, which is the subject of the next section.

Reflection

1. What is the median household income of the clients whom you serve? What discretionary income do they have in that household to devote to law products and services?

2. When do your clients pay for your products and services—by flat fee in advance, under retainer, when billed, or on account, and if on account, with or without security and interest? Why did you choose that method? Would another method make your clients more able to afford your products and services?

3. What percentage and gross amount of your billed services remain uncollectible? What are the reasons for your uncollectible accounts, and what percentage and gross amount of your billed services go uncollectible for each reason?

4. Would changes in your fee arrangements reduce your uncollectible accounts? If so, then how would those changes affect the willingness of clients to enter into fee arrangements with you?

5. What would be an optimum percentage and gross amount of uncollectible accounts? What factors are you considering in so determining? Do you currently maintain an optimum percentage and gross amount of uncollectible accounts?

6. What communications do you make with clients who are unable or unwilling to pay for your products or services after your engagement?

7. Do you offer your clients alternative fee arrangements? Have you ever surveyed your clients regarding their preferred fee methods?

PRICING SERVICES
Affordability
Value
Transparency
Choice
Accountability

B. Value

The associate continued to reflect on the embarrassing session with the silver-haired estate-planning client whose bill the managing partner had withdrawn. Why had the associate so missed the mark with his work, when he had done good work exactly as the other partner had assigned it? The associate decided to ask the assigning partner about it. He took a day to gather his list of questions and think of the right approach to the partner. Then he headed down the hall to the partner's office. The partner looked up from her desk and smiled when the associate walked in. The associate asked if the partner had a minute, and she nodded. He then summarized the event with the managing partner and silver-haired client.

The partner remained silent, listening respectfully to the associate. When the associate finished explaining the event, the partner smiled again, asking the associate what he thought they should do. The associate said that he would like to know more about the silver-haired client's matter so that he could better judge whether he had done as required. The partner took a couple of minutes to outline why she had asked the associate to research the estate-planning issue. The associate acknowledged that the work seemed appropriate. He then asked the partner if she would tell him more about the size of the estate and the difference that the research issue could have made to the client's goals. The partner hesitated but only for a moment. She then pulled a file from her drawer, set it on her desk, turned it toward the associate, and opened it.

The associate felt instantly that he had just stepped across a divide toward becoming responsible to the firm and its clients. He later recalled the moment with even more appreciation. The partner had shown him the schedule of the client's assets and their values. She had and the associate had discussed how much the research issue had at stake in financial terms and what might be a reasonable research budget. They had also briefly discussed the client's financial means. The partner admitted that she had not communicated to the client adequately the value of the associate's work and had not discussed with the client or the managing partner the cost of the work and the best payment mechanism. Indeed, the partner admitted that she had given the client no choice in the research matter at all, despite that she usually did estimate costs for clients. The partner offered to speak with the managing partner about it, even to apologize to the client.

Although the associate was relieved at the outcome, he did not want to repeat the situation. He realized that he and the firm had no procedure in place for associates that would provide the sort of information and ensure the sort of value fit that the associate and estate-planning partner had just discussed. When he asked some of the other associates about it, they just stared blankly back at him as if they, too, had never before thought of the problem. The associate vowed never to take another project without asking the partner who assigned the work for the kind of information that the estate-planning partner had just provided. He knew now that he needed to fit pricing to value in every project, a fit that he had assumed incorrectly that others somewhere within the firm were making.

~

The solo practitioner met an associate from a large firm for lunch one day. They had met briefly and exchanged business cards months earlier at the local bar's Law Day function. On this occasion, the associate had asked to meet with the solo practitioner to discuss the question of valuing law products and services. The associate's inquiry had intrigued the solo practitioner. She felt that she already had a clear sense of the value of many of her products and services. One of the best parts of her work was seeing its immediate impact on the lives and welfare of her clients. Value was especially apparent in her family law work but also in her collections defense, foreclosure defense, and other areas. The practitioner had no clear sense of the value of large-firm products and services. She imagined that the corporate and relatively wealthy clients whom the large firm served were less concerned with value.

Yet the practitioner realized while reflecting on the associate's lunch invitation that she did some things the value of which was highly uncertain. Many of the wills, powers of attorney, and provisional guardianship papers that she prepared were clearly only hedges against a future that none of the clients hoped to realize. Her clients wanted to live, remain healthy, and care for their spouses and children. They did not want to see how valuable their wills, powers of attorney, or provisional guardianship papers were to their family because doing so would involve their own demise. Yet as the practitioner thought about it, she realized more of why her clients paid for these services anyway. They were receiving something of immediate value, and that was peace of mind and confidence in their own responsibility. The practitioner's insight led her to change some of her products, services, and practices to clarify and emphasize for her clients the peace-of-mind value of those products and services.

The practitioner learned from her lunch with the large-firm associate that value was also important to the large firm's work. One or two of the associate's stories amused her, although she could see how painful the value lessons were that the associate had learned. She just never would have thought of billing any of her clients for hours and hours of work that her clients had not authorized and the value of which they did not understand. The practitioner had never had that liberty. She could see, too, that the associate wanted to learn more about pricing law products and services. She could hardly believe how little he knew about the actual cost of his work or even its value to the firm's clients. He seemed to have little sense of what other firms were doing and charging, too, when by contrast she had learned a lot about the local market for her law products and services. She liked the associate, though, and agreed to meet him again for lunch next time they had another practice issue to discuss. She also liked that he paid the bill for lunch.

~

Price depends in large part on value, or more accurately, on value and the client's *perception* of value. As to actual value, effective lawyers fit the quantity and quality of their services to what the clients have at stake in the representation. For the client, the starting point for determining a fair price is not really the market for products and services. The determinant is primarily the value that the client will realize from the product or service. The market may have set the price well above or below the value of the client's interest. The market price does not matter as much to the client as the value that the product or service provides. The product or service may be expensive or inexpensive as lawyers quote its price. If the value of the client's interest does not justify the client's purchasing the product or service at its market price, then the informed client should forgo the product.

For example, just because a client can get a will drafted inexpensively does not mean that the client will purchase a will, if the client does not value a will. On the other hand, in the most obvious of cases, murder charges bearing the prospect of life imprisonment justify the client's complete sacrifice of other financial goals, save possibly only an interest in providing for one's family upon conviction. The value of law products and services necessary to supporting a land development, starting a joint venture, or acquiring a valuable asset are nearly as obvious. One simply takes the economic value of the activity and weighs in a proportional cost for the necessary law products and services. No one would think of forgoing law products and services in any of those transactional situations because doing so would prevent the parties from accomplishing their valued objective. Effective transactional lawyers are generally masters at fitting price to value.

The value of some law products and services, like the above examples, is immediately apparent. A lawyer does not have to convince a real-estate developer trying to draft a joint-venture agreement, or defendant on a murder charge, that they need representation. The question in such cases has more to do with the fair pricing of the law products and services. Market may have more then to do with the price. If the real-estate developer can get the deal documented in a timely and appropriate fashion at one cost from one firm, the developer may be unwilling to pay a significantly higher fee at another firm. On the other hand, if the quality of the representation arguably differs, then the market price adjusts accordingly. The murder suspect who wants the best defense may pay significantly more than the fee for just any defense. In either case, value is not the issue. The clients know that they need representation and know why they need that representation.

Practice Tip

Lawyers sell time. Clients do not always appreciate the cost, necessity, and quality of that time. Most clients have no sense of the years of study and practice a lawyer may need to address a client's matter, no less the complexity of the matter. A reliable way to educate clients about your skill and the complexity of their matters is to inform clients along the way. Document the persistence and technicality of your work for the client. Help the client see the value of your work as the process unfolds.

The value of other law products and services is less apparent, which leads to the question of the client's *perception* of value. In those cases, communicating value is not simply a marketing effort for enterprising lawyers. Communicating value is instead a responsibility of effective lawyers. Consider prenuptial and cohabitation agreements. A well-crafted agreement may help the parties understand and align one another's expectations for the relationship. It may also reveal and confirm benefits, rights, and responsibilities, and opportunities to add greater value to the relationship. Prenuptial and cohabitation agreements can promote the stability and prosperity of relationships, particularly when the parties entering into the relationships do not yet appreciate the complexity and sensitivity of their undertaking.

Enterprising lawyers illustrate for those clients the value of their products and services. You should see now how the subjects covered in Part I on packaging products and services, including fitting an appropriate product or service to the client's specific objectives, support pricing information. Systematic intake procedures that discern, articulate, and confirm client objectives make communications about pricing more meaningful. Product and service value are then more apparent to the client. Clients can make informed and rational pricing choices without biases and stereotypes swaying those choices. Practices and communications that demonstrate value support appropriate pricing.

Do not underestimate the breadth and depth of law product and service value. Lawyers convey value in five general areas within any firm or field. They first help clients identify law product and service needs. The first value is helping the client recognize a law issue and law product or service opportunity. In that sense, marketing to clients adds value by communicating to clients the value that law products and services can add. A second value area lies in the lawyer's initial consultation in which the lawyer helps the client discern achievable objectives and their cost. Planning the work is a third value area in which the client benefits from the lawyer's analysis, resource allocation, and strategies. Executing the work is a fourth value area in which the lawyer draws on teamwork, meeting, negotiation, drafting, advocacy, supervision, reporting, communication, and other skills. A last value area is in completing, documenting, and closing the work.

Practice Tip

Know the fee structures of other lawyers and law firms. For example, keep abreast of the going rate for drunk-driving representation to formulate your own fee structure for the same service. Simply setting fees lower than other lawyers is not a sound way to price services. Low-balling fees below their cost just to keep you busy for a time will soon give you a bad reputation. Lawyers recognize when other lawyers unreasonably undercut markets for common services. Judges, judicial secretaries, and court clerks hear, too, as do some community leaders. Clients can also recognize lawyers who will charge as little as it takes just to get a case, without thought for maintaining the practice. Desperation is not a strategy. Under-pricing services is the road to a practice's demise, not its recovery.

Value may also be contingent and therefore uncertain. The value of some law products and services becomes evident only on the happening of an uncertain contingency or a certain contingency the date of which is uncertain. The value of prenuptial and cohabitation agreements lies in part on uncertain contingencies including the death, disability, or withdrawal of one of the parties to the agreement. Effective lawyers can help clients appreciate the possibility and frequency of uncertain contingencies, and plan for their occurrence, for example, if half of marriages end in divorce and a greater percentage of cohabitation arrangements terminate voluntarily. The pricing point here, though, is not in the value of the planning. The pricing point is in helping clients understand the likelihood of the occurrence as a way for the client to determine the product or service's true value.

Wills, of course, are the classic example. Who needs one, right? The challenge for a lawyer to demonstrate the value of a will is that few clients expect their imminent demise and fewer want to think much about it. Yet the probability of the contingency occurring in which a will would become effective is 100%. The only uncertainty is the timing of the occurrence. Value depends on connecting the will to the timing or probability of the occurrence *or on other benefits that do not depend on those contingencies.* Much estate planning occurs at a time and in a manner in which the greater value is not anticipated relief from a client's imminent demise but the value that the client draws from providing for family and other interests in the event of what is then a still-remote contingency. Clients and their families draw value from estate plans long before death triggers their implementation. Effective estate planners help clients discover and draw on those peace-of-mind and I-care-for-my-family values.

Lawyers must know and communicate the value of their products and services to package, price, and deliver their services effectively. Knowledge of value depends on knowledge of clients, their goals, and interests. Lawyers who price their services without knowing their clients' means, goals, and interests end up with unhappy clients, fewer clients, or no clients. Lawyers must also distribute pricing to be effective. Pricing one product or service to one client at one cost does not mean that the lawyer may price another product or service to the same client at the same cost. One client will value different products and services at different levels even if from the same lawyer, and will also value the same product or service at a different level if provided at a different time by the same lawyer. Different clients will value the same product or service differently. Prices need to reflect value sensitivity. Consider next the question of price transparency.

Reflection

1. How do your clients measure the value of your products and services? Do they use primarily economic or primarily non-economic measures?

2. Have you ever asked or surveyed your clients about the value of your products and services? How would you go about doing so? How might you go about finding out how clients value your products and services other than by client queries and surveys? Could you learn from a focus group?

3. Ignoring for a moment how clients value your products and services, what value do you think that your products and services bring to your clients? Do your clients understand the full value of your products and services? If not, then how might you communicate those values better?

PRICING SERVICES
Affordability
Value
Transparency
Choice
Accountability

C. Transparency

When the associate had started at the firm nearly a year earlier, he had appreciated the fact that he never had to deal with money. He had thought then that he was practicing law as everyone should practice it. He focused entirely on the work while letting others—secretaries, bookkeepers, accountants, the managing partner (he hardly knew who), and of course the clients—deal with the work's financial aspects. His practice was, in a sense, one of blissful financial ignorance. The associate was enjoying the bliss without recognizing the ignorance. The copiers ran, the secretaries showed up, and the firm paid the rent and his paychecks and benefits without the associate having to think about any of the several financial aspects of his work.

No more than halfway through his first year, the associate had already realized that ignorance of the financial aspects of his work was not bliss. It was just ignorance. He had never really thought in law school about the economics of a law firm. His summer clerkships and introduction to the firm had not helped. It was only as his first year at the firm wore on that he began to discern how the revenue that his work generated helped pay the costs of that work. He first learned that the reason that he knew so little about the price to the clients of his work was that the clients were not his from a practical standpoint. The clients dealt solely with the partners who assigned the associate work. The partners, he had gradually learned, were extremely price conscious. The partners, he had discovered, knew what their clients would and would not pay. Money was actually very important at the firm, despite the firm's genteel appearance.

The associate had learned about the clients' price sensitivity when he had heard about the managing partner and other partners cutting the associate's hourly charges to several clients. Evidently, the partners had a price sensitivity by which they were judging the associate's work. The partners did not tell the partners about it directly. The partners were instead just dropping small hints that the associate first thought innocuous but later decided the partners intended to make him more productive. Yet although price and productivity were clearly critical to the associate's future, the associate still did not know the price of his work or the criteria by which the firm measured his productivity, other than gross billable hours. The entrepreneurial aspect of his work was far more than simply bill-the-most-hours. The associate just could not discover the pricing mechanism and productivity criteria.

The associate did not know the price of his work in part because the firm did not advertise it to clients or prospective clients. The associate's interaction with the solo practitioner had made the associate do a little internet research into his own firm's and similar firms' price structures. He had learned nothing. The prices of products and services offered by other firms in other fields to other client demographics was in many cases reasonably transparent. Not for his firm. The associate thought for a time that the partners were intentionally keeping their price considerations from him, perhaps to keep the clients from him. The associate decided instead, though, that the partners did not have a clear sense of the price they should charge for their products and services. Price seemed to be more a question of whether the clients would complain when they got their bills. That was it, the associate decided. The firm did not disclose the price of his work and his partners' work until after they had completed it and billed for it—as strange way to price products and services, the associated concluded.

~

By the end of her first year of practice, the solo practitioner had developed a price schedule for her products and services. She realized in her year-end review of her practices and professional development just how complex her price schedule was. She offered many fixed-fee services, some hourly services under retainer, some hourly services without retainer, and some contingency-fee services. Her pricing had good variety and some flexibility. Yet she was also satisfied that her clients knew where they stood well before they committed to any of her products or services. She had also learned to make her pricing more transparent to prospective clients.

The latter success in transparency had taken some time, effort, and sensitivity. Other lawyers did not generally publish detailed price lists for their products and services, like a restaurant menu. At least, she had never seen one that detailed. Some lawyers did disclose initial pricing, especially retainer fees but also some flat fees for drunk-driving defense, license restoration, and even wills. The practitioner had investigated that pricing to develop her own schedule. Although she had not published her full price schedule on the internet or in any other publicly accessible fashion, she, too, had learned to indicate on her website and in some brochures and business cards some preliminary pricing information. She felt that her practice helped clients and prospective clients believe that she would be transparent and accountable in her pricing for them, even if they could not find out all of her prices for all of her products and services without meeting with her.

When meeting with clients and prospective clients in the office, the practitioner was much more forthright with her pricing. She kept a printed copy of her price schedule handy and would show it to clients and prospective clients at every reasonable opportunity, gladly discussing any product or service on the schedule. At first, price information had seemed like a negative to the practitioner. Gradually, though, she realized that her price schedule was an important tool to expanding her opportunities to provide products and services. Clients and prospective clients did not necessarily know the other products and services that she offered. When they did, they still did not know what those products and services cost. Her price schedule solved both problems. It also made her pricing transparent and her practice price-accountable.

Once in a while, a client or prospective client would ask for a copy of the practitioner's full price schedule. She kept to the practice of declining those requests because she changed her fees from time to time. She also wanted to be able to explain her pricing (including the quality and value of her products and services) when clients learned about it. The practitioner responded to those requests by offering to write down specific prices for products and services in which the clients were interested. Her response helped her learn what other products and services the clients were considering. It also satisfied the clients.

~

Price transparency entails communicating information to clients and prospective clients at a time when they still have the option of purchasing or declining the law product or service. Law products and services carry prices. Clients will pay those prices whether or not the prices are apparent when the clients obligate themselves to pay for the product or service. Simply because products or services have prices does not mean that those prices are transparent to the client or prospective client. Some lawyers price their products and services obscurely, denying clients the opportunity to make informed decisions whether to purchase the product or service. Obscure pricing is at the root not only of many client misunderstandings (even grievances and lawsuits) but also of lost sales and services.

Practice Tip

Solo practitioners must know fixed fees. Fixed fees may have a bad rap in larger firms. Yet a fixed fee is just that, a fixed fee. Fixed fees can be quite conducive to cases where you can readily quantify the requisite time. Cases inevitably involve uncertainty. Yet a no-asset divorce where both parties with no children desire early resolution has fewer risks and could be a good candidate for fixed fees. Fixed fees are above all transparent.

One prominent stereotype that lawyers must overcome is that lawyers have outsize incomes made from huge markups on legal services. In fact, lawyers make responsible incomes in practices that depend on individual client service. Enterprising lawyers communicate to clients that their products and services depend on the lawyer's skilled and committed work on the client's behalf—on the lawyer's concerted attention to the details of the client's individual matter. Effective lawyers not only hold to the high standards required for ethical billing but also communicate those high standards to clients as a pricing advantage. Transparent pricing and value are keys not only to selling products and services but to getting bills paid.

Transparency is thus a significant issue in pricing law products and services. Transparency is such an acute issue because clients, both corporate and individual, question and even fear the affordability of law products and services. Opaque or obscure pricing does not concern clients when they know that the products or services they are purchasing are readily affordable. When was the last time you questioned the bill at the dry cleaner's or deli? Insurers cover the cost of other goods and services like healthcare products and services, making price information unimportant to consumers. By contrast, when consumers are uncertain that they can afford the product or service, the product's cost is likely greater, and the consumer will bear the full cost without insurance, consumers tend to require more price information. Clients do not generally consider lawyers inexpensive. Because clients already suspect that lawyers are expensive, they prefer more, not less, price information.

Lawyers have reasons for obscure pricing. Some reasons are legitimate and others illegitimate. Lawyers may wish to adjust pricing to clients' ability to pay, maintaining a kind of price flexibility. When done to assure affordability and access to representation, flexible pricing has legitimacy. When done to charge a rich client more than the product or service's fair value, flexible pricing is illegitimate. Lawyers may also wish to price obscurely to frustrate potential competitors from undercutting those prices. Doing so runs the risk instead of frustrating clients and prospective clients. Price obscurity to garner sales to uninformed clients who cannot afford the products and services is sharp practice. Some lawyers are uncomfortable speaking with clients about pricing, not wanting to embarrass clients who may not be able to afford the products and services. Tradition (practices without reason) also plays a role in price obscurity.

> *Practice Tip*
>
> Law firms write down unreasonably excessive associate time charges to reasonable levels. Fewer solo practitioners have that luxury. Solo practitioners are unable to spread the loss among partners and associates who are more efficient. From day one, hour one, the solo practitioner needs to provide efficient client service. Establishing a reasonable fixed-fee schedule that accounts for unpredictable variances in the cost of the work can help the solo practitioner become more of the master of the practitioner's own fate.

Some lawyers regard transparent pricing as more business-like than professional. Transparent pricing, though, can be highly professional. Agreement over the price for a product or service, or the pricing mechanism, is part of the foundation of the professional relationship. Effective lawyers inform clients of the price or pricing mechanism, using that understanding to build the trust and confidence on which other aspects of the relationship will depend. Much of the lawyer-client relationship can involve highly uncertain contingencies such as how an opposing party will react or a judge will rule. Transparent pricing removes one substantial potential uncertainty. As already suggested immediately above, obscure pricing (a surprisingly high bill at the end) can destroy a client's opinion of the quality and value of a lawyer's products and services even when the client obtains an otherwise favorable outcome of the matter. Transparent pricing lends its own value even when the client's outcome is less favorable.

Effective lawyers price transparently in several ways. Public advertising of the initial price of consultation is highly appropriate. Public pricing gives clients access to you. The public pricing may simply start with the phrase "free initial consultation." That offer, though, may be particularly appropriate only for contingency-fee matters. To avoid misleading other non-contingency-fee clients, public pricing may require that limitation to "free initial consultation on personal-injury matters." Disclosing some fixed fees in public pricing, such as "uncontested divorce $500/bankruptcy $750" can increase a client's willingness to meet with a lawyer not only for those products and services but for other products and services not publicly priced. Public pricing of some products and services encourages clients to trust that a lawyer offers other fixed-fee disclosed-up-front pricing.

Practice Tip

New associates and their managing partners need not fear partner write-downs. An experienced lawyer may require just three hours for work that a new lawyer requires 20 hours. The managing partner's perspective can be to credit the associate for persevering even while refusing to bill the client for more time than an experienced lawyer would have required. New associates may need time to learn processes. Well-managed firms finance that training rather than passing it on as a direct cost to clients.

Technology can help a lawyer provide more detailed up-front pricing to increase client pricing information and confidence. Of course, lawyers can respond to client telephone calls with pricing information, after advertising "call for price information." Lawyers can also use email replies to email price inquiries. Website advertising can invite clients to make both price inquiries, as in "call or email for price information." Some lawyers go one technological step further, staffing online chat services to share price information. Each of these technologies can carry confidentiality, conflict-of-interest, and truth-in-advertising concerns. This book does not instruct in those specifics. Investigate what other lawyers are doing in making their pricing sufficiently transparent. Then, when you have discerned the extent and method of your pricing disclosures, investigate the ethics and conduct rules applicable to your chosen pricing practice. Consider next a section on providing choices for clients.

Reflection

1. Choose two or three companies offering services available near you that you have used at least once. How do those companies communicate the price of their services? When in the service transaction do you learn the price? Can you learn the service price without communicating in person with a company representative? Can you compare one company's price with the price of another company offering the same service?

2. Search the internet for information about the price of products and services offered by qualified lawyers. What information are you able to obtain generally? What information are you able to obtain about the price of products and services that you also offer?

3. How else can you find out about the prices other lawyers charge for products and services that you also offer? Try to establish a range of prices charged by other lawyers for each of your more common products and services, whether by internet search, networking, or other lawful means.

4. How do you communicate the price of your products and services to clients or prospective clients? When do you communicate the price of your products and services to clients or prospective clients? What price information can your clients or prospective clients learn about your products and services without direct contact with you?

5. When do you obscure pricing from clients? Why do you do so? Are those reasons legitimate or illegitimate?

6. How do you think making your pricing more transparent would affect your practice?

D. Choice

The associate liked the sense of authority that he held and exercised as a lawyer. Who wouldn't? He was knowledgeable. People should listen to him. Clients should listen to him, especially. The associate knew that about which he wrote and researched. The longer he worked for the firm, the more authoritative he felt, and the more authoritative were his law writings. The opinions and advice that he expressed in correspondence and memoranda became sharper, stronger, and clearer. As it did so, the associate grew in confidence. He noticed that even the secretaries were now listening to him, taking his orders. Previously, they had done pretty much as they thought best, even with his projects.

Then, the associate had a curious thing happen. He had one of his relatively rare client meetings without a partner present. The associate had been presenting the client with the associate's conclusion, justifying it with his research and counsel. The associate knew that the client really only had one choice, which involved retaining the firm to protect and defend some significant intellectual-property rights. Doing so was going to be expensive but almost certainly worth it, the associate had been explaining. The associate knew that the partner had already approved his approach with the client's matter. The partner's absence made the associate assume that the client would readily accept the associate's conclusion and approve the firm's additional work.

To the associate's surprise, the client did not do so. Instead, when the associate finished, the client had simply said that the client was not going to do what the associate proposed. The two of them sat silent just long enough to make the stunned associate uncomfortable. He could feel his face redden unwillingly. He instantly regretted that the client had noticed. The associate started to explain again why the client really had no other logical choice but to retain the firm for additional work. This time, though, the client cut off the associate in mid-sentence, repeating that the client was not going to do what the associate concluded.

Affronted by the client's cutting him off, the associate quickly and smugly asked the client what the client was then going to do. The associate figured that the client would have no idea and so would realize the client's folly in not accepting the associate's advice. Instead, the client had just as quickly shot back at the associate that the client's role was not to propose legal options. The associate was to propose the options. After all, the client had added, the associate was the lawyer, and the client was the client. The client got to choose, while the lawyer got to propose and price options. If the associate was not ready yet with his work despite having called the meeting, then the client would return later when the lawyer had completed his work in earnest, the client concluded. The client then rose, bowed slightly to the lawyer, and left the office.

~

The solo practitioner watched from the back of the restaurant as the associate entered, spotted her at the back table, and approached her from across the restaurant. The associate looked so weighted down, the practitioner thought, as if he took himself too seriously. She smiled to try to cheer him up, deciding to keep the lunch mood light. She rose, they greeted briefly, and they sat. Without even asking her how she was doing, the associate began complaining to her about an arrogant client with whom he had been dealing. Without revealing the client's identity, and while keeping all other confidences, the associate related to the practitioner the story of the client who had refused to follow his advice, had demanded options and prices, and walked out on him. The associate paused, expecting the practitioner to commiserate with him over unreasonable clients.

The practitioner instead also paused, saying nothing. She was thinking about her approach not only to the issue of client conduct and relationships but also of her professional relationship to the associate. The associate was treating her as a professional peer, not a protégé or mentor. In each of their few meetings, he had always seemed to her a little condescending, as if he thought he knew more about law and its practice than she did. Yet she just connected that attitude with the firm at which the associate worked. She felt that the associate accepted her as a peer rather than treating her as a subordinate. The practitioner also felt, though, that the associate was now trying to draw her into an attitude that the partners at his firm shared with the associate—an attitude that she decidedly did not share. She was not in the habit of complaining about clients. So she decided to follow her first thought about the lunch, which had been to keep the mood light.

The practitioner smiled at the associate, made a quick excuse for the associate's client, and tried to change the subject. The associate waited for the practitioner to pause but, when she did, resumed his complaint about the client. So the practitioner listened. When the associate finished his complaint, the practitioner said simply that it sounded like the client wanted options. So did her clients, the practitioner added. She explained that whenever she prepared for a significant client meeting, she tried to develop at least two and often several options, and to ready the price information for each of them. The practitioner was describing a practice that she had learned over the course of her first year in practice, although she had discovered much earlier (in law school) that clients value their autonomy and that she also did so.

The associate did not seem to hear the practitioner's thoughtful rejoinder to his complaining. Instead, the associate lamented that clients did not seem to appreciate the complexity of law and the skill the associate took to advise them. The practitioner, who had been smiling again at the associate's seriousness, laughed involuntarily at the associate's last comment. Her laugh stopped the associate, who gave her a questioning look. The practitioner apologized and explained that she had been thinking of something. She changed the subject quickly. They finished the lunch talking about things other than law practice. When the bill came, the practitioner insisted on paying for it. She was not sure that she wanted another lunch meeting with the serious associate and did not want to feel as if she needed to reciprocate. His seriousness seemed to have a little too much arrogance in it.

~

Clients value their autonomy in everything that they do including interacting with lawyers. Individual clients have families, values, commitments, and communities through which they share their lives and process their decisions. So do the representatives of corporate clients. The significance, risk, and complexity of law matters do not mean that clients cede their autonomy to lawyers to make decisions for them. Medical conditions confront patients with significant decisions involving high personal risk, substantial uncertainty, and highly technical issues, and yet patients still value their ability to have and make choices over their medical care. Indeed lawyers ensure that doctors provide patients with informed consent over medical procedures. Law matters are significant, risky, and complex but no more so than medical-care decisions. Clients need, value, request, and deserve autonomy support from their lawyers.

Clients face particularly acute autonomy issues when purchasing law products and services. Law matters are often obscure and complex. Clients often have little or no law knowledge. Clients must rely heavily on their lawyers for advice and evaluation of their matters. They will often not perceive that they have options unless the lawyer tells them so. If the client does perceive that the client has options, then the client may still not understand those options without the lawyer's advice. Effective lawyers recognize and address the autonomy crisis that clients face, primarily by offering options and information enabling clients to evaluate and choose wisely among those options.

Because clients value their autonomy, and because clients often do not understand their legal matters sufficiently, choice is important to clients. Autonomy depends on choice. A client cannot claim independence and self-governance when a lawyer presents no options. A take-it-or-leave-it approach leaves the client dependent on the lawyer's one offering. Probably, few law matters truly present only one option. Most if not all law matters leave at least some room for pursuing different goals through different strategies meant to achieve different interim objectives. Even where circumstances strictly limit or circumscribe goals, strategies, and objectives, lawyers and clients may be able to allocate at least some of the tasks necessary to pursue those goals, strategies, and objectives.

Steps to Take

Some prospective clients, especially in consumer-law services, will already have conducted extensive research online into the legal issue they face. They may have already read about possible solutions. These clients may regard their preliminary knowledge and plan as reliable, when you would know that they are not reliable. Explore prospective clients' knowledge and expectations, and their sources for that knowledge and those expectations. Help them evaluate the reliability of those sources. Explain why you believe your specific course of action is better. Help clients make choices informed by reliable information.

Clients value choice in evaluating lawyers' offers of products and services in part because they find choices elsewhere. Choice is everywhere, in every offer of products or services outside of law products and services. Clients can choose to which schools they send their children, which of 100 cable- or satellite-television stations to watch, and where they will eat for dinner. They choose their cell-phone companies, motor-vehicle insurers, and news providers. Clients choose their dentists, oral hygienists, and hairdressers. They choose their churches and synagogues, parishes and priests. They choose their music and medicines. In this environment of choice, the lawyer who offers nothing but a single product or service at a single price for the client's specific need runs the risk of failing to serve the client.

Choice is especially important on price. Some law matters present few if any strategic options. Yet even where strategic options are limited, and perhaps especially where those options are limited, clients should have price options. As just mentioned, lawyers may be able to develop price options by offering to divide tasks between lawyer and client or perform less than all aspects of the matter, especially but not solely in transactional matters. Unbundling law products and services into their discrete components can give clients price options. The entire legal-service-provider industry builds on the possibility, wise or not, that individuals can self-represent in at least some of the tasks related to their law matters.

Lawyers may also be able to develop price options by offering different quality levels of products and services within the basic standard of competence. Not every product or service needs all of the bells and whistles. For example, Appendix C includes three different process models, process choreographies, or event-driven process chains, involving a client seeking a cohabitation agreement. Each model describes a different level of client service for the same cohabitation-agreement product. The process models intimate the lawyer's different cost of producing each of those three same products with different quality level. The first agreement the process model designates as "bells and whistles," the second a basic plan, and the third an automated product. The first product involves three lawyer-client meetings, the second product one lawyer-client meeting, and the third product only lawyer review without meeting. The firm could price each product at significantly different levels to meet varying demand.

Choice is important not only on price but on product and service options. Enterprising lawyers develop a spectrum of offerings limited only by their sensitivity to clients' needs and interests, and the complexity of the law project. A following section on law-project management helps illustrate the broader range of product-and-service offerings for any one project. Choice on price and product-and-service options gives an enterprising lawyer an advantage over other providers while also developing new client-service populations.

Choice is also important to the individual lawyer or law firm because clients certainly have choices among lawyers. Corporate clients especially, but individual clients, too, evaluate multiple proposals for law products and services from different lawyers and law firms. They also evaluate proposals for law-related products and services from non-lawyer entities including accounting firms, business consultants, and title companies. The more choices that lawyers and law firms offer clients in law products and services, and law-related products and services, the greater more lawyer expertise clients can acquire to address their needs and interests, and pursue opportunities.

Steps to Take

Know the extensive-choice paradox. Choices are good for clients but only up to a point. Too many choices can leave a client unable to decide concerning a specific product, service, or plan of action. Do not overload clients with unnecessary options. Consider a dealer's offer of two identical cars, one black and one white. If the customer chooses one over the other, then the choice may have satisfied the customer who chose the more desirable alternative. However, if the dealer offers red, orange, blue, and green cars, too, then the customer's choice becomes more difficult due to the additional options. Offer choice, just not too many.

From the lawyer's standpoint, offering price options depends on the lawyer's ability to vary the four variables through which lawyers price products and services. As mentioned above in the section on affordability, experienced lawyers know how to estimate the cost of products and services based on price's four components. First, price is a function of the scope of a project. The broader is the scope, the higher the price. Client and lawyer can vary the scope of the work to generate price options. Second, price is a function of the resources (lawyer time, assistant time, administrative time, travel, expert consultants or witnesses, etc.) necessary to devote to accomplishing the matter's objective. The more resources are necessary, the higher the price. Again, though, resource allocation implies choices. Clients can often choose the amount of resources to devote to the law matter.

Third, price is a function of the risk of the work, whether the lawyers can discern and quantify all potential costs in advance of the price agreement. The more risk that a law matter carries, the higher the price. Finally, price depends to some degree on project timing. The shorter the time frame within which the client requires the project completed, the higher the price. If the client can accept longer time frames, then the lawyer may be able to offer a lower price option.

Lawyers can communicate choices on pricing, products, and services to clients from the beginning to the end of the professional relationship. Consider these examples:

- Print and other media advertising can convey ranges of services while stating or implying ranges of prices;
- Websites present especially rich opportunities to convey a firm's willingness and ability to price to meet client interests and abilities;
- Networking opportunities give lawyers the opportunity to discuss in person price choice, sensitivity, and flexibility;
- Office visits by prospective clients give law firms opportunities to provide brochures, signage, and in-person discussion of price, product, and service options;
- Intake systems can alert and communicate price, product, and service options to clients;
- Initial meetings are a critical juncture at which lawyer and client should clearly articulate service-level agreements after exploring price, product, and service options;
- Status reports can readily include information on pricing, product, and service options;
- Closing meetings and communications can reinforce the client's experience that the lawyer and firm are price sensitive and able to offer future pricing options.

Pricing choices are important to providing effective law services. The perception that lawyers set the price and clients pay it, leaving the clients no choice, may do more to prevent clients from seeking law products and services from lawyers than any other single factor. Clients' inability to choose and thus to some degree to control pricing may have more to do with lawyers failing to serve clients who need law products and services than any other factor. Effective lawyers give due attention to pricing choices. Consider next another important factor, accountability, in meeting client pricing needs and expectations.

Reflection

1. Why develop and communicate price options? What difference do you think price options make for clients? What difference do you think offering price options would make in the development of your law practice?

2. What law matters offer the greatest opportunity for flexibility in the level of product, service, and pricing? Where, in other words, do lawyers have the greatest opportunity to account for the client's available resources and price products and services within those resources?

3. What law matters offer the least opportunity for flexibility in the level of product, service, and pricing? Are there any law matters where the lawyer cannot offer any pricing option?

4. What makes some law matters, like certain litigation, more difficult to price? What makes other law matters, like certain transactional matters, easier to price? Do you think that with study of your experiences and the experiences of other lawyers, you could make reasonably accurate predictions of cost for most if not all products and services, and price accordingly?

5. When, optimally, would you communicate price options? How, optimally, would you communicate price options?

E. Accountability

Over his first two years, the associate had developed a keen sense of his accountability to both the firm. In fact, he accounted for every tenth of an hour. At first, the practice of tracking his time and activities down to the tenth of an hour had bewildered the associate. His life up to that point, including the jobs he had held, had required of him nothing close to that same level of accountability. Once he adjusted to the monotony of routinely recording the detail of his work in steady increments, the associate's bewilderment shifted to burden. The burden of timekeeping was greatest when the associate knew that he was not meeting his hourly quota. When he exceeded the quota, timekeeping took on a strange kind of joy.

The associate's sense of accountability to clients was not so keen. The associate did gradually develop a sense of how some clients felt about his work. For the most part, that information came through the firm's partners. A partner would occasionally let something slip about a client being unhappy with the project or the firm's billing. The partners did not seem to aim those quips at the associate, though, as if expecting him to change his conduct. Rather, the comments seemed incidental, as if the partners were just annoyed enough at the client's dissatisfaction that they could not help expressing their annoyance. At first, the associate had thought it odd that he got no direct client feedback. Gradually, though, the associate realized that his only accountability was to the firm, not to the client. He was on the hourly billing treadmill.

The only exception that the associate encountered was when one client began requiring budgets with each assignment. The associate discovered the client's requirement when a partner tired of preparing the budgets and delegated the task to the associate. The associate had never thought in advance about a project's discrete tasks or how long each task on one of the client's projects would take. He felt instead that his estimates were pure guesswork. He nonetheless listed what he thought might take place on the client's project, making rough guesses about how long each task might take. The associate turned the budget in to the partner and never thought of it again until the partner delegated another budget-preparation to him. Each time the associate prepared a budget, he wondered whether he ought to be billing for it.

~

The practitioner had the strongest bond of accountability to her clients. She did not always get it right the first time. In by far most cases, her sound intake, consultation, and documentation practices kept her on course and her clients satisfied with her products and services. In the rare case, though, she would discover that she had not met a client's needs. Sometimes, the cause turned out to be confusion over the client's objectives, more often confusion on the client's part but on one or two occasions the practitioner's own misunderstanding. On other occasions, they had understood and agreed on the objectives but simply had not carried them out because of unforeseen fortuities. In either case, the practitioner would immediately try to make the situation right.

For example in one case, the practitioner had thought that a non-citizen client had wanted her legal status reviewed, when as it turned out the client had been more concerned about the security of her children in the event of her sudden arrest for deportation. It had taken the practitioner a second consultation to draw out the client's deeper objective, but as soon as she had done so, the practitioner quickly prepared a limited power of attorney for a relative's guardianship of the child, satisfying the client. In another instance, the practitioner's work forming a limited-liability company had failed to procure funding for a client's business. In a second consultation, the practitioner and client had discerned that rather than a limited-liability company, the client needed a joint-venture agreement, which the practitioner had promptly provided.

The practitioner wanted to know how her clients felt about her work. Early on in her practice, the practitioner had developed a system of sending electronic messages to each client 30 days and 90 days after she completed their matter. Her 30-day follow-up simply ensured that the client had received everything that the client needed relating to her representation and was satisfied that the matter had closed. Her 90-day follow-up was more like a customer-satisfaction survey, gently asking clients to let her know if she had failed in any way to meet their needs or if she could improve her next service to them. She seldom got responses to either message, other than brief messages of appreciation. When she did get a response indicating any level of dissatisfaction, she acted right away. She had not had to refund any fees, but she had twice offered to do so. In each instance, the clients instead accepted revised products.

As a result, the practitioner never had any significant disputes over pricing, billing, or value. Her clients seemed to accept that she was accountable to them. The practitioner also appreciated that her clients were accountable to her for payment. She expected their accountability as a measure of respect for her and her products and services, and as a matter of self-respect for the clients. Accountability worked both ways, and her clients knew it. Most of her practice involved fixed fees in advance, retainer fees, or contingency-fee work, so that collecting on accounts would not have been a major practice issue. Yet where she did bill clients, she received payment on nearly all of those accounts. For the most part, the only accounts receivable that she carried were family-law matters where she and her client anticipated fee-shifting at the matter's conclusion or payment out of divided property.

~

Accountability is critical to effective law practice. An effective lawyer gives account to the client. Lawyers do not practice for the benefit of lawyers. Lawyers practice to benefit clients. Law is a service profession. Lawyers serve clients. Clients do not serve lawyers. Lawyers must demonstrate that their service considers the client's interests as primary. To give account is to prove the wise commitment of resources to the client's interests, particularly that the lawyer spent those resources in the most efficient and effective manner possible toward achieving the client's objectives. Lawyers are accountable when they are able to show clients that they have given due consideration to the costs of their work in order to minimize those costs as they maximize the value of their products and services to their clients.

Enterprising lawyers act accountably toward clients in several different explicit ways at several different stages of a representation. A lawyer is accountable when:

- communicating and explaining pricing options in written form and orally before a client engages the lawyer;
- reducing a representation agreement to an understandable writing shared with and approved by the client in advance of the engagement;
- including sufficient detail in the representation agreement or subsidiary service-level agreements so that the client understands and can approve the manner in which the lawyer will convey value to the client;
- performing the work according to law project management guidelines developed and refined to control and minimize project costs;
- communicating project status with the client at appropriate stages in appropriate detail, in order that the client remain sufficiently informed to make sound decisions;

- providing accounts timely and with sufficient description and detail for the client to evaluate the cost, scope, and progress of the work;
- documenting completion of interim and final work promptly in a manner that secures for the client the benefit of the work;
- filing and recording documents with third parties timely to secure the client's rights;
- releasing personal property, monies, and accounts to clients promptly with accompanying documentation giving clients their full use; and
- providing closing statements and other indicia that the client's matter has concluded finally and properly.

Consider further just one of the above examples. A lawyer can include in every fee agreement a section titled "Client's Specific Concerns" in which the lawyer may list actions, features, or courtesies that the individual client values and to which the lawyer agrees to commit. Agreeing to meet specific concerns can quickly improve the client's price-to-value ratio. Even if the client identifies no specific concerns, the lawyer has communicated to the client that the lawyer was prepared to tailor the product or service to the client's interests and commit in writing as a matter of contract to supplying that product or service. Accountability includes not only making and keeping specific promises but also expressing the willingness to make and keep specific promises even when the client requests none.

Practice Tip

Communicating with clients timely is the single greatest way to show them respect and accountability. Do not leave your office until you have returned all client calls for that day, even if your return call is simply to say that you will reach them tomorrow. Communication helps clients recognize that you support, believe, and will advocate for them. Even when you lose a client's contested matter, your communication with and respect for the client can satisfy the client with your service.

An enterprising lawyer may elect to provide another level of price accountability by detailing in an hourly fee agreement the hours the lawyer expects each task to take and the anticipated associated fee. A projected-cost agreement helps clarify client expectations while helping the lawyer measure progress against expectations as the work proceeds. The client gets both a performance promise and price projection. The client and lawyer can even build in additional value when detailing the work and projecting the cost. Projected-cost agreements create a results-driven and client-driven process. The lawyer then works to produce the performance while gauging the cost against the anticipated price. Projected-cost agreements provide both flexibility and accountability. They also tend to generate lawyer-client communications whenever the lawyer sees costs substantially exceeding projections, inducing another form of accountability.

Steps to Take

Developing a projected-cost agreement not only helps the client but also is a practice-development tool. By detailing and tracking the progress of various stages of a case, you further develop for future clients specific aspects of that type of case. You improve at what you do. Develop a systematic way to track your own improvement over time. Catalog in a special file the small adjustments you make as you plan and assess your work. That process and catalog can help you justify fixed-fee and other pricing arrangements.

Benchmarking lawyer performance against client measures also communicates accountability. A benchmark is an established measure against which the parties to an agreement can determine whether the party promising performance, in this case the lawyer, has performed. Review your representation agreement for whether and how it communicates that you will provide those values to your client. Your representation agreement states the basis for the fee and how the parties will calculate the fee. It should also state the scope of the representation and how either party may terminate the representation. Yet does it state how the client will be able to measure your performance against the client's benchmarks? A fee agreement that benchmarks the lawyer's performance against measures that the client accepts communicates accountability.

Consider for example a fixed-fee agreement to form a nonprofit organization for the client and qualify the organization as tax exempt. The fee agreement could include a clause that some of the fee or the entire fee is contingent on the organization's receipt of Internal Revenue Service approval as a tax-exempt organization. If in the usual case the risk of IRS rejection is low and dependent primarily on following through promptly with the process, then an effective lawyer could easily benchmark final performance against IRS approval. Fee waiver is unnecessary for benchmarking but nonetheless an impressive commitment to accountability. The lawyer could benchmark interim performance against state approval of filed articles, tender of draft bylaws, submission of the completed application form, response to IRS inquiry, and other interim stages of the work.

Benchmarking can be especially useful in distinguishing your law products and services from the products and services of other lawyers and professionals. Benchmarking can connect your values and work more closely to your client's values and work. Other more-creative client benchmarks could include your firm's commitment to be:

- green, occupying efficient buildings while limiting waste and environmentally damaging products, activities, and travel, and contributing to environmentally sensitive causes;
- diverse, increasing and valuing the contribution and representation of differently situated individuals in the firm's work and community engagement;
- socially consciousness, remaining aware of, and attending and contributing to the needs and interests of, all members of the community;
- culturally engaged with the arts, education, and other programs and activities that enrich the cultural fabric and design aesthetic of the community;
- sustainable, adopting employee and workplace policies and practices that are responsible to each individual and their family members, and to future generations;

- innovative, continually investigating, assessing, and improving work processes over time to generate new value to clients and community;
- stable, ensuring continuity of personnel and services while planning for emergencies to reduce or avoid service interruption;
- technological, being early evaluators and adopters of efficiency-generating systems, software, and equipment to increase client value;
- accessible, sharing the firm's professional-development programs with clients to help clients generate new skills and efficiencies; and
- reputable, ensuring that the firm's public profile constantly enhances the client's own reputation within the client's community.

The keys to accountability are to discover your clients' interests and then define readily measureable benchmarks against those interests. Beyond identifying the requisite stages of the work, as in the above example, time is another common benchmark. Clients often need or desire prompt performance. From experience with other professionals, some clients will doubt or even fear a professional's failure to perform timely. Benchmarking performance against the client's time constraints demonstrates accountability. A fee agreement or service-level agreement can readily include the client's time constraints for stages of the representation or final delivery. Promise performance within a certain time. Parties can readily measure time.

Practice Tip

A seasoned lawyer who had practiced for 30 years entered the conference room where the local prosecutor held pretrials. Lawyers waiting for the prosecutor's attention filled the room. One of them asked the seasoned lawyer whether he was keeping busy. The seasoned lawyer joked, "Plenty busy. Answering all those grievances takes a lot of time." Attorney Grievance Commissions are no joke. Disgruntled clients occasionally complain to the Grievance Commission when they feel that their lawyer did less than an acceptable job. Responding to a grievance is urgent, serious, expensive, and time-consuming work. Sound practices save that money and time.

Other benchmarks can include the lawyer's reporting to the client the status of the matter at specific intervals or after specific stages. Benchmarking can include the lawyer's providing documentation of the accomplishment of certain tasks or the occurrence of certain events, with the documentation to be in a certain form within a certain time of the event. The more complex the work, the more detail the parties can negotiate as to the appropriate benchmarks. Yet even in a simple representation performed on a fixed fee, the lawyer's willingness and ability to promise to the client that the lawyer will perform in measureable ways meeting the client's needs communicates accountability.

Practice Tip

How fixed are fixed fees? The answer may depend on the client and situation. For example, a lawyer may have a fixed-fee price that requires up-front payment. The lawyer may waive the up-front requirement for a reliable former client who desires the new service at the fixed-fee price but asks to pay over three months. Few lawyers would send the former client away. Fixed fees do not preclude letting the client know that you can be flexible and are reasonable.

The critical accountability, though, is the ratio of price to value. While price-to-value accountability can be the hardest to build into a representation agreement, from the client's standpoint price to value is also often the most worthwhile accountability. In fixed-fee, value-based, and contingency agreements, the value lies on the performance side. The benchmarks should be like those examples stated just above, on the interim and final objectives of the representation, time for performance, and manner of communication. In hourly or other flexible-pricing agreements, the value lies on both the performance side and price side. The parties must establish benchmarks not only on performance, as above, but also on price.

Accountability on price implies that the lawyer has adopted a set of attitudes and will employ a set of practices that place the client first.

Clients know that hourly fee agreements reward lawyers for inefficiency. The lawyer's fee increases as the lawyer takes more time rather than less time to complete the client's project. Fixed, contingency, and value-based fees avoid this reverse price-incentive problem. Yet lawyers can still build some accountability into hourly fee agreements. Budgets are one example. A lawyer who offers a project budget takes a first step toward accountability. The lawyer who agrees to communicate in advance when departing from a budget provides another level of accountability. The lawyer who agrees to disincentives for budget departures (reduced rates or forgone bonuses, for instance) demonstrates another level of accountability.

At root, accountability suggests that the lawyer will be frugal with the client's money, not in affecting the quality of the work but as to the practice style of the lawyer. Frugality of the right type is an asset in conducting a law practice. It enables a lawyer and firm to conduct affordable work that others could not. Frugality touches first on the practice's cost structure. Cost structure includes such keys as the size, location, and cost of the practice's office or other physical space. For clients, small offices, shared offices, home offices, and leased conference sites, rather than sumptuous offices, can be good things. Cost structure includes the cost and efficiency of the practice's technology, through such advantages as software as a service and cloud computing. The point here is not to identify these practice-management specifics but to recognize that frugality can demonstrate accountability.

Effective lawyers also seek and welcome feedback on performance, from clients and others. Ongoing client-satisfaction surveys are essential for continually refining and improving your services, and to the success of the services that you deliver. No matter how you deliver your services, you can find ways to assess and refine those services. Appendix D includes a template client-satisfaction survey. You can modify any of its items to fit your practice. Shorter surveys yield more-frequent responses, while longer surveys can provide greater insight. Accumulate and analyze responses in a spreadsheet or database that enables you to sort the data to distinguish systemic from individual-client problems. Modify surveys frequently enough to gain the insight that will improve your practice.

Consider offering a different survey to every client at three points: (1) after initial intake; (2) during your service; and (3) when your service concludes. Use the initial survey to evaluate the client's expectations and preferences, familiarity with the law, legal system, and lawyers, and the client's knowledge of the client's own problem. The initial survey may reveal value that you can add to the client's matter including additional contacts, meetings, information, and services. Use the ongoing-work survey to identify potential problems before they interfere with the client relationship. Use the closing survey to identify individual and systemic issues in how effectively you served the client, and to build or regain the client's confidence in your services.

A last aspect of accountability is what a lawyer should do when the lawyer has not performed as promised. Effective lawyers ensure that clients have the opportunity to communicate satisfaction or dissatisfaction with the product or service. Whether simple or elaborate, formal or informal, effective lawyers provide time, space, and means for clients to communicate their reaction to the performance. When a lawyer has not met reasonable client expectations of performance, the lawyer should remedy the situation promptly. Be accountable to clients.

Reflection

1. Consider various services that others provide to you. How accountable does each service provider appear to you as to the service's quality, timeliness, and price? How (and how well) does each service provider communicate its accountability to you?

2. Think of an instance when a service provider had not performed for you as expected. How did the failure come to your attention? What, if anything, did the service provider do to remedy the failure? How did the event affect your willingness to use the service provider again?

3. Having now reflected as just above, do you recognize that you choose service providers based at least to some degree on their accountability to you? Can you think of an instance when you refused to retain an unaccountable service provider?

4. How accountable are you in your law practice? Using some of the examples in this section for ideas, make a list of how you might improve your accountability. Then, rank the items on your list in terms of both significance to your client and achievability to you. Work today on the number one item in each ranked list.

Part III

Delivering Services

When he had joined the firm three years earlier, one of its assets that the associate had most appreciated was its address. His firm occupied the top floor of the premier office tower in the city. To the associate and others, everything about the location spoke quality, success, and exclusiveness. New clients, he had been sure, felt like they had finally arrived—had made it—when they entered the firm's premier office suite and retained the firm. The associate had certainly felt that way when he joined the firm. No organization could occupy such premier space without having been successful. To secure and maintain the address would have taken a substantial financial commitment over a long term, both of which (money and longevity) would have been key indicators of success.

Three years later, though, the associate was no longer so sure about the address. He had learned how high costs affect the work of the firm.

He had seen how high costs influenced the hours the partners expected the associates to work, the incentives the firm maintained maximizing its revenue, the relationships of partners to partners and partners to associates, and so many other critical aspects of the firm's work. The associate realized now how high costs limited the community's access to the valuable products and services of the lawyers within the firm. The associate was convinced that the managing partner had filled the firm with smart people who exhibited good intentions. Yet he also had seen how the firm's cost structure including in particular its expensive address inhibited those good intentions. Revenue simply had to be king.

Oddly, the associate now also realized how the firm's premier office suite limited the ability of the associate and other lawyers within the firm to engage the community's diverse needs and populations. So much of what the firm's lawyers did seemed to center on the firm's offices. The associate could tell that many clients would have preferred meeting and working elsewhere. When he had first joined the firm, he had taken such pleasure in the firm's sumptuous offices that he had hardly noticed clients' reactions when he invited them magnanimously to come in for a consultation. Now, though, he noticed their hesitation. The associate had even taken to reassuring clients that the firm would stamp their ticket for free exit from the building's parking structure. Even the firm's premier corporate clients seemed to want more client-centered work. One of the firm's corporate clients had requested that the firm's lawyers actually work on the corporate client's site.

The associate had finally realized how inflexible the firm's premier office space had become. He noticed how other lawyers just seemed to flow through, work within, and move about the community with so much greater ease than his firm's lawyers. The associate knew several lawyers who shared office space with other lawyers and some who even worked from their homes and cars without a permanent office. He had assumed at first that they were all new lawyers who could not afford a decent permanent office. The associate had gradually noticed, though, that the mobile lawyers were actually a good cross-section of the bar, some new, while others senior. Several were outstanding lawyers who lacked nothing in resource or skill. Even more intriguing, some had premier corporate clients like the associate's firm. Times, the associate concluded, were changing.

~

By the beginning of her fourth year in practice, the former solo practitioner (now the managing partner of a five-lawyer firm) was certain that she had made some wise choices along the way. Her first and biggest decision had been one that she had initially doubted more than all others. She had chosen as her first office a small space in a suite of street-level offices in which several other lawyers worked. Others had recommended that she open her own office, taking a larger space into which she could grow as her clientele developed. Office brokers had even shown how she could have afforded to do so.

Yet as a new solo practitioner, she had wanted to maintain flexibility in her cost structure and commitments so that she could go where her practice took her and clients wanted her. Low-cost, flexible, shared space suited her more than the higher cost and longer commitment of a multi-year lease. As it turned out, she had been able to add small offices to her own space in the same suite when her small firm grew. The short-term commitment had grown into a somewhat longer-term commitment but one that remained at low cost. Offices look so permanent and stable. She had learned instead that new offices were constantly under development while lawyers and other suite-holders constantly come and go. Her timing in this dynamic real-estate market had been impeccable. She had occupied low-cost, flexible, and appropriate office space over a relatively long term.

Her office suite was not even located in one of the premier office buildings in the downtown business district. That choice, too, had proven wise. Parking was at a premium (difficult to find and costly when found) in the downtown business district. Traffic was more congested. While the courthouse was downtown, and downtown had its own special energy, she had figured that her clientele might find her services more accessible in one of the several mixed districts that ringed downtown. Costs for space and parking were also lower in those near-downtown areas. Once again, her instincts had proven right. She found it easier and quicker to reach her suburban and rural clients. They found it easier and quicker to reach her. Her location seemed to connect well with both individual and corporate clients, urban and suburban clients, high income and low income, and young and old.

When she took on two more associates in her third year, she had also not hesitated to locate one of them in a different office in a district on the opposite side of downtown. The other associate worked almost solely from her suburban home. The practice's files were electronic, stored in the cloud, meaning that all five of the practice's lawyers could access the same files from any location. The practitioner had also elected early to treat her software systems as services rather than licensed products. That strategy meant that each lawyer in her firm could not only access files anywhere but could run the firm's software anywhere. One of her biggest concerns—constantly purchasing expensive new hardware and software—had evaporated. The firm did not even purchase hardware. Each lawyer had brought his or her own desktop, laptop, e-reader, or smart phone to the firm.

The practitioner realized in retrospect that nearly every one of her decisions had gone against the conventional law-firm wisdom but been consistent with how she sensed her practice ought to operate. She was thankful that she had stuck to her guns (as her mother would say). The results were deeper than her practice's efficiency and the access afforded her clients, mobility of her lawyers, and timeliness and quality of their collective work. The results had just as much to do with the identity and culture of her firm. In just a little more than three years, other lawyers knew her practice to be a fair, meaningful, and satisfying place to work. She could now see herself bringing new lawyers and their clients into her practice over the ensuing five years. She only needed to start planning for it.

~

Delivering law products and services is a different subject than packaging and pricing products and services. A lawyer could be good at discerning the right service to offer the right client population at the right price and yet fail at effective practice if the lawyer had an inadequate sense of how to deliver that service. In the end, law practice is all in the delivery. Providers of products and services in other fields will tell you the same thing. If you cannot bring the product or service to market, then you have nothing to offer. Success requires more than differentiating your law product and service offerings into market niches. You must also have *cost-leadership* strategies. All of a lawyer's hopes, dreams, and designs of making a decent living while serving others come to nothing unless the lawyer can deliver. Every practicing lawyer has been there, ready with all of the plans while wondering about the capacity to deliver.

Delivering law products and services has something substantive, authentic, and even physical about it. Delivery takes not just thought but action. An effective lawyer must be in motion. Yes, the mind must work, but so must the hands, voice, feet, and heart. Effective lawyers put things in motion and not just randomly or haphazardly but with precise design and intention. Delivering a law product or service as packaged and priced requires efficient action. Lawyers are not process engineers by training but are by practice and experience. They must know how law projects come together, in what order and with what design and resources. They must be able to motivate others and accomplish the work themselves to precise specifications.

Practice Tip

Running a successful law practice begins with controlling overhead. New associates in law firms have a harder time than solo practitioners do seeing how overhead costs affect a law practice. That effect is as simple as the adage that the pennies you save on overhead, you put in your pocket and your client's pocket. Overhead does not provide returns to you or your clients.

This Part III on delivering law products and services thus features project-management principles. Project management is a field that few lawyers actually study and even fewer law schools teach. That omission is surprising. Lawyers are constant project managers. They also train to research and assess before acting. More lawyers should be more aware of project-management practices. Enterprising lawyers who put into practice sound principles of project management can gain efficiencies that enable them to serve new client populations. Project management can be critical to a lawyer's ability to offer new products and services at lower cost in a way that makes those products and services affordable for new client populations.

Law practices depend on sound processes. According to process modelers, a sound process is one that defines the client and recognizes the client's priority. That priority may sound obvious, but some firms operate for their partner-owners rather than for the clients. Sound processes also define process outcomes. We ought not to do things just for the doing, but rather, for the getting them done—for *deliverables.* Sound processes identify the inputs necessary to produce the outcomes and the input suppliers. A sound process then (the critical part) documents requirements for the procedure's activities. What is it that we do, and how do we do it? Sound processes measure and monitor interim and final results to improve processes, setting new goals. Finally, sound processes allocate the resources to make the process work. Lawyers have an intuitive sense of these process steps. Express study can produce significant improvement.

Steps to Take

Consider the typical project-management tool as applied to tangible businesses like manufacturing. Abstract these well-developed management concepts. Then apply them to *service project management,* a specialized body of knowledge that requires applying a specific set of skills in service rather than manufacturing businesses.

For example, lawyers develop core competencies. Study of work processes can help you discern what those core competencies are and how they relate to producing value for your clients in line with your firm's strategic vision. Core competencies relate to a firm's mission. Firms do things well because they value them, devoting systems and resources to their improvement. Effective firms involve internal and external process owners in the improvement of core processes. Core competencies also relate to the competitive environment in which the firm operates. If other firms perform the same competencies just as well, then the firm may do better to refer away or contract out that work, to devote greater resources to developing other core competencies.

Practice Tip

Maintain an office. Client meetings require an office. You can meet clients at their homes, a local library, or the hospital. Meeting in non-traditional ways and settings will put off some clients. When you meet clients in non-traditional settings, treat the meeting place as you would an office, ensuring confidentiality and coming prepared with technology.

Delivery of law services requires not just process modeling and project management but also organizational development. Effective lawyers work within effective organizations, creating, managing, and influencing those organizations. Innovative lawyers influence their firms through strategies that shape the processes of those firms in positive directions with lasting effect. Lawyers wield that influence most productively through an appreciative-inquiry form of action research. They first recognize that members of a law firm share a vision for the work, while also sharing firm culture and norms. Every action that an effective lawyer takes to influence positively the firm's vision, culture, and norms must first appreciate the history and power of the members' collective action. While lawyers can and should act provocatively to influence positively a firm's norms, they do so best when beginning with appreciation and working collaboratively.

A lawyer's delivery of a law product or service must also entail a client's access to law, order, peace, prosperity, and justice. Efficient delivery is not enough. Law products and services do not stand alone as diversions, recreations, or attractive baubles. They have function. Their function is to order clients' lives, business, property, and affairs, to make them stronger, safer, more prosperous, and more productive. Law products and services must therefore be accessible, available widely to persons of all means at all times for all matters. In the American experiment, exclusiveness of law products and services is simply not an option.

Practice Tip

Sharing office space with other lawyers can work well. Keep in mind, though, that clients judge you by the company you keep. Share space with lawyers of good reputation. If you are newer to practice, then even the slightest thing can tarnish your new reputation.

The delivery of law products and services must also be mobile. It must move and flow within and through the affairs of clients where those affairs occur rather than exclusively in a certain office, district, or courthouse. Delivery must also be timely, for if delivery is not timely, then delivery can mean nothing and even worse than nothing. A law product or service provided too late for the event can leave the client worse off than ever for having relied to the client's detriment on a timely delivery.

Practice Tip

Controlling overhead requires sensitivity, not ruthlessness. Avoid being pennywise but pound-foolish. Overhead incurred to improve business cards, stationery, websites, and other details that convey your practice's quality image may be well worth it. Keep things looking professional.

Finally, law products and services inevitably carry with them aspects of the lawyer's identity. Law entails professional relationship. An effective lawyer imparts more than paper, more than product, and more than principle. Effective lawyers impart professional character and integrity. Their products and services imply future services and relationship, when the client's confidence in that implication can be more important than current product or service. Consider these five aspects of delivering law products and services, the efficiency with which the lawyer must work, access that the lawyer must provide for clients, mobility of the work, its timeliness, and the identity through which the lawyer acts. Begin with a consideration of efficiency.

Reflection

1. Think of a home-delivery service of any kind. What need does it fulfill? How else could the service's recipients receive the same service

other than by home delivery? To whom does home delivery make the service accessible?

2. Think of a service not delivered to homes but that could in theory be delivered to homes. Why do service providers not make home deliveries of that service?

3. Rank in order of significance to clients these five factors affecting the delivery of law products and services: (a) the lawyer's efficiency in delivering the product or service; (b) the client's access to the product or service; (c) the lawyer's mobility relating to the work; (d) the timeliness of the product or service's delivery; and (e) the identity of the lawyer providing the product or service.

A. Efficiency

The managing partner had gathered the associates for a rare meeting. Evidently, the managing partner had been meeting with a business consultant of some kind to review the firm's practices. All of the partners except the managing partner were conspicuously absent from the meeting with the associates. The newest associate, now a two-year veteran at the firm, took note of their absence. That the managing partner never mentioned the other partners or any role that they might have in the initiatives that the managing partner discussed at the meeting confirmed for the newest associate that the partners were not buying what the managing partner was selling the associates. The newest associate would wait and see, but the proverbial handwriting was on the wall that this initiative would simply be another like the failed ones that had gone before.

It was too bad, the newest associate thought, because this initiative seemed to him to have more promise than some of the earlier ones that the managing partner had presented (usually by memoranda) over the previous two years. The associate had been reading a little about law firm and other organizational management, some of it in the bar journals but some also on the internet and in some books that he had picked up online. The associate entertained no illusions about affecting how the firm did its business. Who was he but the firm's most junior associate? No partner, not even the senior associates, had ever shown any interest in his thoughts about the firm's management—not that he had ever tried seriously to express them. As he thought about it, he realized that his curiosity about management issues probably worked to assuage his growing sense that the firm might be imploding.

In any case, this meeting had been about systems that might help the firm improve its business processes. The managing partner's announcement had surprised the newest associate, who had never heard any partner at the firm talk either about the business of the firm or describe anything that they did as a process. The managing partner had forgotten the precise terms for the new initiative but said the terms were not important. The managing partner said that he wanted the associates to try to define the things that they did repeatedly on each new project—to break processes down into parts that the firm did over and over on each new matter. The managing partner then wanted the associates to measure the resources they devoted to each part, analyze whether they were using the right resources, propose improvements in resource allocation, and finally to propose ways to control the next projects to ensure that improvements remained in place.

To the newest associate, the managing partner's initiative sounded like some of the things that he had been seeing in the management literature. Unfortunately, the way that the managing partner had presented it seemed to give the initiative no chance. Why assign process investigation to associates, the newest associate wondered? He had already surmised the answer, though, which was the other partners' reluctance to change anything having to do with the firm's management. The firm's management probably served the partners too well as it stood, even if that management did not seem to serve its dwindling client base or, for that matter, its weary associates so well. The newest associate had half a mind to see what that solo practitioner thought about this business-process idea. He had heard that she had taken on some associates of her own.

~

Three-plus years in, and the solo practitioner was no longer a solo practitioner. Near the end of her first year of practice, the solo practitioner had begun to realize that she had more work than she could handle. She had simultaneously realized that she understood enough about that work and how to manage it that she just might make a good manager of other lawyers. For the entire second year of her law practice, the solo practitioner had studied business processes and, more specifically, law project management. No, she did not need law office management help. She was figuring out those basics—office lease, office equipment, staffing, payroll, accounts, billing, website—just fine from her network of professionals and other resources. The learning curve was steep but manageable.

Instead, the solo practitioner had been looking beyond the usual law-office-management fare to confront some deeper issues that back in law school she had learned law firms faced. Those issues had to do with the way that law firms packaged, priced, and delivered their products and services. She wanted her work to be different from what she had heard and read was challenging law firms. She wanted her work to serve clients, really to serve them, and to do so in a way that reached more clients at lower cost while making her a decent living. The solo practitioner had found many answers (not all the answers, but many answers) just beyond where it seemed that other lawyers were looking. She had found answers by using her critical-thinking skills, challenging assumptions not about the law and facts of her clients' matters (well, she did plenty of that critical thinking, too) but about the practice of law.

One of her best discoveries had to do with law project management. The solo practitioner had first stumbled on the continuous-improvement literature, how one defines the task goal, locates the resource measurements, analyzes those resources to improve allocations, and then controls to ensure consistent implementation of the improvement. The continuous-improvement literature was hard not to stumble over insofar as it was so prevalent, at least outside of law firm management. Yet law project management had been the real key to applying continuous improvement to her work as a solo practitioner.

She had learned to chart a tasks timeline for each of her products and services and then to study the timeline for improvements.

For a while, it had been hard going. She had spent many nights and a couple of weekends just on the first chart, starting with one of her simplest products. The effort had shown her that even her simplest product or service had several more steps than she had imagined. That discovery was alone a revelation. Law work presented many more opportunities to delegate, outsource, or share work than she had imagined before she completed her first decent project-management timeline. Once she was satisfied that her chart represented each step of what she actually did, she went back over each step, asking how she could increase her efficiency and reduce her cost in delivering the product. The result was a series of incremental improvements in the first product that she studied.

Each improvement was small, but together the several improvements made a big difference. The solo practitioner found that she could cut her time and cost of producing the product, while actually increasing its consistency and quality in small respects. She had then asked how she could ensure that each improvement remained in place, finding simple cross-checks, developing checklists, and isolating necessary review and supervision. The overall result was that she had greater confidence than ever in the product, which she was now producing easily at a lower cost. Each of her next product and service analyses took less time. When she was done with all of her core products and services, and found her practice busier and more profitable than ever, she knew she had the management acumen to hire her first associate. She hired two, and within a little over another year, she had hired two more.

~

Delivering law products and services entails efficient processes in actually producing the law product or offering the law service. Lawyers must be efficient to deliver affordable law products and services. Efficiency suggests more than the simple ability to complete assigned work. Efficiency is normative. Efficiency suggests that a lawyer can do work in a time and manner that meets reasonable expectations as to the resources expended. The more work that a lawyer produces in less time and with less expense, the greater is the efficiency of the lawyer. Consistent delivery of law products and services requires efficiency. Inefficient lawyers cannot deliver products and services consistently. Inefficiency decreases the predictability, increases the cost, and reduces the reliability of the product or service.

Delivering law products and services need not be inefficient. The saying goes that watching a legislature make law is like watching a butcher make sausage. Lawyers, though, have more control than individual legislators when producing law products and services. Lawyers can design and implement work plans with a much greater degree of predictability and precision. Certainly, law work has variables. Every work does. Yet law work also has patterns. Much of what lawyers do is according to routines, protocols, and patterns built on substantial experience. Delivering law products and services involves a relatively high degree of predictability. Predictability lends itself to studying and improving efficiencies.

Practice Tip

Improve efficiency by thinking outside the box. Practitioners building practices have options galore. Consider providing services at a corporate client's site one day a week. Answer law questions at a flat reduced fee at a local township hall once a month. Possibilities abound. People, businesses, and organizations need law services. Make your niche available, accessible, and affordable services.

Lawyers increase efficiency when they use law project management effectively. Lawyers can estimate project costs informally. They do so all of the time, intuitively. Every practicing lawyer carries a clock in the mind, gauging the work's progress against the estimated or available time and against project deadlines. Most lawyers make those judgments on the fly, constantly, using experience accumulated and skills honed over years of practice. One of the challenges for a lawyer entering a new field is that the lawyer will lack reliable estimates of the time each part of the work will take. Every lawyer knows that subject knowledge is important. Lawyers must know the law. Yet process knowledge is also important. Lawyers must constantly judge a work's progress. They ordinarily do so drawing intuitively on an undefined body of process knowledge.

When a lawyer instead records and analyzes project tasks using explicit analytic systems, the lawyer can find efficiencies in the ordering of tasks and assigning of resources. Business-process modelers call those improvement *process orchestrations* or *process choreography*. A *process model* describes the steps that an organization uses to produce a product or service, and the relationship of those steps to one another. Each step models the activity, while the process model orders the activities capturing their relationship to one another in accomplishing the business objective. The process model makes explicit the sequence of steps, like algorithms, that personnel have developed over time to accomplish a business objective. In social and cognitive psychology terms, process models help a lawyer build new cognitive schema or scripts for reliable practice. Experienced lawyers process automatically using ingrained professional schema, scripts, and heuristics that they no longer recognize explicitly. Those lawyers may not even readily be able to articulate those scripts.

Steps to Take

When first forming a new practice or entering a new practice area, organize, model, record, and analyze every activity you undertake. Make the practice of modeling and studying your activities a continual development tool. Make it the first thing that you do each day. Make your processes progressively smoother and therefore easier to undertake.

Process models grew out of studies of *workflow*. Workflow studies emphasized the physical route of papers or other products. Process models emphasize integrated, staged functions, particularly where paper or other physical product is not present. Process models can look like flow charts. Advanced process models can diagram the activity states of various personnel, departments, systems, or other entities as they work in parallel, series, or independently to accomplish the business objective. A well-designed process model meets what modelers call the ACID test of atomicity, consistency, isolation, and durability. Personnel or automation should be able to complete each step in the model, transfer the process consistently to another stage, not interfere with other steps, and produce results that survive failures in other system processes.

Process modeling offers another advantage in that it helps you discern your practice's business rules. A *business rule* is different from a process. It is a policy or constraint by which your practice operates, that your practice's processes must accommodate. Obvious rules include ethical constraints like not accepting matters that create conflicts of interest or require practice in a jurisdiction in which you are not licensed. Yet other rules, like those arising out of your strategic vision, professional commitments, practice knowledge, and business efficiencies, can be just as important to the success of your practice. Process modeling helps identify these rules for study and refinement. For instance, you might find that you have implicit business rules regarding core competencies (to accept matters only in certain fields), compensation (requiring contingency fees of no less than 25%), accounts receivable (requiring retainer fees), case handling (to serve discovery requests with the complaint where allowed), and prompt work processing (to open mail immediately on receipt).

Process modeling follows a method that begins with your firm's organization, mission, vision, and strategies. Strategies help guide your selection of specific new products and services within your firm's mission and vision. Research into available data and using empirical study of interviews should then help define the process-design goals for a specific new product or service. The design phase then represents the specific activities and their relationships to one another. You then, in a step modelers call *platform selection,* assign the personnel functions and technologies to implement the process. The implementation phase includes testing of the process results. The deployment phase includes training the personnel. Operation and control ensure that the process follows the design.

Once an organization creates a process model by observing and recording those activities, the organization can then prescribe those same steps for future similar processes. Lawyers and firms constantly train new lawyers and staff in these processes, although few do so using explicit process models. Process models aid in training. Lawyers constantly employ these analytic systems and methods, but for the most part they do so only intuitively. Effective lawyers do so explicitly, making analysis of their work transparent and accountable. Effective lawyers study and control their work processes. Continual performance assessment is a natural and necessary part of any professional practice. Even experienced lawyers make errors due to over-confidence barriers and planning fallacies. Effective lawyers self-study their processes and performance, as an aspect of accountability to clients. Process models help them do so by making the automatic processing explicit.

Prescription for new or inefficient employees, though, is not the only or necessarily the primary use for a process model. A process model also helps the organization explain and justify the process, including its integrity, timing, and cost, to others such as lawyers may often do for clients. Moreover, a process model also permits the organization to study and improve the process. Analytic systems like process models that encourage a lawyer to define the process, identity quantitative measures for process components, analyze those components for optimal use of time and resources, improve those allocations, and control those variables during process implementation lead to system efficiencies. Process models help organizations identify data to collect to improve processes. System efficiencies lead to lower, more affordable prices. See three process-improvement studies in Appendix E.

If you have not done so already, then consider making a law process model for your most common product or service. Create it in table form. Along the top of the table, list each stage involved in producing the product or completing the service. In separate boxes for each stage, first define the stage, then articulate the cost measures (time, expense) for the stage, analyze those cost measures, discern and record improvements, and state how you would control those improvements to ensure that they remain in place. When you are satisfied that you have a sense of how to use process models to improve your work processes, then try developing another model for your next-most-common product or service, until you have developed a set of models for each of your common products or services.

Process models can help lawyers build project-management plans for complex law matters and then use those plans to negotiate price, performance, and schedule with the client. Individual process models track the time and resources necessary to complete tasks. Accumulating those process models into a single project-management plan can define the costs for a specific project. It can also help determine performance parameters and appropriate schedule. A project-management plan can also record risks involving project costs and delay. See Appendix F for two examples of project-management plans and schedules with risk disclosures.

Use project-management plans to communicate and negotiate with clients to provide maximum value to minimum price. Gain the client's commitment to the specific aspects and costs of the project. Use the project-management plan to validate the project's scope, cost, and particulars with the client. Effective lawyers welcome client participation in planning performance, particularly with sophisticated clients who understand processes but also with unsophisticated clients. When a client sees the detail and complexity of a lawyer's work, and how deliberately the lawyer plans and studies it, the client will appreciate better the lawyer's accountability to the client. Project success entails not just reasonable time, cost, and performance, but client acceptance of the project.

Different organizations have different levels of maturity in their use of project management. Most firms continue to use ad hoc systems while their managers are aware of the benefits of process models and project management. Some firms will have already introduced project-management structures and standards for at least their core activities. More advanced firms would institutionalize project management throughout the firm and will use process models for all repeated activities. The best of firms would integrate their project management and process models into the management of the firm, optimizing efficiency and resources using benchmarking to achieve success consistent with the vision of the firm and measures of its clients.

Process models, or law project management guidelines, are just one tool that lawyers can use to improve efficiency in delivering law products and services. Once an organization develops a process model, the organization can use other principles to allocate resources. Lawyers operate intuitively using the Pareto principle, which is that 20% of the work tends to produce 80% of the work's advantage. The last 80% of the work produces only marginal 20% advantage. Some projects require a lawyer to expend fewer than full resources for full project completion for full advantage. Dispute resolution, whether by trial or alternatives, presents a common example where clients may be unwilling and lawyers unable to expend the full cost of preparation for all contingencies. Effective lawyers distribute limited resources according to the Pareto principle where they produce the greatest advantage. In some cases, 20% of the preparation can get a client 80% of the advantage. Effective lawyers make sound judgments about where to spend limited resources.

Delivering law products and services efficiently also requires innovation. Technology changes constantly. The social and economic environments within which clients live, work, and do their business also change constantly. Other professionals and providers of products and services are changing to meet changing client needs and expectations. The lawyers whom law firms hire are also changing the way that they do and value their work, and balance it with other commitments. These changes all augur change in the way in which lawyers and their firms organize to deliver efficiently their products and services. The following sections explore some of the changes effective lawyers are making in order to improve their delivery of law products and services. Consider access issues next.

Reflection

1. What company makes for you the best example of the most efficient provider of products or services? How do you recognize its efficiency? Which of the following attributes, consistency, quality, timeliness, and price, do you believe depend on efficiency?

2. Taking your example from the prior questions, how do you think that the company made itself so efficient? What education,

training, skills, or experience do you think the company's managers have that most help them improve efficiency?

3. Think now of an example of a company that seems particularly inefficient to you. What education, training, skills, or experience do you think the company's managers lack that most inhibit them from improving efficiency? What other bars do you think exist in that example to improving efficiency?

4. How effective do you believe law firms are at employing analytic systems to improve efficiency? What makes law firms hesitate to improve efficiency using the means that organizations in other fields use?

5. How could you learn more about process efficiency? Identify three steps that you can take within the next month to learn more about improving product-and-service delivery efficiency.

DELIVERING SERVICES
- Efficiency
- **Access**
- Mobility
- Timeliness
- Identity

B. Access

The associate was surprised one day to meet the practitioner in the elevator on the way up toward his firm's office suite. They had not seen one another for months, although the associate had heard that the practitioner had hired associates. The two of them had greeted only briefly when the elevator stopped half way up toward the associate's office. The practitioner stepped off, saying that she was hosting a client conference. The elevator door closed behind her as they both said simultaneously that they should get together. The associate puzzled over what the practitioner had meant by hosting a client conference. The explanation gradually dawned on him. The practitioner must have been renting a conference room from that new office-suites tenant he had heard about coming to their building.

The associate could not at first quite tell why his discovery seemed to so disconcert him. Gradually, as he worked throughout the afternoon, that explanation also dawned on him. The practitioner had found a way to serve her corporate clients in the same building as his firm but without the premier cost. The associate had heard through the grapevine that the practitioner's new associates were doing some corporate work. That news, though a little surprising, had not concerned him. The practitioner's corporate clients must have been emerging new businesses that could not yet afford his firm's services. One of those emerging new businesses must have wanted to use this building to impress someone.

The associate was just drawing some comfort from these inferences on his way down the elevator early that evening when the elevator stopped again at the floor where the practitioner had gotten off earlier that day. Two riders stepped onto the elevator. One was the practitioner, who smiled at the associate and extended her hand in warm greeting, already laughing at how quickly they had seen one another again. As the associate smiled back and laughed with the practitioner, the associate noticed that he recognized the other rider. It was the CEO of one of his firm's premier corporate clients. The practitioner and CEO got off the elevator discussing where they were going to have dinner to celebrate that afternoon's closing.

~

The practitioner knew some of the impediments her clients faced in reaching lawyers. Her pro bono work years ago in law school had taught her the security, comfort, and culture of location. As a law student, she had accompanied faculty members to the indigent clients' places like community centers, churches, soup kitchens, assisted-living facilities, and homeless missions. She had felt uncomfortable, unfamiliar, out of touch, and even insecure in some of those places, in contrast to the rich sense of community that the clients there shared. The diverse clients whom she met there seemed to share unspoken habits of greeting, dress, demeanor, language, time, and relationship. In their familiar places, the clients had an ease about them through which they readily expressed their needs and interests.

The practitioner had seen some of the same clients in places unfamiliar to them, particularly in the law offices, agency offices, and courtrooms to which their law issues took them. The clients behaved differently in those strange places. They were cautious, guarded, and even distrustful. They communicated little, and what they did communicate, they tended to communicate poorly. They behaved as if they knew that they had to assume the unfamiliar language of the unfamiliar place. They exhibited little or none of the hope and optimism that they expressed when in their more-familiar locations. They looked and acted as if they were isolated, alone, without social support.

The practitioner intentionally let these observations influence her choice of office and practice base. She had deliberately chosen a street-level office, one with its own door to the outside, to reduce the sense of exclusion and isolation. She wanted her office to have a physical connection with the community. She wanted her clients to feel as if they could bring their lives with them into her space, which she shared with them as their space. The practitioner also wanted her office located in a transitional community, a district that seemed to catch people between their own place and another place, where the corporate interacted with the individual, the educated with the uneducated, and the secure with the insecure.

The practitioner trusted her clients enough to believe that they, too, valued how their lives should intersect with the lives of others. Her corporate clients valued diversity and sustainability, and so she wanted her practice to support both values. She wanted diversity and sustainability to permeate her practice in ways that made her corporate clients want to hire her for those values. Her individual clients valued social conscience and community service, and so she wanted her practice to carry forward both values. She wanted her practice to speak social conscience and community service in ways that made her individual clients want to hire her for those values. Her practice had to provide access not only by packaging and price but by delivery, in tangible, even physical ways.

The practitioner's decision to let those access points—diversity, sustainability, conscience, and community—guide her delivery of products and services became for her a guiding principle. That principle to locate based on core practice values led her to decide on the location of her first office and second office, and to adopt home-sourcing. Lawyers can practice efficiently wherever they find an office and internet access, she had realized early. Unlike steel manufacturers or nuclear plants, law firms do not need a harbor or rail line, or abundant cool waters. The practitioner had sensed that clients, both corporate and individual, wanted her to impress them in new ways rather than traditional ways with fancy digs and expensive artwork. As it turned out, the growth of her practice proved that she had sensed right.

~

Delivering law products and services entails access. Access can mean several things when it comes to law products and services. Certainly, packaging law products and services in ways that client populations recognize value promotes access to those products and services. Offerings that seem complex, irrelevant, or arcane do not promote access. Pricing the packaged law products and services within reach of those client populations also promotes access. Offerings that appear too expensive or the price of which is unclear do not promote access. Yet beyond packaging and pricing, access also entails aspects having to peculiarly to do with delivery. How and where a lawyer offers a product or service has a lot to do with whether clients can access the product or service.

The lawyer's location is a first consideration. Just as the three rules of real estate are location, location, and location, location also has a lot to do with the effectiveness of a lawyer in reaching the client populations whom the lawyer expects to serve. Discerning lawyers know where their clients live, work, and obtain products and services. They have a keen sense of their community's neighborhoods and their various demographics. Discerning lawyers know how their clients travel and the districts in which and means by which their clients prefer to shop for products and services. Effective delivery of law products and services requires a lawyer to gauge the willingness and ability of clients to reach the lawyer at the locations and by the means through which the lawyer offers products and services.

Practice Tip

Business cards, websites, and telephone message systems remain keys to accessibility. Service is marketing gold. Give a client special attention, and they will sing your praises. Create and maintain a website that explains and defines your services. Ensure that your telephone message system transfers client callers easily to your personal greeting. Ensure that your business card reflects all ways to reach you. Consider your accessibility a financial asset.

For example, not all clients have ready access to transportation. A law office's location on a bus or other mass-transit line can mean a lot to whether certain client populations, particularly but not exclusively low-income populations, can reach a lawyer. Even clients of means may lack personal transportation, such as when elderly, medicated, or physically disabled, or when having lost a license, had it suspended, or never received one. Clients who do have transportation may still find that the cost, inconvenience, or risk of travel and parking discourages access. Clients value their own time, not just the lawyer's time. They also value their safety. Locations that are not just accessible but that are also near, safe, and convenient promote access.

Location can mean more than the client's ability to get to the lawyer's office, though. Location can also carry messages that either encourage and welcome clients or discourage and put them off. Uptown and downtown addresses, and urban and suburban addresses, send different messages. Ease or difficulty of access from the street, presence or absence of security guards or other access control, size and décor of the building lobby and office reception area, and dress and ethnicity of building and office staff all send other messages. Those messages can be cultural (formal or informal, inclusive or exclusive), social (professional, personal, or familial), historical (hidebound, traditional, or innovative), and financial (extravagant or responsible).

Practice Tip

Office location is a challenging issue. Many lawyers want to be right downtown at the county seat. Courthouse locations carry a number of advantages, particularly your quick access to the courthouse but also prestige and professional community. Yet many clients do not like coming to the big city. City traffic, directions, and parking can be daunting, and personal safety and property security questionable. Much recommends a community location.

Enterprising lawyers learn and value the messages that their office locations send to different client populations. A lawyer can use a research program to determine those messages and an assessment to evaluate office locations. The lawyer's research program might include, most directly, formal or informal surveys of, or focus groups for, the client populations. Ask the clients whom you hope to serve where they wish to see you. Research can also include formal or informal surveys of other lawyers and of other non-law service providers to those populations. Find out where the social workers, medical-care providers, and other professionals who already assist your client population are located. Property managers and brokers, while having vested interests, will also have substantial experience in public traffic and consumer preferences. Public information on residential districts and their demographic makeup, traffic patterns, and crime patterns can also help.

Access also involves more than location. A lawyer can have a perfect location and yet be perfectly inaccessible. Wherever their location, effective lawyers make themselves available to clients by the means and at the times most convenient to those clients. They meet with clients who walk in, take telephone calls from clients who call, and read and return email and social-media contacts. For some clients, access entails availability of the firm's lawyers at evening or on weekend hours. Some clients' work schedules prohibit them from taking time off for lawyer appointments. Other clients contend with childcare or eldercare issues. Corporate clients may have global or regional offices in different time zones.

Enterprising lawyers know their clients' access issues and accommodate them accordingly. Purchasers of law products and services can be notoriously difficult to locate and attract because of confidentiality and privacy concerns. Holding a public educational seminar for individuals interested in a divorce or bankruptcy, or suffering domestic violence, for instance, is unlikely to attract potential clients. People tend not to want others to know about their financial and family problems. The market for law products and services can be a hidden market. Finding the right location can be critical to overcoming the hidden quality of the law-product-and-service market.

The enterprising lawyer establishes a presence and identity in the client's location, whether including a physical office, residence, or simply periodic visits. Lawyers find clients when clients see and know lawyers in the clients' places, whether those places are residential or centers of trade, commerce, finance, faith, education, culture, community, recreation, or social service. The lawyer's presence may be physical, engaging the client population directly (without soliciting in violation of conduct rules), or it may simply be by reputation from prior service, charitable service, advertising, or participation in other positive activities. Lawyers communicate access in a variety of ways beyond a physical office.

Access can also certainly include language issues. Corporate clients may have foreign offices or managers whose foreign language counsel must accommodate. Urban, suburban, and rural communities can have large immigrant populations speaking other languages. Even relatively small cities can have insular communities whose members speak only foreign languages. Effective lawyers reach out and into those communities in ways that reassure their members of the availability of translation services. Translation services by telephone or in person through retained consultant or permanent staff are a norm for many law offices. Nonprofit, cultural, faith, and community organizations can also give effective lawyers bridges into those communities through bilingual professional staff.

Ultimately, access entails more than time, place, culture, and language. It entails a lawyer maintaining the right state of mind toward the clients whom the lawyer intends to serve. Effective lawyers exhibit an openness and willingness to reach and serve their clients on their clients' terms, no matter what dimension those terms invoke. Access is a broad and complex issue toward which effective lawyers maintain an acute sensitivity. Deliberate interaction with diverse populations can heighten a lawyer's sensitivity to access issues. Go ahead and make yourself uncomfortable. Place yourself in circumstances that challenge you to see the service world through other eyes. Consider next a closely related issue having to do with a lawyer's mobility.

Reflection

1. Who is the most convenient service provider you visit irregularly (doctor, dentist, optometrist, clothier, dry cleaner, etc.)? What about their location makes them so convenient? What other than their location makes them so convenient?

2. Who is the least convenient service provider you visit irregularly? What about their location makes them so inconvenient? What other than their location makes them so inconvenient?

3. If a non-lawyer member of your family had to visit a lawyer (other than you), what location would be most convenient for that family member? What factors did you consider when answering? Would they come to your office?

4. Try listing 10 access issues that one or more of your clients or client populations face. Then rank those 10 issues in terms of their greatest to least impact on your law practice. In other words, what is most affecting your clients' ability to reach you? Then analyze the top three issues for how you could improve access by eliminating or reducing those three issues.

C. Mobility

The associate had been finding it hard to fill his hours throughout his fourth year of practice. The partners still assigned him work, but they assigned him less work, and that work was taking him less time than it once did. There would have been a day when the associate would have welcomed a respite from the constant pressures of work, but not now, not today. Instead, he dreaded slow days, was eager for new assignments, and was never happier when he had a small backlog of work. Yet those days were fewer and the slow days more. The associate even realized to his disappointment that he had developed several habits to look busy, disguising when he had no work.

Finally, the associate decided to approach the partner whom he most regarded as a mentor, the one who had helped him through some other rough spots at work. The partner first listened intently to the associate's concerns and then started asking the associate questions. The associate was familiar with the partner's questioning style. He had expected her to draw something out of him more than to tell him what she thought. Her gentle interrogations were a large part of why the associate felt that she was his best mentor within the firm. Yet the associate was surprised when the partner questioned why he was interested in more assignments. He had thought that his problem was exactly that and nothing other. The associate left his brief meeting with the partner more puzzled than ever.

The phrase that stuck with the associate after the meeting was when the partner had asked him whether he getting *out and about.* The associate had laughed at the phrase when the partner used it, thinking at first that she meant that he needed better balance in his life, maybe a hobby or recreation, when his own diagnosis was that he needed more work, not less. The partner had not laughed in return. She had not even smiled. Nor did the partner seem to mean that he needed a hobby or recreation. Her questions that followed had focused on the associate's connections within and outside of their community. The partner had ended the meeting asking the associate to think about those connections.

The partner had also used the phrase *generating work,* a subject that the associate had yet to consider seriously. The associate was not naïve. He had heard long ago that firms valued rainmakers. He knew that it would benefit the firm and him if new clients came to him for their work. The associate felt that he had developed the skill and maybe even a little bit of a reputation for prompt, high-level, even sometimes masterful work. He had thought that his place at a premier firm and the high quality and general timeliness of his work would have won over clients. The associate had even seen a little of that influence, when a client occasionally asked him to do extra work that a partner had not anticipated or assigned.

The associate had just not thought much about getting out and about to generate work. He had certainly not made any such deliberate plan. The associate had always felt that the firm's office was his practice base, not the business or social community. He felt that he was being productive only when he was at work in the firm's office. The associate realized then that he believed that his success depended on attracting new clients to the firm's office. The firm's office was where things got done. He still believed that was true, that rainmaking meant getting new clients to come to his office, where he could convince them of his premier skills. He looked around his office.

The associate's secretary brought in the mail as the associate was musing about these things. As he sorted through it, he was surprised to notice his practitioner acquaintance (the one who leased conference space in his building) on the cover of a local business journal. The cover photograph showed local business leaders celebrating a charity auction's success. The associate thought that the practitioner—a relatively new and young lawyer, although also now the managing partner of a small firm—looked a little out of place among the other business leaders. Then he noticed the division manager of one of his firm's best corporate clients standing next to the practitioner.

~

The practitioner jumped at the offer. Her firm had been doing bits and pieces of work for a major corporate client that also employed other local, national, and international law firms. The practitioner had met the client's corporate counsel at a conference on business innovation in another city. They had spent much of the conference together after they realized that they were from the same locale. The connection had led to the small assignments that the practitioner's firm had done for the major corporate client.

Now, the corporate counsel had offered the practitioner the use of an office on the corporation's site. The corporate counsel had encouraged the practitioner to have the firm's lawyers use the office at any time, particularly though not necessarily exclusively for the corporation's work. The corporate counsel had just said that the office would be available for the firm's general convenience.

The practitioner had ensured that her firm's lawyers used the loaned office nearly daily since. Sometimes, one of the firm's lawyers would just drop by the loaned office for an hour, while picking up or dropping off certain of the corporate client's work. At other times, the practitioner or one of the firm's other lawyers was in the loaned office all day, working on the corporate client's matters but also doing other work. As a result, the practitioner and her associates had gotten to know more of the corporate client's business, culture, and staff. The practitioner could see that her associates now understood and even served the client better. The corporate counsel's innovation had worked.

The practitioner's technology decisions choosing cloud storage, software as a service, and other mobile operations had enabled her firm's lawyers to use the loaned office without interrupting the firm's work. They were all able to communicate instantly by webmail, cell phones, and videoconferencing. They could all access files remotely and work on documents simultaneously from remote sites. The practitioner had long encouraged her associates to work wherever they found it most convenient for themselves and their clients, sometimes at home, sometimes on the road, other times at community locations, and often at the clients' locations—nursing homes, community centers, and business offices.

The corporate client's loaned office simply confirmed what the practitioner had long sensed, that effective practice occurred as much or more outside of the firm's offices as it did in the offices. The practitioner had the sense of her firm's work flowing in and through the community more than the work having a single home base. She loved that sense of flow and community connection, valued that sense more than many other things about her practice. It was what made her encourage her associates to join community boards, volunteer for community projects, join business associations, and attend conferences and events. She wanted the public to see her lawyers using their skills all over the community, yes, in the highest places (the mayor's task forces, the arts council) but especially in the low places where the community most needed law products and services.

~

Mobility is an important factor in the effective delivery of law products and services. Mobility begins with a lawyer's ability to move from site to site while accomplishing work at each site or in transit. Law offices are not the center of client universes. Clients have their own place of operation and, like the other product suppliers and service providers on whom they depend, must also operate at other sites.

Clients move and expect lawyers to move also. Lawyers can connect with and serve clients in more efficient manner when they are able to come to the client, meet the client halfway, or otherwise move about while accomplishing their work.

Mobility may be as simple as working at the client's location. More law firms are loaning lawyers to corporate clients, having their lawyers work on the client's site. Lawyers visit headquarters, manufacturing plants, and regional offices of corporate clients. They visit hospitals, nursing homes, foster-care facilities, and residences of individual clients. For some clients, the only service is home service. Effective lawyers are simply more mobile in accomplishing their work, ready, willing, and able to serve their clients where their clients need the service. If there was once was a day when lawyers beat a path from their office to the courthouse and back, and traveled nowhere else, that day is long gone.

Not all mobility is efficient. Lawyers know too well that hours spent traveling to court, depositions, and other locations can keep a lawyer away from productive work. Efficiency in mobility depends on the ability to work away from a home base, meaning that it depends on mobile technology. Lawyers use laptop computers, e-readers, and smart phones to access electronic communications, store and retrieve cloud-based files, and use mobile software. They use portable printers to produce finished documents on site and mobile projectors to display those documents and other presentations. Battery-based mobile technology allows lawyers to work at anytime anywhere that they can obtain a reliable mobile signal while also producing and displaying finished work. Technology and work processes no longer tie lawyers to their desks or even to their firms' intranet. A mobile-practice briefcase is not an embarrassment but a mark of innovation and distinction.

Practice Tip

A new litigator, advocating for the father in a child-custody hearing, told the judge that she wanted to keep the mother from moving to another state. The judge replied, "We live in a portable society. Boundaries do not exist anymore. A global world is our future." The judge's words reflect how clients increasingly think about law services. You must be all about the mobile needs of your clients. Does the client want you at the client's office? Does the client want you meeting by videoconference to save money? Service, mobility, and accessibility form an equation that reaches and satisfies clients.

Of course, enterprising lawyers build efficiency into their mobility not only with mobile technology but also by wise planning of routes and scheduling of work. Travel to worksites can bring a lawyer closer to other worksites and client-contact opportunities at other sites. Clients do not generally expect their lawyer to stop by in person with draft documents or for brief discussions. The lawyer who does so on routes planned for efficiency can provide a high level of personal service beyond the client's expectations. A lawyer must use mobility efficiently. Mobility can create efficiencies across several clients and client projects. Travel that would be inefficient for one client or project may be highly efficient for several clients or projects.

Mobility is not limited to the lawyer's physical movement from work site to work site. Firms use document-sharing technology and videoconferencing for simultaneous collaborative work among their lawyers who are located in different offices or working from remote sites. Document-sharing services, readily available through major internet companies, not only make lawyers mobile but also change the way that lawyers can work. Two or more lawyers working simultaneously on a document can coordinate its development. They teach and learn from one another, and correct one another's mistakes. Collective work on a document speeds work processes. Individual lawyers do not obsess over producing perfect work before handing over a document to another lawyer or to a client for review.

Document-sharing services also enable lawyers and clients to share in the development-and-review process while working at separate locations. Clients can even test draft provisions while the lawyers continue other parts of the collective work, further increasing efficiency. To further increase client participation and access from remote locations, enterprising lawyers use file-sharing services giving clients secure remote access to anything that the lawyer makes available to them in their virtual files. Lawyers also use internet-based video services to communicate and work with clients from different locations.

Mobility, though, also requires a lawyer's willingness to move about and provide service to and from remote sites. The key is in conceiving properly of the delivery of law products and services. Producing law products and supplying law services does not require substantial industrial equipment, complex fabrication or assembly, or long supply chains. Law offices are not factories, central locations to bring together labor and materials to manufacture and assemble products. Today, with information retrieval, telecommunications, and video-communication available almost anywhere, law offices are more conveniences for lawyers and (sometimes) clients than they are necessities to what lawyers produce.

Mobility is also more than physical and technological. Mobility is also social, technical, and professional. Lawyers who move between communities, cultures, and demographic categories and classes gain social insight, discernment, and perspective. They are then able to use those social skills and perspectives to their clients' advantage. When lawyers move between industries, trades, and businesses, they gain technical insight, discernment, and perspective. They are then able to use those technical skills and perspectives to their clients' advantage. When lawyers move among professions, they gain professional insight that they then use to their clients' advantage.

Practice Tip

The practitioner found that mobility included expanding ideas for law products and services. The practitioner started to volunteer legal services for members of a local Indian tribe. Soon, the tribe had hired the practitioner to handle its legal work.

The mobile lawyer delivers higher quality products and services more efficiently than the sedentary lawyer whose office is the literal and figurative center of the lawyer's world. While often convenient for the lawyers, law offices can also readily become obstacles to the efficient delivery of services. Effective lawyers rise from their desks, leave their offices, and engage clients and community, valuing mobility as a key ingredient to delivering more services more efficiently. You will see effective lawyers at business gatherings, involved in government matters, on school boards, and at community events. You will see them involved in fundraising, faith gatherings, and volunteer and nonprofit work.

Mobility is also more fitting to human nature and preferences than sedentary work, healthier not only for law firms and clients but also for lawyers. People simply thrive when in motion. Mobility is not something for lawyers to dread, like yet another expectation of ever-more-demanding clients. Rather, movement between places and among people stimulates a lawyer's curiosity, interest, motivation, ambition, and senses. When lawyers can work from multiple locations, including office, home, school, client's location, an attractive community library, and maybe even when traveling with family, their work lives become integrated with their community life and take on added flavor and dimension. Mobility is a key ingredient to the effective delivery of law products and services because it is a lawyer and client's natural state. Consider next another key ingredient, timeliness.

Reflection

1. Think of two mobile services that, until recently, were available only at the service provider's location. How much more or less complex do you think mobilizing those services was than it would be to mobilize a lawyer's services?

2. Where do you work most? Where do you work best? Name three locations that you would like to work if your work was completely mobile as to location.

3. Where would your clients most like to see you work? Name three locations that your clients would like to see you available, other than your main office.

4. What is the one thing that you miss most, insofar as your ability to be productive, when not in the office? What could you and your firm do to make that factor mobile?

5. What mobile technology or tool would you most like to acquire? List your top three mobile-technology tools that you do not currently have but think would improve your work. Then locate a lawyer who

uses each technology. Inquire of the lawyer about how well that tool works and what steps the lawyer took to adopt it.

D. Timeliness

The associate had run into a bad string of events and just could not seem to shake them. It had started with getting a project out late. The partner who had assigned it to the associate had told the associate when the partner needed it back. The associate had duly calendared the assignment's due date and then returned to other work. He had figured that he would start the assignment two days before it was due, thinking that it was about a day-and-a-half project. He made a note on his task list to begin the assignment on that date.

In the meantime, the associate would do other work with nearer deadlines or work that he just preferred to do over the partner's assignment even though the assignment had a nearer due date. By now, after years of practice, the associate trusted his ability to estimate the complexity of assigned work. He was more than used to working against deadlines. Deadlines were now completely embedded in his nature. He needed deadlines to do most any work. The associate took no work without asking for and calendaring a due date. When the assigning partner would not or could not give him a deadline, he would calendar a due date out a ways anyway and bide his time before beginning the work. The associate thought of his practice as letting assignments ripen on the vine, as a master grower might. Practice should have a reflective pace to it, he had always thought. The more time one took, the more value one conveyed, right?

This time, though, the associate had underestimated the time that it would take him to finish the partner's work. The associate's lapse was completely uncharacteristic. Because he was seldom if ever late with work, the associate figured that the partner would forgive him. He also figured that the partner would let him know if the due date was a hard deadline. The associate then took another two days beyond the deadline to complete the work. When he was done, he made sure to print it out and hand-deliver it to the partner.

To the associate's disappointment, the partner had waved him away at the office door, saying simply that it was too late. The associate had paused for a moment at the door before offering the work again, starting to reassure the partner about the value of the associate's work. The partner had interrupted him and just said again, without even looking up from his work, that the client had needed it yesterday. The associate had to turn and walk silently back to his desk with the rejected work.

That one event had led to a cascade of similar events. The two extra days that the associate had taken for the partner's work had cost the associate needed work time on three other projects. Despite doing his best to get back on top of the work, the associate had missed two other deadlines and had fallen further behind on other due or soon-due work. Worse, once he got severely behind, the associate found himself distracted by the time pressure. Tasks that he could previously have done quickly with little thought now seemed to take hours of arduous labor.

The associate got so depressed with constantly being behind in his work that he began to groan and complain to his secretary. At first, the secretary tried some consoling words. When the associate continued to gripe, the secretary said nothing, ignoring him. When the associate continued to moan days later about the constant deadlines, the secretary told the associate that he was paying the penalty for procrastinating. The associate blew up at the secretary, denying that he had ever procrastinated. The secretary got up and walked out. Back in his office, the associate thought about what the secretary had said. The secretary was right, the associate decided. He had been a procrastinator since day one.

~

The practitioner loved the energy of practice. She particularly enjoyed that it constantly encouraged her to take immediate action. She likened her days to playing tennis, constantly hitting balls back over the net for someone else to act. The practitioner wanted to keep every ball in the other court. As soon as she could act, she did act. She really did not believe in deadlines. Oh, she calendared due dates just like any other lawyer. Yet rather than work backward from deadlines, leaving herself just enough time to complete each project before its due date, she worked forward from assignments.

In retrospect, the practitioner could tell that the way that she thought about and timed her work had been one of her greatest successes in serving more clients more efficiently. Her standard line with clients from her first day of practice had been to tell them when they could expect her to complete their project (in two hours, two days, etc.) rather than to ask them when they wanted or needed it finished. The practitioner's estimates usually pleased and often surprised her clients. Many times, the practitioner had heard clients laugh and make small jokes, when she had indicated that she would have the work finished well in advance of when the clients expected it. Yet she routinely met her estimates, to the surprise, satisfaction, and reassurance of her clients.

From the moment she had hired her first associate, the practitioner had made her timing system an integral part of her firm's work. She called her system *work against assignment* (WAG) in contrast to other firms' *work against deadline* (WAD). Liking the sound and secondary meanings of the two words, she would remind her associates to WAG, not WAD, and then laugh good-naturedly about it. To the practitioner, though, the timing of work was no laughing matter but instead a core part of her success. The system enabled her firm to get work out to clients more quickly than other firms. Repeatedly, she had head other lawyers speak about deadlines. She had also worked from time to time with co-counsel from other firms. Most of them seemed to use deadlines to schedule their work.

The practitioner wanted instead to deliver products and services as soon as she could provide them. She felt that in doing so, she could move on to other productive work, making her more efficient. Looming deadlines just tended to stress and discourage her. She felt much more creative and energized when she could tackle work as soon as it was available. She found that her initiative stimulated more initiative. By working against assignments, the practitioner found her able to say yes to additional work, without having to be cautious to save time to meet those looming deadlines. She realized that she was filling with new work what otherwise might have been gaps or interludes in her productive time.

The practitioner realized, too, that she was both a starter and a finisher. She had learned early on in her law practice that starting a new project is the hardest moment because it is fraught with uncertainties over how long the work will take and difficult it will become. So she had developed the practice of starting work immediately on assignment, even if starting meant simply opening a new word-processing file and putting a title on the document. She also adopted the practice of completing work, even when it meant choosing among alternatives that the client would only finalize later. She found that completed (still not finalized) documents were easier to evaluate than incomplete products. When orienting and encouraging her new associates, she added that phrase—be a starter and finisher—to her WAG-don't-WAD jingle. The practitioner did not want to seem like a taskmaster. These practices were not mechanistic drills. They were instead unleashing her associates' best energy and work.

Working against assignments also gave the practitioner time to share draft documents soon enough before they were needed for her firm to make any unanticipated revisions. Her early-delivery system had saved her firm and its clients much embarrassment and trouble on more than one occasion. Early completion also gave her and her associates time to reflect on and improve the work. The practitioner could hardly count the number of times that she had finished a project but then returned to improve it as additional thoughts occurred to her looking back on the completed work. She and her associates were not only working more quickly. They were also working better.

~

Every lawyer knows that the timeliness of law products and services is a critical ingredient to their effective delivery. So much of a lawyer's work depends on the lawyer performing to the client's timetable, or to timetables established by rule or regulation, court or agency, opposing party or counsel, or other third party. Many products or services delivered late have no value whatsoever. Lawyers must timely prepare and deliver wills, powers of attorney, purchase offers, liens, restraining orders, answers, motion responses, appeal briefs, and dozens of other documents. Clients' families, finances, and futures can depend on the lawyer's timely delivery of work. Law products and services are not critical in the sense of medical care or even social services. Yet they can have their direct and indirect effects on those critical needs and on virtually everything else that keeps clients' lives in reasonable peace, prosperity, and order.

Practice Tip

A lawyer's greatest service is communicating the right information in a timely manner. Some services, like answering a complaint, demand timely service. Other services do not appear to demand timeliness. Yet lawyers can substantially improve their services by treating those other matters with appropriate urgency. The client who wishes he or she was not paying for legal services in the first place should at least have the satisfaction of your treating their work as a priority.

While every lawyer knows the importance of timely performance, though, lawyers sometimes do not appreciate the several ways in which the timing of work can increase or decrease client confidence and value. Unfortunately, some lawyers have a notorious reputation for untimely work. The public reputation of lawyers generally in that respect is probably not high. A general expectation of slow delivery may be one of the main reasons (after cost) that members of the public hesitate to consult lawyers. The public expects timely delivery of pizzas and pharmaceuticals, not necessarily law products. A sense of uncertainty over the timing of the delivery of a law product or service undermines a client's ability and willingness to rely on the lawyer. Clients develop contingency plans or choose other options over law services.

By contrast, prompt delivery of law products and services increases client confidence and value. While some lawyers are notorious for delay, even among their professional colleagues, clients know other lawyers to be exceedingly prompt, reliable, and timely. Prompt and timely delivery increases clients' ability and willingness to rely on a lawyer's products and services. Some clients who have sound alternatives to law products and services, including self-help and self-representation, will nonetheless rely on their lawyer knowing that the work will be prompt and timely. A lawyer can garner more work that clients would have others perform or would do for themselves, when the lawyer's performance is quicker than the alternatives. Speed counts, particularly in transactional work but also in personal, family, and litigation matters.

Practice Tip

The first question a new lawyer working at a law firm should ask the partner who assigned the project is when the partner expects the new lawyer to complete the work. The second question the new lawyer should ask is how much time the project should take. The questions are actually independent. Both questions are critical.

As the above illustrations show, how a lawyer times work can also affect the lawyer's productivity. Timeliness is not simply a matter of satisfying client needs or beating client expectations. Timeliness is also a matter of the quantity and quality of work that a lawyer produces. Timing the delivery of a law product or service has a lot to do with balancing time and quality. Effective lawyers strike the right balance, as the section on quality also indicates. They also conceive properly of the way to prioritize, order, and execute work, as other sections also illustrate.

Just because a lawyer need not deliver a product or service until a distant future date does not mean that the lawyer should not deliver the product or service earlier. Some law products and services carry instant protective value. Remote or immediate contingencies can arise in nearly every client situation. Consider the following more-obvious examples:

- A young parent may not need a will with a guardianship designee for quite some time, but who knows the moment of one's own demise?
- An elderly client may not need a power of attorney for patient care for another few months, but who knows the moment of one's own delirium?
- A joint-venture agreement next month might satisfy a client's anticipated co-venturer, but who knows whether a more attractive co-venturers than the client might arise?
- A purchase agreement next week might satisfy the seller from whom the client hopes to buy, but who knows whether another buyer might make a better offer?
- A lender client's financing statement filed tomorrow may be sufficient, but who knows what other financier or tradesperson's liens might file today?

When it comes to timing, habits count. Procrastination does not merely increase the likelihood of untimely delivery of law products and services. It also reduces a lawyer's efficiency. Lawyers are naturally and wisely cautious, precise, and oriented to detail. Beyond those laudable attributes, though, some lawyers become perfectionists. There is no perfect product. Obsessing over the contents and quality of work does not routinely make work better. It may actually make the work worse. The obsessive lawyer over-thinks matters, by control eliminates collaboration, and by delay eliminates client review, comment, and revision. Obsession may also make the work late.

Practice Tip

The practitioner's job is to learn the urgency of the project to the client and to meet that urgency and expectation with results. A simple call to the client or writing a brief letter updating the matter's status reassures the client while developing trust. Try not billing the client for those brief letters. Describe the activity but write on "no charge" on the bill for those updates. The goodwill this practice builds will be worth far more than few dollars the charges would have earned.

Timing involves more than the right attitudes and execution. It also involves planning. Effective lawyers plan and know the shortest timeline through even a complex process. Like constructing a building, lawyers must do much law work in a certain order. In ordinary litigation, investigation precedes the complaint, which precedes service, which precedes discovery, which precedes motions, which precede trial, which precedes judgment, which precedes post-judgment appeals and collections. Effective lawyers are repeatedly triggering the next stage at the earliest opportune moment, knowing that their failure to do so can increase the overall project timeline from a few months to years.

Complex transactional work proceeds in the same way. Deliberate planning of timelines through complex transactional processes is nearly a necessity, not a luxury. Effective transactional lawyers know the critical timelines, whether for start-ups, mergers, acquisitions, reorganizations, or dissolutions. They plan their work and initiate the work of others accordingly, to bring the work to completion within the shortest responsible timeline. Prompt completion of complex work makes the reputations and even careers of individual lawyers. The failure to complete complex work within reasonable timeframes breaks lawyers and law firms, not to mention clients.

Some experts at time management and work flow suggest that multi-tasking is a myth because each individual project requires concentration. A lawyer can focus on only one thing at a time, when law work demands focus. As a result, it is easy to think of law work as a pipeline through which only one project can pass at a time. In that manner of thinking, a lawyer must prioritize work and then do the priority work before moving to other work, ever conscious of looming deadlines and deadlines piling on deadlines. Yet effective lawyers find ways to initiate work promptly, delegate portions of it, share its progress with other lawyers and with clients, recruit and rely on inside and outside support at critical junctures, and generally increase the speed, quantity, and smooth flow of work. In an odd sense, time managed in this manner allows for multiple dimensions.

Timing and timeliness are simply critical to delivering reasonable-cost effective law products and services. Time is a far greater consideration than most lawyers make it in their work processes. Lawyers know that projects have deadlines. Yet they often do not consider the full effect and value of timing, both to their own work processes and to their clients' interests. Timeliness has much more to do with effective delivery of law products and services than simply meeting another deadline. Consider one last factor having to do with the delivery of law products and services, the lawyer's identity.

Reflection

1. Think of a product or service that you once received late. What effect did its late delivery have on you and others? How did its late delivery affect your opinion of the product supplier or service provider?

2. What is the timeliest delivery of a product or service that you can identify? What makes timeliness so important to the effectiveness of that product or service? Are your law products and services any less important?

3. How do you conceive of the timing of your law work—as a series of deadlines like the associate in the first vignette above in this section or more like opportune tasks to initiate and complete immediately like the practitioner in the second vignette?

4. Identify from the above discussion three reforms having to do with how you manage time within your projects that could help you increase the speed, quantity, and complexity of your work. What is the first step you could take to institute each of those three reforms?

E. Identity

The associate knew that he had reached a crisis that would either end his law career or produce its catharsis. His last couple of years at the firm leading up to his rejection for partnership and termination of employment had been especially difficult. He had felt that his chances of making partner were decent, but at the same time he had known that he was not the kind of rainmaking partner the firm valued and needed. Something had been lacking in the way that the associate had gone about his work at the firm or, more accurately, gone about his career and professional development within the firm's business and management structure.

The associate had not been enterprising in his work, he realized now, as much of his hours and skill as he had given it. The firm's partners were entrepreneurial in some sense that he was not, although those partners had completely failed to convey to him just what entrepreneurial skills they were exercising. The associate had failed, when to that point in his life he was not accustomed to failing. The experience had left bitterness in his soul that scared him more than the financial uncertainty attendant on job loss. He had to find a way to get over it, or that bitterness he knew would be his deeper undoing.

Yet in another sense, the associate felt that he had landed somewhat on his feet. First, even if he did not have the entrepreneurial spirit that he might need to create and sustain productive employment, he had still honed some valuable skills. He had also gotten to know many of the mid-level managers and much of the inner workings of the community's corporate network. Even if he was not in any sense a player in that network, he nonetheless knew his way around it. The firm had also been reasonably generous in the way that it had offered the associate separation—well alright, required his resignation. He had some time to find a new direction, which he knew that he needed badly.

Each of these considerations played a role in the associate's accepting an invitation to meet with the practitioner whom he had gotten to know over the past few years, to discuss a possible new venture. They met over lunch in the same place that they had first met years earlier. The associate first told the practitioner some of the details of his separation from the firm and what he had learned about himself and his work in the process. Even as he spoke, the associate realized how arrogant he must have seemed to the practitioner the few times that they had met previously. The practitioner filled the associate in on how her firm had grown and a little of why she felt that it had been successful.

After they had finished their meals, the practitioner told the associate that she had a business proposition that she would like him to consider. She was planning a title company and wanted someone with the associate's kind of experience and contacts to manage the company, particularly its work flow and client contacts. Was he interested enough to think about it? The associate did not hesitate to say that he was interested—very interested. He also did not hesitate to ask the practitioner why she thought that he could do any better running a title company than he had done trying to make partner. The practitioner smiled at the associate's humility. She knew then that the associate was exactly the right professional for the job, ready to learn how to be enterprising.

~

Years into her law practice, the practitioner knew that she had somehow acquired her own professional identity and one that she knew served her well. She would not exactly call it her style (as an image consultant would call it) or brand (as a marketing consultant would call it). The practitioner had recognized way back in law school that some lawyers and professionals in other fields just had a certain set of distinct characteristics that were in some part shared by other excellent professionals but also in some part entirely their own. It surprised the practitioner that she might soon begin to count herself among them in that one respect, that something largely internal to herself was working in her favor in expanding her influence.

The practitioner's consciousness of her own identity (if one could call it that) had recently enabled her to make a subtle shift from managing her firm's practice to managing her firm's growth and, beyond that, the growth of other productive interests. The entrepreneurial skills that she had developed in her solo practice and then parlayed into forming and managing a small firm were the same skills that she was now beginning to use in other new ventures. She was starting a title company as a natural extension of work that her firm was already doing. The practitioner was also developing concepts and exploring ventures for business-consulting, management-services, and property-management firms.

The practitioner loved the creativity and energy of her work. Her husband supported her ambition at every step. She knew that he trusted her ability to keep her priorities and life in balance. The two of them were enjoying their daughter as much as ever. In fact, her marriage, family, and community activities and interests were an important part of her professional identity. She drew constant inspiration in her professional work from her non-professional activities, just as she drew lessons from her work for her non-work activities.

The practitioner's enterprise had larger connections than simply law products and services or even than simply work. For the practitioner, enterprise was like a 1,000-piece puzzle in which she was constantly putting together an ever-larger picture that included herself and her family, clients, and community, a picture that already had its own design that she need only discover. Her endeavor took insight and perseverance, occasionally even struggle, but was also constant joy as long as she remembered the cause and grace of it all. The practitioner knew to whom to look for wisdom and discernment, and whom to thank. In the end, she knew that passionate professional identity comes from one's core understanding and commitment. She had found the source and guide in the practice wilderness.

~

Each of the sections in this book, and particularly those in this third part on delivering law products and services, has suggested that the lawyer's identity remains a key part of the overall equation. While packaging, pricing, and delivering law products and services requires entrepreneurial practices, those practices in no sense diminish the personal aspects of those products and services. Law remains personal in some qualities to both the client and lawyer. Law knowledge is action logic, useless without its sound application based on discerned and articulated meanings and commitments. A lawyer's core enterprise is to connect law to the client's commitments through the lawyer's own professional identity and experience. Who supplies the law product and service, and what is that professional's identity, still matter to clients. Lawyers may study, standardize, and commoditize law products and services, but they still deliver those services to clients through interpersonal interaction and intrapersonal discernment.

Professional identity means the sum total of the lawyer's professional knowledge, skills, and ethic, but particularly as that sum distinguishes the lawyer from other professionals offering similar products and services. Identity is something outward, how others recognize a person. Identity is also something inward, how the person's character and attributes shape and form how others see them. The character of a professional lies peculiarly in the professional's expert knowledge, expert skills, and professional ethics—head, hands, and heart, if you will. Professional identity involves all three dimensions.

Steps to Take

Image and identity can mean everything to a lawyer in some circumstances. A truly excellent lawyer will not only act consistent with core personal and professional values but also appear to so act. Conduct a personal-values assessment to truly understand your values. Then develop a concrete plan to make your values evident in your expression and appearance.

Lawyers share aspects of professional identity. Lawyers ought usually to have at least some similar characteristics, attributes, and commitments that distinguish them from non-lawyer professionals. To some degree, they should think, speak, and act alike at least out of those core commitments that identify law as a profession. A client should be able to recognize core aspects of shared professional identity in the client's lawyer. Lawyers know what that shared identity is, in the commitment to offer sound products and services meeting the requirements of the law and in the client's interest, based on sound data gathered after reasonable investigation. This book need not define that identity. Law schools inculcate it, making American lawyers individual responsible agents of a marvelously successful republican democracy.

Yet to thrive within the current economic, social, political, and technological environment, lawyers must acquire and share another aspect of professional identity, which is that of entrepreneurs, to be enterprising. Lawyers and firms are certainly moving in that direction. They are more concerned than ever before with cultivating their individual skills and organizing their firms in ways that will enable them to reach and serve more clients. Law firms now employ training managers and professional-development directors to ensure the currency of their lawyers' skills. Lawyers and firms operate ancillary businesses training their clients' officers, directors, managers, and systems engineers in governance, compliance, employment, tax, intellectual-property, and other law areas. Lawyers are learning to adopt a professional identity that includes responsible enterprise as a core characteristic.

On the other hand, professional identity is not a cookie cutter. While sharing core commitments forming one's professional identity, each lawyer also carries distinct professional identity. Each lawyer has a distinct way of carrying out the profession's productive and stewardship roles. No lawyer is exactly like another. Distinguishing professional identity can legitimately mean funny bowties, or cute shoes and lipstick, or catchy 1-800 numbers, particularly for clients who draw value from distinct image. Law issues can easily dehumanize clients. Distinct professional identity can reassure those clients that even in law, individual experience, character, conduct, and personality matter. If a client cannot distinguish the client's lawyer from other lawyers, then what hope does the client have that the lawyer will recognize, support, and validate the client's individual character, conduct, and experience?

Yet distinguishing professional identity also means more than funny bowties or cute shoes and lipstick. It does not necessarily mean a catchy 1-800 number. Distinct professional identity has more to do with embedded value messages than it does with outward appearances. Clients can be incredibly discerning, not always about their own matters but often about their own lawyers. Soon enough, consumers see through outward appearances to a product supplier or service provider's core value. Because of the personal significance of law issues, a client's discernment of lawyer value can come more quickly and acutely than is the case with non-law products and services.

Steps to Take

Be careful not to appear to be a salesperson when networking strategically. Each individual in any networking event offers you something in your practice development. Even if they are not "buying" (and few are in networking events), they may have a helpful concept from which you can learn. They may have a resource such as shared office space. They may simply be a good listener and inquirer whose skills help you learn about your own professional identity and development. Networking is not client intake. It is an opportunity to share and learn.

So, think of professional identity not so much as *style* (as an image consultant might identify it) or *branding* (as a marketing consultant might have it). Style and branding are both meaningful concepts and can be excellent tools. As to style, would you rather have some than none? As to branding, would you rather have potential clients know you? Image and marketing consultants have much to offer. Yet their greater offering is when they help a lawyer discern the value messages that the lawyer needs to convey to serve clients effectively. Law products and services have enormous value, not simply in securing, preserving, or saving one's prosperity but also in creating personal, corporate, and community wealth, order, and liberty.

One reliable way to communicate a value message is to discern and publicize its relevant measures. Do not attempt to define yourself. Avoid advertising your attributes, particularly by using adjectives and adverbs. Doing so wastes the opportunity to communicate value. Every lawyer could claim to give *special* attention, *aggressive* representation, or *timely* advice. When you have three seconds of your website reader's attention, *excellence* as an advertising theme will not distinguish your services from the services of other providers claiming the same quality. Adjectives and adverbs also invite negative contrasts. Your claim to timely and aggressive representation may trigger your reader's suspicion about late and lax advice.

Instead, create and communicate values that distinguish your law products and services. Where lawyer-conduct rules and client confidentiality permit them, specifics like major clients represented, major transactions facilitated, major cases resolved, and special jury verdicts can help. Aggregated data from client surveys, like very high percentages of satisfied clients, can distinguish. Client testimonials can help. Teaching specific courses in specific programs can demonstrate niche skills. Awards and appointments can demonstrate the confidence that others have in your reputation, service, and skills. Publications can distinguish.

Steps to Take

Research can readily lead you to lists of action words in advertising. Avoid cliché terms and phrases. Consider using a consultant to conduct real-time client research with eye-tracking software to see where your clients look when they see your design. Use the results to modify your online and off-line marketing materials.

Most significantly, identify the specific value of your specific services that you provide, where you believe that others may not provide equivalent value. If you serve a corporate market for which price is the greatest sensitivity, then communicate your price-sensitive practices of providing flat fees or estimates, budgets, and performance benchmarking. If you serve a working clientele for whom office hours are significant barriers to service, then communicate your evening and weekend hours. If you serve a consumer clientele for whom location is the access issue, then communicate your online videoconference availability and availability for local on-site consultations. Yes, advertise specific products and services that meet specific needs where those products and services are unusual or unique, but also communicate unusual or unique pricing and delivery features. Link the value that you have created to your identity.

The point is simply that effective lawyers give thought and take action to strengthen and amplify their professional identity, particularly as it relates to client value. Professional identity develops whether a lawyer likes it or not. As in all other things, some degree of responsible self-reflection can improve one's professional identity. Think of it: you probably know of a lawyer or other professional who seems unconscious about how others regard them. Unconsciousness can be a good thing when it comes to avoiding self-absorption, arrogance, and preening. Yet unconsciousness can also be a bad thing when a little bit of self-insight could substantially improve the lawyer's character and, with that improvement, the lawyer's performance and productivity.

Steps to Take

Investigate and track how you have provided a service over the course of your practice and why you changed its content, price, and delivery. Did you refine one law product or service into two or more products or services? If so, what external forces or internal advantages caused you to do so? When you identify what you have done and why you changed it, you begin to see new possibilities to market products and services in new ways before they become mainstream.

Enterprising lawyers connect their professional identity to value messages. They do so by every ordinary action they take in the course of their law practices. Daily effective practice of the kind described throughout this book communicates value in itself, winning client converts who spread your value message. Yet enterprising lawyers also deliberately develop and convey consistent value messages through a variety of communication means. They do so electronically by email, social media, websites, tweets, and blog posts. They do so with print brochures and newsletters, and in print media. And they do so in person, participating in all kinds of professional, social, and personal forums.

When effective lawyers spread their value message into their communities, whether among individuals or through families, for-profit corporations, non-profit organizations, and government agencies, they do so with special purpose. Even and especially when commoditized into affordable and standardized law products and services, law practice has service, not profit, as its core mission. Particularly when it comes to projecting professional identity, profit can be one of those things (like other pleasures) that recede quickly when pursued directly. The ability of lawyers and firms to profit from their practice depends first and last on service. No lawyer or firm long survives without at least to some degree putting service ahead of profit. Those lawyers who find innovative and responsible new ways to serve will also find profit.

Finally, the professional identity of enterprising lawyers does not necessarily stop with traditional law products and services. Law is not a bounded profession, like dentistry or veterinary services. Enterprising lawyers are perfectly capable of taking back law-related services that law firms have long since ceded to title companies, banks, accountants, social workers, social and government agencies, public-interest organizations, and other non-law-firm entities and non-lawyer professionals. Many lawyers are also capable of offering business, marketing, professional-development, information-technology, product- and service-development, and other services beyond law-related services. Lawyers know *how* to be enterprising, to create new productivity and profit centers not just for themselves but for their clients. They simply need to know that they can be, naturally are, and *must be* enterprising.

Set longer-term enterprise goals whether new client populations, associates, partners, locations, fields, or ancillary businesses. Discern the successful professionals whom you most admire, and then discern why you admire them, grounding your enterprise goals in your interests and passion. Envision where you would like to be in your enterprise not just in one year but in three years and then in five years. Make your vision specific, achievable, and challenging. Work backward from those visions, picturing and recording each major step in monthly, quarterly, or semi-annual increments. Set one, two, or three objectives that will accomplish each step. Then identify the people who and organizations that can help you reach each of those objectives, finally planning how to engage those people and organizations in your plans. Identity happens to some of us, while others of us plan for and earn it. Make your identity one of engagement and enterprise.

Reflection

1. Locate and review a local business newspaper or online journal for lawyer advertisement. Which law firms advertise in that non-lawyer business forum? Why are those firms advertising and not other firms? How do their products and services relate to the advertiser audience? How (with what words and images) do the firms convey their value message?

2. Locate and review a local general newspaper or online forum for lawyer advertisement. Which law firms advertise in that general non-lawyer forum? Why are those firms advertising and not other firms? How do their products and services relate to the advertiser audience? How (with what words and images) do the firms convey their value message?

3. Think again of the lawyer advertisements to two different non-lawyer audiences that you just reviewed. How effective do you think those messages are? Are they positive in the sense of conveying that lawyers can make clients more prosperous, or are they negative in the sense that lawyers can keep clients from becoming less prosperous?

4. What value message would you most like to convey to your clients? What single words or short phrases do you think would evoke that value? What images would do so?

5. What is your professional character? What distinguishes you from other lawyers? How does your professional character connect with the value message that you articulated in answering the prior question?

6. Collect on your desk a printed image of everything that the non-lawyer public sees about you on a regular basis including at a minimum your website home page, letterhead, and business card, plus any advertising. How effectively do they communicate your professional identity? How could you improve them?

7. Identify three other activities that you can start today to continue to reflect productively on your professional identity.

Conclusion

The law profession faces an unusually clear divide in the views of its future. Commentators like Richard Susskind in *The End of Lawyers?* predict diminishing markets for ordinary law practitioners, in which sole practices and small and large firms struggle to survive. From popular, professional, and academic sources, one hears dire news of too many lawyers and the coming shakeout within legal education and demise of longstanding law practices. The criticism supports proposals to close law schools, end bar exams, and open law services to unlicensed providers. On the other hand, practitioners like Stephanie Kimbro in *Limited Scope Legal Services: Unbundling and the Self-Help Client* see new opportunities to serve more clients through mobile offices, virtual practices, new delivery methods, and new pricing structures, without fundamental regulatory reforms. These practitioners trust that the profession can save itself. They hesitate to kill the goose laying the golden eggs, when changes in practices can increase the benefit for everyone.

The critics, while sensing important trends, give insufficient attention to certain fundamentals. Markets grow when their participants—buyers and sellers, or if you prefer, all members of the community dependent on one another—are more productive. Increasing the productive capacity, wisdom, and ambition of market participants increases both individual and overall welfare. Abundance results from wise faith committing ambitions, education, and other resources to social and material prosperity. Education in law is education in helping others find social forms, controls, and practices that promote human flourishing. No education—not engineering, medicine, accounting, manufacturing, public administration—stands a greater immediate prospect for helping others do more good than law education.

If lawyers, law firms, and law schools get law practice right, then the market for law products and services should expand significantly, enabling many more practitioners to succeed, whether solo or in small or large firms. Unstable fiscal, monetary, political, and population trends in a technological, information, and global age have not made law less significant but more significant, to individuals, families, organizations, communities, and agencies. Others wring hands over the future of law practice. Responsible leaders should not. The effective packaging, pricing, and delivery of law products and services are more possible and important than ever before. Lawyers have greater opportunity to do more good works more effectively than at any other time in history.

Lawyers help clients become and remain productive. Lawyers are economic drivers, helping their clients break up their unplowed ground, seed the soil with new ventures, manage their crops responsibly, and harvest their riches to re-invest in new fields. Lawyers help broken clients create new entities, lives, and families. They help mature and productive clients manage growth and share wealth. They help aging clients bless succeeding generations. Lawyers ensure the social conscience, law compliance, risk management, responsible trade, and sound governance of their clients' enterprises. Lawyers make others enterprising.

This book should have reflected that effective lawyers are also enterprising. Indeed, in important respects, effective lawyers are *enterprises.* They develop their own set of approaches, products, and practices that are so distinctly effective and their own that they become their own brand. Now, *brand* is a marketing word, and this book is decidedly not about marketing. Marketing is a commercial concept. Lawyers, while a significant part of commerce (in some respects the most significant part because commerce depends on lawyers), are fundamentally not commercial actors. They are fundamentally professional actors, with a unique and uniquely important role facilitating the security, liberty, and productivity of others. Yet lawyers must be enterprising to reach sufficient numbers of underserved clients with effective products and services.

To be enterprising means to give attention to those attributes and activities that influence the course and shape of the enterprise in which one engages. The enterprise of a lawyer maintains as its fundamental focus the efficient, affordable, and effective serving of clients having need for law products and services. Thus, lawyers act wisely and responsibly when they give attention to the things that make them efficient, affordable, and effective in reaching and serving those clients. Enterprises survive and prosper through the kind of practices that this book describes in its three parts on packaging, pricing, and delivering law products and services. While visceral reactions can sometimes be right, and handy heuristics that short-circuit laborious processes can often serve us well, the entrepreneur must still give productive thought to the enterprise.

Entrepreneurs are not simply visionaries who see a new venture. They are also systems designers and analysts who discern the critical components and measures for those ventures. Entrepreneurs have a sense of mission about what they do. They articulate the mission with clarity and simplicity. Entrepreneurs communicate and build a sense of urgency about accomplishing the mission. They get others involved, leading visibly. Entrepreneurs locate and communicate simple measures of progress toward the goal. They base judgments on valid and reliable data. Entrepreneurs foster innovation that will achieve the organizational goal, quantifying what constitutes successful innovation. They draw vision from paradox and find opportunity in ambiguity and chaos. They fail productively with a learner's appetite for challenge and renewal.

Lawyers are a particular kind of entrepreneur. Each of the three parts of this book addresses five components for a successful law venture. When packaging a law product or service, an enterprising lawyer gives careful thought to the population to serve, its objectives, the products and services that will meet those objectives, how to fit the product or service to individual clients within those populations, and what quality level to provide in the service. When pricing a product or service, the enterprising lawyer gives thought to what clients within those populations can afford. The enterprising lawyers also considers the efficiency with which the lawyer must act to keep the product or service affordable, the pricing's transparency to the client, the choices that the client deserves among products and services, and the accountability that the lawyer has as to pricing and affordability. When delivering a product or service, the enterprising lawyer gives thought to the client's access including the lawyer's location, mobility, and flexibility, and the timely delivery of the product.

Effective lawyers keep each of these components and measures in mind as they daily discern, develop, package, price, and deliver law products and services. Turning law practice into a productive enterprise is no less complex than doing so for many other enterprises. A law license alone is not a guarantee of successful enterprise. The law license is, well, a license—a permission to embark on an enterprise. The enterprise is, well, an enterprise—a complex endeavor having discernible components the study and reform of which will improve the enterprise. Entrepreneurs are simply those who embrace enterprise, who see their work as endeavors worth innovating, expanding, and improving. Lawyers have every reason to see themselves as entrepreneurs and their work as enterprising. The work of lawyers has such great value as to warrant expansion and improving.

Lawyers and those who employ them often say that law schools do not prepare law students for the practice of law. In response, law schools rightly focus on research and writing skills, clinical work, advocacy skills, teamwork tasks, and other practical forms of education. Yet the real work of lawyers that law schools do not teach and law firms do not understand sufficiently well are the processes through which lawyers package, price, and deliver law products and services. Lawyers can complete entire careers without once ever developing or even seeing a work-process chart of the kind that is routine in other enterprises, or researching how to serve under-served and emerging client populations.

The consumer-credit crisis of a few years ago, and the new law services that its casualties required, may for many of those casualties be a thing of the past. The still-present mortgage-foreclosure crisis, and the new law services its casualties require, may someday soon also be past. We may hope that the legions of soldiers presently returning from active-duty service and the law services that they require may also soon be victorious history. Yet with a continuing jobs slump in the face of continuing climbs in the cost of higher education, a student-loan crisis and, with it, a vast need for new law services looms. Fiscal cliffs, monetary crises, natural disasters, political crises, security crises, and other foreseen and unforeseen regional, national, and international developments will demand new law products and services.

Our hope is that this book will inform and inspire lawyers to greater enterprise and, through it, to greater service in the face of emerging law needs. The future of the great American enterprise depends on lawyer inspiration and success. Lawyers can and should be remarkable in their innovation and insight. They should also be courageous and generous. We must not lose faith as a profession. We should instead turn our peculiar analytic skills and social ambitions to our own practices to enlarge their influence. Nothing ventured is nothing gained. Our individual and collective success depends on our own expertise applied with action borne of faith.

About the Authors

Nelson Miller is a professor and associate dean at the Grand Rapids campus of Thomas M. Cooley Law School, a tax-exempt nonprofit and the largest law school in the nation. Before joining Cooley, Dean Miller practiced civil litigation for 16 years, representing individuals, private and non-profit corporations, government agencies, public schools, and public and private universities. He pursued and defended multi-million-dollar civil cases in products liability, personal injury, airliner and helicopter crashes, civil rights, securities, employment, real estate, and business disputes. He is an editor and author of 12 books and dozens of articles on law practice, civil procedure, torts, ethics, and legal history, philosophy, and education. The State Bar of Michigan recognized Dean Miller with the John W. Cummiskey Award for pro-bono service.

Michael J. Dunn is a visiting professor at the Grand Rapids campus of the Thomas M. Cooley Law School teaching skills and practice courses, and directing the Access to Justice Clinic. Before joining Cooley, Professor Dunn practiced law for 25 years, while also earning a Master's Degree in Business Administration. He is a veteran of both large and small firm practice, and a frequent contributor of book chapters and bar-journal articles for practitioners. We know Professor Dunn best for his decade-long radio show "The Lawyers" with co-host Professor Curt Benson.

John Crane is former CEO of The Center for Life Improvement, LLC, a strategic career planning consulting company. Currently, he is the founder and CEO of Practice Reinvention Solutions, LLC, a relationship, experience, evaluation, visibility, and research firm focusing on service businesses. He has published numerous books and articles, and frequently speaks to professional organizations on client development and comprehensive service evaluations. His versatile education and experience includes fields from law and business to predictive analytics and health psychology.

Bibliography

Law Practice

ABBOTT, IDA O., THE LAWYER'S GUIDE TO MENTORING (National Assn. for Law Placement 2000);

ADKINS, ANDREW Z., III, THE LAWYER'S GUIDE TO PRACTICE MANAGEMENT SYSTEMS SOFTWARE (American Bar Association Law Practice Management Section 2009);

ANDRUS, R. BLAIN, LAWYER: A BRIEF 5,000 YEAR HISTORY (American Bar Association 2009);

BARBER, DAVID H., SURVIVING YOUR ROLE AS A LAWYER: A PROGRAM TO REDUCE STRESS AND IMPROVE PRODUCTIVITY (Law Distribs. 1983);

BATDORF, TIMOTHY D., THE LAWYER'S GUIDE TO BEING HUMAN: HOW TO BRING WHO YOU ARE TO WHAT YOU DO (iUniverse Inc. 2007);

BAUMLE, AMANDA K., SEX DISCRIMINATION AND LAW FIRM CULTURE ON THE INTERNET: LAWYERS AT THE INFORMATION AGE WATERCOOLER (Palgrave Macmillan 2009);

BLOMQUIST, ROBERT F., LAWYERLY VIRTUES (Vandeplas Pub. 2008);

BOCK, HEATHER, & ROBERT RUYAK, CONSTRUCTING CORE COMPETENCIES: USING COMPETENCY MODELS TO MANAGE FIRM TALENT (American Bar Association 2007);

CAIN, GEORGE H., TURNING POINTS: NEW PATHS & SECOND CAREERS FOR LAWYERS (American Bar Association 2010);

COOPER, CHARLES, LATER IN LIFE LAWYERS: TIPS FOR THE NON-TRADITIONAL LAW STUDENT (Fine Print Press 2d ed. 2012);

CULLEN, ROBERT W., THE LEADING LAWYER: A GUIDE TO PRACTICING LAW AND LEADERSHIP (LegalWorks 2008);

DOWNEY, MICHAEL P., INTRODUCTION TO LAW FIRM PRACTICE (American Bar Association 2010);

DUFFEY, WILLIAM S., JR., & RICHARD A. SCHNEIDER, EDS., A LIFE IN THE LAW: ADVICE FOR YOUNG LAWYERS (American Bar Association 2009);

Edmonds, David, *Training the Lawyers of the Future – A Regulator's View*, 45/1 THE LAW TEACHER 4 (2011);

ELEFANT, CAROLYN, & NICOLE BLACK, SOCIAL MEDIA FOR LAWYERS: THE NEXT FRONTIER (American Bar Association 2010);

ELWORK, AMIRAM, STRESS MANAGEMENT FOR LAWYERS: HOW TO INCREASE PERSONAL AND PROFESSIONAL SATISFACTION IN THE LAW (Vorkell Group 3d ed. 2007);

ENNICO, CLIFFORD, THE PARTNER TRACK: HOW TO GO FROM ASSOCIATE TO PARTNER IN ANY LAW FIRM (Kaplan Pub. 2009);

FURI-PERRY, URSULA, FIFTY UNIQUE LEGAL PATHS: HOW TO FIND THE RIGHT JOB (American Bar Association 2009);

FURI-PERRY, URSULA, YOUR FIRST YEAR AS A LAWYER REVEALED: SECRETS, OPPORTUNITIES, AND SUCCESS! (Jist Works 2010);

GALBENSKI, DAVID, UNBOUND: HOW ENTREPRENEURSHIP IS DRAMATICALLY TRANSFORMING LEGAL SERVICES TODAY (Lumen Legal 2009);

GIBSON, K. WILLIAM, HOW TO BUILD AND MANAGE A PERSONAL INJURY PRACTICE (American Bar Association 3d ed. 2012);

GOLDBERG, GERALD G., PRACTICAL LAWYERING: THE SKILLS YOU DID NOT LEARN IN LAW SCHOOL (Kaplan Pub. 2009);

GRANFIELD, ROBERT, & LYNN MATHER, PRIVATE LAWYERS AND THE PUBLIC INTEREST: THE EVOLVING ROLE OF PRO BONO IN THE LEGAL PROFESSION (Oxford Univ. Press 2009);

GREENE, ARTHUR G., THE LAWYER'S GUIDE TO GOVERNING YOUR FIRM (American Bar Association 2009);

GULLETTE, LYN COBIN, & WILLIAM R. GULLETTE, DIFFICULT CLIENTS—DEDICATED ATTORNEYS: PRACTICAL PSYCHOLOGY FOR EFFECTIVE IN-THE-TRENCHES REPRESENTATION (Bradford Pub. 2005);

HERMANN, RICHARD L., FROM LEMONS TO LEMONADE IN THE NEW LEGAL JOB MARKET: WINNING JOB SEARCH STRATEGIES FOR ENTRY-LEVEL ATTORNEYS (LawyerAvenue Press 2012);

HERMANN, RICHARD L., MANAGING YOUR LEGAL CAREER: BEST PRACTICES FOR CREATING THE CAREER YOU WANT (American Bar Association 2011);

KAUFMAN, GEORGE W., THE LAWYER'S GUIDE TO BALANCING LIFE AND WORK (American Bar Assn. 2d ed. 2006);

KENN, DEBORAH, LAWYERING FROM THE HEART (Aspen Pubs. 2009);

KIMBRO, STEPHANIE L., LIMITED SCOPE LEGAL SERVICES: UNBUNDLING AND THE SELF-HELP CLIENT (American Bar Association 2012);

KIMBRO, STEPHANIE L., VIRTUAL LAW PRACTICE: HOW TO DELIVER LEGAL SERVICES ONLINE (American Bar Association 2011);

KOWALSKI, MITCHELL, AVOIDING EXTINCTION: REIMAGINING LEGAL SERVICES FOR THE 21ST CENTURY (American Bar Association 2012);

LAURITSEN, MARC, THE LAWYER'S GUIDE TO WORKING WITH SMARTER KNOWLEDGE TOOLS (American Bar Association 2011);

LE VAN, GERALD, LAWYERS' LIVES OUT OF CONTROL: A QUALITY OF LIFE HANDBOOK (Le Van Co. 1993);

LEVIT, NANCY, & DOUGLAS O. LINDER, THE HAPPY LAWYER: MAKING A GOOD LIFE IN THE LAW (Oxford Univ. Press 2010);

LITOWITZ, DOUGLAS E., THE DESTRUCTION OF YOUNG LAWYERS: BEYOND ONE L (University of Akron Press 2005);

LUBAN, DAVID, LAWYERS AND JUSTICE: AN ETHICAL STUDY (Princeton Univ. Press 1988);

LUNDIN, STEVEN C., & JAMES K. ARNOLD, YOUR PATH TO A REWARDING WORK LIFE (Charthouse Learning Corp. 1997);

MAYSON, STEPHEN, MAKING SENSE OF LAW FIRMS: STRATEGY, STRUCTURE AND OWNERSHIP (Blackstone Press 1997);

MILLER, BARBARA, THE LAW FIRM ASSOCIATE'S GUIDE TO CONNECTING WITH YOUR COLLEAGUES (American Bar Association 2010);

NELSON, SHARON D., HOW GOOD LAWYERS SURVIVE BAD TIMES (American Bar Association 2010);

NEWELLHORTON, AMY, LAWYERS WORKING TO END HOMELESSNESS (American Bar Association 2006);

REEVES, ARIN N., THE NEXT IQ: THE NEXT LEVEL OF INTELLIGENCE FOR 21ST CENTURY LEADERS (American Bar Association 2012);

RHODE, DEBORAH L., PRO BONO IN PRINCIPLE AND IN PRACTICE: PUBLIC SERVICE AND THE PROFESSIONS (Stanford Univ. Press 2005);

RUBENSTEIN, HERB, LEADERSHIP FOR LAWYERS (American Bar Association 2d ed. 2008);

SCHUTT, MICHAEL P., REDEEMING LAW: CHRISTIAN CALLING AND THE LEGAL PROFESSION (IVP Academic 2007);

SIMMONS, JEFFREY R., LIFE, LAW, AND THE PURSUIT OF BALANCE: A LAWYER'S GUIDE TO QUALITY OF LIFE (Maricopa County Bar Assn./American Bar Assn. 2d ed. 1997);

STEFANCIC, JEAN, HOW LAWYERS LOSE THEIR WAY: A PROFESSION FAILS ITS CREATIVE MINDS (Duke Univ. Press 2005);

SUSSKIND, RICHARD, THE END OF LAWYERS? RETHINKING THE NATURE OF LEGAL SERVICES (Oxford Univ. Press 2008);

TAMMINEN, JULIE M., LIVING WITH THE LAW: STRATEGIES TO AVOID BURNOUT AND CREATE BALANCE (American Bar Assn. 1997);

TIGAR, MICHAEL E., NINE PRINCIPLES OF LITIGATION AND LIFE (American Bar Association 2009);

TONSING, DENNIS J., 1000 DAYS TO THE BAR—BUT THE PRACTICE OF LAW BEGINS NOW: HOW TO ACHIEVE YOUR PERSONAL BEST IN LAW SCHOOL (William S. Hein & Co. 2003);

TRAUTZ, REID F., THE BUSY LAWYER'S GUIDE TO SUCCESS: ESSENTIAL TIPS TO POWER YOUR PRACTICE (American Bar Association 2010);

WILLIAMS, JOAN C., FAIR MEASURE: TOWARD EFFECTIVE ATTORNEY EVALUATIONS (American Bar Association 2d ed. 2009).

Business and Management

ALDRICH, CLARK, THE COMPLETE GUIDE TO SIMULATIONS AND GAMES: HOW THE MOST VALUABLE CONTENT WILL BE CREATED IN THE AGE BEYOND GUTENBERG TO GOOGLE (Pfeiffer 2009);

BARLOW, JANELLE, & CLAUS MOLLER, A COMPLAINT IS A GIFT (Berrett-Koehler Pub. 1996);

BASARAB, DAVID, PREDICTIVE EVALUATION: ENSURING TRAINING DELIVERS BUSINESS AND ORGANIZATIONAL RESULTS (Berrett-Koehler Pubs. 2011);

BINMORE, KEN, PLAYING FOR REAL: A TEXT ON GAME THEORY (Oxford Univ. Press 2007);

BROWN, PETER MEGARGEE, & ALEXANDRA STODDARD, FIGURE IT OUT: A GUIDE TO WISDOM (The Lawbook Exchange 2010);

BUNZEL, TOM, TOOLS OF ENGAGEMENT: PRESENTING AND TRAINING IN A WORLD OF SOCIAL MEDIA (Pfeiffer 2010);

CARTWRIGHT, EDWARD, BEHAVIORAL ECONOMICS (Routledge 2011);

CHABRIS, CHRISTOPHER, & DANIEL SIMONS, THE INVISIBLE GORILLA: HOW OUR INTUITIONS DECEIVE US (Broadway 2011);

COLLINS, JIM, GOOD TO GREAT: WHY SOME COMPANIES MAKE THE LEAP… AND OTHER'S DON'T (HarperBusiness 2001);

COLLINS, JIM, GOOD TO GREAT AND THE SOCIAL SECTORS: A MONOGRAPH TO ACCOMPANY GOOD TO GREAT (HarperCollins 2005);

DIAMOND, PETER, & HANNU VARTIAINEN, EDS., BEHAVIORAL ECONOMICS AND ITS APPLICATION (Princeton Univ. Press 2007);

DIXIT, AVINASH K., & BARRY J. NALEBUFF, THE ART OF STRATEGY: A GAME THEORIST'S GUIDE TO SUCCESS IN BUSINESS AND LIFE (W.W. Norton & Co. 2008);

DRUCKER, PETER F., MANAGING FOR RESULTS (Collins 1993);

DWECK, CAROL S., MINDSET: THE NEW PSYCHOLOGY OF SUCCESS (Ballantine Books 2007);

FERCH, SHANN RAY, & LARRY C. SPEARS, THE SPIRIT OF SERVANT LEADERSHIP (Paulist Press 2011);

FERRAZI, KEITH, NEVER EAT ALONE – AND OTHER SECRETS TO SUCCESS, ONE RELATIONSHIP AT A TIME (Doubleday 2005);

FRENCH, WENDELL L., & CECIL H. BELL JR., ORGANIZATION DEVELOPMENT: BEHAVIORAL SCIENCE INTERVENTIONS FOR ORGANIZATION IMPROVEMENT (PrenticeHall 6th ed. 1999);

GLADWELL, MALCOLM, BLINK: THE POWER OF THINKING WITHOUT THINKING (Back Bay Books 2005);

GLADWELL, MALCOLM, OUTLIERS: THE STORY OF SUCCESS (Back Bay Books 2011);

GODIN, STETH, LINCHPIN: ARE YOU INDISPENSABLE? (Penguin Group 2010);

GOETSCH, DAVID L., & STANLEY B. DAVIS, QUALITY MANAGEMENT FOR ORGANIZATIONAL EXCELLENCE: INTRODUCTION TO TOTAL QUALITY (Prentice Hall 6th ed. 2010);

GOLDRATT, ELIYAHU M., & JEFF COX, THE GOAL: A PROCESS OF ONGOING IMPROVEMENT (North River Prods. 3d ed. 2004);

HAMMOND, JOHN S., RALPH L. KEENEY, & HOWARD RAIFFA, SMART CHOICES: A PRACTICAL GUIDE TO MAKING BETTER DECISIONS (Crown Business 2002);

HAVEY, MICHAEL, ESSENTIAL BUSINESS PROCESS MODELING (O'Reilly Media 2005);

HOLYOAK, KEITH J., & PAUL THAGARD, MENTAL LEAPS: ANALOGY IN CREATIVE THOUGHT (A Bradford Book 1996);

HUNTER, DALE, STEPHEN THORPE, HARNISH BROWN, & ANNE BAILEY, THE ART OF FACILITATION: THE ESSENTIALS FOR LEADING GREAT MEETINGS AND CREATING GROUP SYNERGY (Jossey-Bass 2009);

JOSEPHSON, MICHAEL S., & WES HANSON, THE POWER OF CHARACTER: PROMINENT AMERICANS TALK ABOUT LIFE, FAMILY, WORK, VALUES, AND MORE (Josephson Institute & Unlimited Pub. 2004);

JOSEPHSON, MICHAEL S., THE BEST IS YET TO COME (Josephson Institute of Ethics 2002);

JOSEPHSON, MICHAEL S., YOU DON'T HAVE TO BE SICK TO GET BETTER! THOUGHTS ON BEING A BETTER PERSON AND LIVING A BETTER LIFE (Josephson Institute of Ethics 2001);

KEOHANE, NANNERL O., THINKING ABOUT LEADERSHIP (Princeton Univ. Press 2010);

KEELY, DOUG, THE MARK OF A LEADER (INSPIRING STORIES OF ORDINARY PEOPLE WHO HAVE DONE EXTRAORDINARY THINGS) (The Mark of a Leader 2007);

KELLOGG, RONALD T., FUNDAMENTALS OF COGNITIVE PSYCHOLOGY (Sage Pubs. 2007);

KIYOSAKI, ROBERT T., RICH DAD POOR DAD: WHAT THE RICH TEACH THEIR KIDS ABOUT MONEY THAT THE POOR AND MIDDLE CLASS DO NOT (Plata Pub. 2011);

KLEIN, FREADA KAPOR, GIVING NOTICE: WHY THE BEST AND THE BRIGHTEST LEAVE THE WORKPLACE AND HOW YOU CAN HELP (Jossey-Bass 2008);

LATHAM, JOHN, & JOHN VINYARD, BALDRIDGE USER'S GUIDE: ORGANIZATION DIAGNOSIS, DESIGN, AND TRANSFORMATION (John Wiley & Sons 3d ed. 2008);

LEGUALT, MICHAEL R., THINK: WHY CRUCIAL DECISIONS CAN'T BE MADE IN THE BLINK OF AN EYE (Simon & Schuster 2006);

LEHRER, JONAH, HOW WE DECIDE (Mariner Books 2010);

LENCIONI, PATRICK, THE FIVE DYSFUNCTIONS OF A TEAM: A LEADERSHIP FABLE (Jossey-Bass 2002);

LUNDIN, STEPHEN C., & JAMES K. ARNOLD, PERSONAL ACCOUNTABILITY: YOUR PATH TO A REWARDING WORK LIFE (Charthouse Learning Corp. 1997);

LUNDIN, STEPHEN C., HARRY PAUL, JOHN CHRISTENSEN, & KEN BLANCHARD, FISH! A PROVEN WAY TO BOOST MORALE AND IMPROVE RESULTS (Hyperion 2000);

MAXWELL, JOHN C., THE 21 INDISPENSABLE QUALITIES OF A LEADER: BECOMING THE PERSON OTHERS WILL WANT TO FOLLOW (Thomas Nelson 2d ed 2007);

MEDINA, JOHN, BRAIN RULES: 12 PRINCIPLES FOR SURVIVING AND THRIVING AT WORK, HOME, AND SCHOOL (Pear Press 2009);

MEREDITH, JACK R., & SAMUEL J. MANTEL JR., PROJECT MANAGEMENT: A MANAGERIAL APPROACH (John Wiley & Sons 7th ed. 2010);

PAUL, RICHARD W., & LINDA ELDER, CRITICAL THINKING: TOOLS FOR TAKING CHARGE OF YOUR PROFESSIONAL AND PERSONAL LIFE (FT Press 2002);

PETERS, TOM, THRIVING ON CHAOS: HANDBOOK FOR A MANAGEMENT REVOLUTION (Alfred A. Knopf 1988);

PINK, DANIEL H., A WHOLE NEW MIND: WHY RIGHT-BRAINERS WILL RULE THE FUTURE (Riverhead Trade 2006);

PINK, DANIEL H., DRIVE: THE SURPRISING TRUTH ABOUT WHAT MOTIVATES US (Riverhead Trade 2011);

PINTO, JEFFREY K., PROJECT MANAGEMENT: ACHIEVING COMPETITIVE ADVANTAGE (PrenticeHall 2007);

RABE, CYNTHIA BARTON, INNOVATION KILLER: HOW WHAT WE KNOW LIMITS WHAT WE CAN IMAGINE—AND WHAT SMART COMPANIES ARE DOING ABOUT IT (AMACOM 2006);

READY, ROMILLA, & KATE BURTON, NEURO-LINGUISTIC PROGRAMMING FOR DUMMIES (For Dummies 2d ed. 2010);

SCHEDLBAUER, MARTIN, THE ART OF BUSINESS PROCESS MODELING: THE BUSINESS ANALYST'S GUIDE TO PROCESS MODELING WITH UML & BPMN (The Cathris Group 2010);

SCHWARTZ, HUGH, A GUIDE TO BEHAVIORAL ECONOMICS (Higher Education Pubs. 2008);

SELIGMAN, MARTIN, FLOURISH: A VISIONARY NEW UNDERSTANDING OF HAPPINESS AND WELL BEING (Free Press 2011);

SHENK, DAVID, THE GENIUS IN ALL OF US: NEW INSIGHTS INTO GENETICS, TALENT, AND IQ (Anchor 2011);

SMITH, EDWARD E., & STEPHEN M. KOSSLYN, COGNITIVE PSYCHOLOGY: MIND AND BRAIN (Prentice Hall 2007);

SMITH, TIM J., PRICING STRATEGY: SETTING PRICE LEVELS, MANAGING PRICE DISCOUNTS, & ESTABLISHING PRICE STRUCTURES (South-Western Cengage Learning 2012);

STEVENS, ROBERT E., DAVID L. LOUDON, BRUCE WRENN, & PHYLIS MANSFIELD, MARKETING PLANNING GUIDE (3rd ed. The Haworth Press 2006);

STONE, DOUGLAS, BRUCE PATTON, SHEILA HEEN, & ROGER FISHER, DIFFICULT CONVERSATIONS: HOW TO DISCUSS WHAT MATTERS MOST (Penguin 2010);

SUMMERS, DONNA C.S., QUALITY (Prentice Hall 5th ed. 2010);

THALER, RICHARD H., & CASS R. SUNSTEIN, NUDGE: IMPROVING DECISIONS ABOUT HEALTH, WEALTH, & HAPPINESS (Penguin 2009);

WATSON, JOEL, STATEGY: AN INTRODUCTION TO GAME THEORY (W.W. Norton & Co. 2d ed. 2008);

WESKE, MATHIAS, BUSINESS PROCESS MANAGEMENT: CONCEPTS, LANGUAGES, ARCHITECTURES (Springer Berlin Heidelberg 2007);

WRIGHT, ROBERT, NONZERO: THE LOGIC OF HUMAN DESTINY (Vintage 2001);

ZENGER, JOHN, JOSEPH FOLKMAN, & SCOTT EDINGER, THE INSPIRING LEADER: UNLOCKING THE SECRETS OF HOW EXTRAORDINARY LEADERS MOTIVATE (McGraw-Hill 2009).

Law and Education

ARTHUR, JAMES, & KAREN BOHLIN, EDS., CITIZENSHIP AND HIGHER EDUCATION: THE ROLE OF UNIVERSITIES IN COMMUNITIES AND SOCIETY (Routledge 2009);

BALL, ARNETHA F., MULTICULTURAL STRATEGIES FOR EDUCATION AND SOCIAL CHANGE (Teachers College Press 2006);

BALLIET, BARBARA J., & KERRISSA HEFFERNAN, THE PRACTICE OF CHANGE: CONCEPTS AND MODELS FOR SERVICE LEARNING IN WOMEN'S STUDIES (Stylus Pub. 2000);

BATTISTONI, RICHARD, & WILLIAM E. HUDSON, EDS., EXPERIENCING CITIZENSHIP: CONCEPTS AND MODELS FOR SERVICE LEARNING (Stylus 1997);

BEAN, JOHN C., & MARYELLEN WEIMER, ENGAGING IDEAS: THE PROFESSOR'S GUIDE TO INTEGRATING WRITING, CRITICAL LEARNING, AND ACTIVE LEARNING IN THE CLASSROOM (Jossey-Bass 2011);

BERG, GARY A., LOW-INCOME STUDENTS AND THE PERPETUATION OF INEQUALITY (Ashgate 2010);

BRUNER, JEROME, THE CULTURE OF EDUCATION (Harvard Univ. Press 1996);

BROOKFIELD, STEPHEN D., TEACHING FOR CRITICAL THINKING: TOOLS AND TECHNIQUES TO HELP STUDENTS QUESTION THEIR ASSUMPTIONS (Jossey-Bass 2011);

BROOKFIELD, STEPHEN D., THE SKILLFUL TEACHER: ON TECHNIQUE, TRUST, AND RESPONSIVENESS IN THE CLASSROOM (Jossey-Bass 2d ed. 2006);

BUDD, JOHN M., HIGHER EDUCATION'S PURPOSE: INTELLECTUAL AND SOCIAL PROGRESS (University Press of America 2008);

BURGAN, MARY, WHAT EVER HAPPENED TO THE FACULTY?: DRIFT AND DECISION IN HIGHER EDUCATION (Johns Hopkins Univ. Press 2009);

BUTIN, DAN W., SERVICE-LEARNING IN HIGHER EDUCATION: CRITICAL ISSUES AND DIRECTIONS (Palgrave Macmillan 2005);

CHAN, ADRIENNE S., & DONALD FISHER, EDS., THE EXCHANGE UNIVERSITY: THE CORPORATIZATION OF ACADEMIC CULTURE (UBC Press 2009);

CHRISTENSEN, CLAYTON M., & HENRY J. EHRING, THE INNOVATIVE UNIVERSITY: CHANGING THE DNA OF HIGHER EDUCATION FROM THE INSIDE OUT (Jossey-Bass 2011);

CURRY, LYNN, & JOHN F. WERGIN, EDUCATING PROFESSIONALS: RESPONDING TO NEW EXPECTATIONS FOR COMPETENCE AND ACCOUNTABILITY (Jossey-Bass 1993);

CUYJET, MICHAEL J., MARY F. HOWARD-HAMILTON, & DIANE L. COOPER, EDS., MULTICULTURALISM ON CAMPUS: THEORY, MODELS, AND PRACTICES FOR UNDERSTANDING DIVERSITY AND CREATING INCLUSION (Stylus Pub. 2011);

DEWEY, JOHN, EXPERIENCE AND EDUCATION (Free Press 1997);

DEWEY, JOHN, HOW WE THINK (FQ Books 2010);

DICK, WALTER, LOU CAREY, & JAMES O. CAREY, THE SYSTEMATIC DESIGN OF INSTRUCTION (Allyn & Bacon 7th ed. 2011);

FALLOWS, STEPHEN, & STEVEN CHRISTINE, INTEGRATING KEY SKILLS IN HIGHER EDUCATION: EMPLOYABILITY, TRANSFERRABLE SKILLS, AND LEARNING FOR LIFE (Routledge 2000);

FARNSWORTH, KENT A., LEADERSHIP AS SERVICE: A NEW MODEL FOR HIGHER EDUCATION IN A NEW CENTURY (Rowman & Littlefield Pubs. 2006);

FRIEDLAND, STEVEN, & GERALD HESS, TEACHING THE LAW SCHOOL CURRICULUM (Carolina Academic Press 2004);

FRIEDLAND, STEVEN I., & JEFFREY SCOTT SHAPIRO, THE ESSENTIAL RULES FOR BAR EXAM SUCCESS (West 2008);

GAGNE, ROBERT M., & KAREN L. MEDSKER, THE CONDITIONS OF LEARNING: TRAINING APPLICATIONS (Wadsworth 1995);

GARDINER, LION F., REDESIGNING HIGHER EDUCATION: PRODUCING DRAMATIC GAINS IN STUDENT LEARNING (Jossey-Bass 1994);

GEYH, CHARLES, WHAT'S LAW GOT TO DO WITH IT? (Stanford Univ. Press 2011);

GITLOW, ABRAHAM, AMERICA'S RESEARCH UNIVERSITIES: THE CHALLENGES AHEAD (Univ. Press of America 2011);

GOTTLIEB, KARLA, & GAIL ROBINSON, A PRACTICAL GUIDE TO INTEGRATING CIVIL RESPONSIBILITY INTO THE CURRICULUM (Community College Press 2007);

HESS, FREDERICK, ET AL., THE POLITICALLY CORRECT UNIVERSITY: PROBLEMS, SCOPE, AND REFORMS (Aei Press 2009);

HESS, GERALD F., STEVEN I. FRIEDLAND, MICHAEL HUNTER SCHWARZ, & SOPHIE SPARROW, TECHNIQUES FOR TEACHING LAW 2 (Carolina Academic Press 2d ed. 2011);

JOHNSON, BRIAN T., & CAROLYN R. O'GRADY, EDS., THE SPIRIT OF SERVICE: EXPLORING FAITH, SERVICE, AND SOCIAL JUSTICE IN HIGHER EDUCATION (Anker Pub. Co. 2006);

JUNCO, REYNOL, & JEANNA MASTRODICASA, CONNECTING TO THE NET.GENERATION: WHAT HIGHER EDUCATIONAL PROFESSIONALS NEED TO KNOW ABOUT TODAY'S STUDENTS (National Assn. of Student Personnel Admins. 2007);

KAHLENBERG, RICHARD D., REWARDING STRIVERS: HELPING LOW-INCOME STUDENTS SUCCEED IN COLLEGE (The Century Foundation 2010);

KARABEL, JEROME, THE CHOSEN: THE HIDDEN HISTORY OF ADMISSION AND EXCLUSION AT HARVARD, YALE, AND PRINCETON (Mariner Books 2006);

LASSON, KENNETH, TREMBLING IN THE IVORY TOWER: EXCESSES IN THE PURSUIT OF TRUTH AND TENURE (Bancroft 2003);

LE BRUN, M., & R. JOHNSTONE, THE QUIET (R)EVOLUTION: IMPROVING STUDENT LEARNING IN LAW (Law Book Co. 1995);

LISMAN, C. DAVID, & IRENE E. HARVEY, BEYOND THE TOWER: CONCEPTS AND MODELS FOR SERVICE LEARNING (Stylus 2000);

LITOWITZ, DOUGLAS E., THE DESTRUCTION OF YOUNG LAWYERS: BEYOND ONE L (Univ. of Akron Press 2005);

MACFARLANE, BRUCE, THE ACADEMIC CITIZEN: THE VIRTUE OF SERVICE IN UNIVERSITY LIFE (Routledge 2006);

MAHARG, PAUL, TRANSFORMING LEGAL EDUCATION (Ashgate 2007);

MARTIN, JAMES, & JAMES E. SAMELS, TURNAROUND: LEADING STRESSED COLLEGES AND UNIVERSITIES TO EXCELLENCE (Johns Hopkins Univ. Press 2008);

MARTIN, RANDY, UNDER NEW MANAGEMENT: UNIVERSITIES, ADMINISTRATORS, AND THE PROFESSIONAL TURN (Temple Univ. Press 2011);

MERRIAM, SHARAN B., & ANDRE P. GRACE, THE JOSSEY-BASS READER ON CONTEMPORARY ISSUES IN ADULT EDUCATION (Jossey-Bass 2011);

MUNNEKE, GARY A., HOW TO SUCCEED IN LAW SCHOOL (Barron's Educ. Series 4th ed. 2008);

NODDINGS, NEIL, EDUCATING FOR INTELLIGENT BELIEF OR UNBELIEF (Teachers College Press 1993);

PARKS, SHARON DALOZ, BIG QUESTIONS, WORTHY DREAMS: MENTORING EMERGING ADULTS IN THEIR SEARCH FOR MEANING, PURPOSE, AND FAITH (Jossey-Bass 10th anniversary ed. 2011);

POPHAM, W. JAMES, UNLEARNED LESSONS: SIX STUMBLING BLOCKS TO OUR SCHOOLS' SUCCESS (Harvard Educ. Press 2009);

POST, ROBERT C., DEMOCRACY, EXPERTISE, AND ACADEMIC FREEDOM (Yale Univ. Press 2012);

RANDALL, VERNELIA, PLANNING FOR EFFECTIVE LEGAL INSTRUCTION: A WORKBOOK (Carolina Academic Press 2011);

REDFIELD, SARAH E., THINKING LIKE A LAWYER: AN EDUCATOR'S GUIDE TO LEGAL ANALYSIS AND RESEARCH (Carolina Academic Press 2d ed. 2011);

RESNICK, DANIEL P., & DANA S. SCOTT, THE INNOVATIVE UNIVERSITY (Carnegie Mellon Univ. Press 2004);

RILEY, NAOMI SCHAEFER, THE FACULTY LOUNGES: AND OTHER REASONS YOU WON'T GET THE COLLEGE EDUCATION YOU PAY FOR (Ivan R. Dee 2011);

RUCH, RICHARD S., & GEORGE KELLER, HIGHER ED, INC.: THE RISE OF THE FOR-PROFIT UNIVERSITY (Johns Hopkins Univ. Press 2003);

SALT, VULNERABLE POPULATIONS AND TRANSFORMATIVE LAW TEACHING: A READER (Carolina Academic Press 2011);

SALTMARSH, JOHN, & EDWARD ZLOTKOWSKI, EDS., HIGHER EDUCATION AND DEMOCRACY: ESSAYS ON SERVICE-LEARNING AND CIVIC ENGAGEMENT (Temple Univ. Press 2011);

SANDEEN, ARTHUR, ENHANCING LEADERSHIP IN COLLEGES AND UNIVERSITIES: A CASE APPROACH (Charles C. Thomas Pub. Ltd. 2011);

SCHACHTER, MADELEINE, THE LAW PROFESSOR'S HANDBOOK: A PRACTICAL GUIDE TO TEACHING LAW STUDENTS (Carolina Academic Press 2003);

SCHAUER, FREDERICK, THINKING LIKE A LAWYER: A NEW INTRODUCTION TO LEGAL REASONING (Harvard Univ. Press 2009);

SEDBERRY, STEVEN R., LAW SCHOOL LABYRINTH: A GUIDE TO MAKING THE MOST OF YOUR LEGAL EDUCATION (Kaplan Pub. 2009);

SHULMAN, LEE S., THE WISDOM OF PRACTICE: ESSAYS ON TEACHING, LEARNING, AND LEARNING TO TEACH (Jossey-Bass 2004);

SKEMP, RICHARD R., INTELLIGENCE, LEARNING, AND ACTION: FOUNDATION FOR THEORY AND PRACTICE IN EDUCATION (John Wiley & Sons 1979);

SLAUGHTER, SHEILA, & GARY RHOADES, ACADEMIC CAPITALISM AND THE NEW ECONOMY: MARKETS, STATE, AND HIGHER EDUCATION (Johns Hopkins Univ. Press 2009);

SMITH, BARBARA LEIGH, JOHN MCCANN, & ALEXANDER W. ASTIN, REINVENTING OURSELVES: INTERDISCIPLINARY EDUCATION, COLLABORATIVE LEARNING, AND EXPERIMENTATION IN HIGHER LEARNING (Jossey-Bass 2001);

SMITH, DARYL G., DIVERSITY'S PROMISE FOR HIGHER EDUCATION: MAKING IT WORK (Johns Hopkins Univ. Press 2011);

SMITH, FRANK, THE BOOK OF LEARNING AND FORGETTING (Teachers College Press 1998);

SMITH, WILSON, & THOMAS BENDER, EDS., AMERICAN HIGHER EDUCATION TRANSFORMED, 1940-2005: DOCUMENTING THE NATIONAL DISCOURSE (Johns Hopkins Univ. Press 2008);

STELLJES, ANDREW D., SERVICE-LEARNING AND COMMUNITY ENGAGEMENT: COGNITIVE DEVELOPMENTAL LONG-TERM SOCIAL CONCERN (Cambria Press 2008);

STEVENS, DANNELLE D., & JOANNE E. COOPER, JOURNAL KEEPING: HOW TO USE REFLECTIVE WRITING FOR LEARNING, TEACHING, PROFESSIONAL INSIGHT AND POSITIVE CHANGE (Stylus Pub. 2009);

STEVENS, ROBERT BOCKING, LAW SCHOOL: LEGAL EDUCATION IN AMERICA FROM THE 1850S TO THE 1980S (Lawbook Exchange 2001);

SULLIVAN, WILLIAM M., ANNE COLBY, JUDITH WELCH WEGNER, LLOYD BOND, & LEE S. SHULMAN, EDUCATING LAWYERS: PREPARATION FOR THE PROFESSION OF LAW (Jossey-Bass 2007);

TALASKA, RICHARD A., ED., CRITICAL REASONING IN CONTEMPORARY CULTURE (State Univ. of New York Press 1992);

TANAKA, GREG, THE INTERCULTURAL CAMPUS: TRANSCENDING CULTURE AND POWER IN AMERICAN HIGHER EDUCATION (Peter Lang Pub. 2007);

TAYLOR, MARK C., CRISIS ON CAMPUS: A BOLD PLAN FOR REFORMING OUR COLLEGES AND UNIVERSITIES (Knopf 2010);

THELIN, A HISTORY OF AMERICAN HIGHER EDUCATION (Johns Hopkins Univ. Press 2d ed. 2011);

THOMSON, DAVID I.C., LAW SCHOOL 2.0: LEGAL EDUCATION FOR A DIGITAL AGE (LexisNexis 2009);

TIMPSON, WILLIAM M., TEACHING DIVERSITY: CHALLENGES AND COMPLEXITIES, IDENTITIES, AND INTEGRITY (Atwood Pub. 2003);

TOMA, J. DOUGLAS, MANAGING THE ENTREPRENEURIAL UNIVERSITY: LEGAL ISSUES AND COMMERCIAL REALITIES (Routledge 2011);

WARD, KELLY, FACULTY SERVICE ROLES AND THE SCHOLARSHIP OF ENGAGEMENT: ASHE-ERIC HIGHER EDUCATION REPORT (Jossey-Bass 2003);

WILDAVSKY, BEN, THE GREAT BRAIN RACE: HOW GLOBAL UNIVERSITIES ARE RESHAPING THE WORLD (Princeton Univ. Press 2d ed. 2010);

ZACHARY, LOIS J., THE MENTOR'S GUIDE: FACILITATING EFFECTIVE LEARNING RELATIONSHIPS (Wiley 2000).

Law and Society

BEAN, JONATHAN, RACE AND LIBERTY IN AMERICA: THE ESSENTIAL READER (INDEPENDENT STUDIES IN POLITICAL ECONOMY) (Univ. Press of Kentucky 2009);

BERMAN, GREG, JOHN FEINBLATT, & SARAH GLAZER, GOOD COURTS: THE CASE FOR PROBLEM-SOLVING JUSTICE (New Press 2005);

BERMAN, HAROLD J., LAW AND REVOLUTION: THE FORMATION OF THE WESTERN LEGAL TRADITION (Harvard Univ. Press 1983);

BRADNEY, ANTHONY, LAW AND FAITH IN A SCEPTICAL AGE (Routledge-Cavnedish 2009);

BURNHAM, WILLIAM, INTRODUCTION TO THE LAW AND LEGAL SYSTEM OF THE UNITED STATES (West 2006);

CENTNER, TERENCE J., AMERICA'S BLAME CULTURE: POINTING FINGERS AND SHUNNING RESTITUTION (Carolina Academic Press 2000);

CHARLES, J. DARYL, RETRIEVING THE NATURAL LAW: A RETURN TO MORAL FIRST THINGS (William B. Eerdmans Pub. Co. 2008);

DEMINT, JIM, & J. DAVID WOODARD, WHY WE WHISPER: RESTORING OUR RIGHT TO SAY IT'S WRONG (Rowman & Littlefield Pubs. 2007);

DORE, ISAAK, THE EPISTEMOLOGICAL FOUNDATIONS OF LAW (Carolina Academic Press 2007);

DUNOFF, JEFFREY L., & JOEL P. TRACHTMAN, RULING THE WORLD?: CONSTITUTIONALISM, INTERNATIONAL LAW, AND GLOBAL GOVERNANCE (Cambridge Univ. Press 2009);

ELKINS, ZACHARY, TOM GINSBURG, & JAMES MELTON, THE ENDURANCE OF NATIONAL CONSTITUTIONS (Cambridge Univ. Press 2009);

FOX, HELEN, WHEN RACE BREAKS OUT (Peter Lang 2009);

GARDNER, HOWARD E., MIHALY CSIKSZENTMIHALYI, WILLIAM DAMON, & HOWARD GARDNER, GOOD WORK: WHEN EXCELLENCE AND ETHICS MEET (Basic Books 2002);

GARVEY, JOHN H., WHAT ARE FREEDOMS FOR? (Harvard Univ. Press 2000);

GEORGE, ROBERT P., MAKING MEN MORAL: CIVIL LIBERTIES AND PUBLIC MORALITY (Oxford Univ. Press 1995);

GILMORE, GRANT, THE AGES OF AMERICAN LAW (Yale Univ. Press 1979);

HALPIN, ANDREW, & VOLKER ROEBEN, THEORISING THE GLOBAL LEGAL ORDER (Hart Pubg. 2009);

JOHNS, MARGARET Z., THE UNITED STATES LEGAL SYSTEM: AN INTRODUCTION (Carolina Academic Press 2d ed. 2006);

KAVANAGH, EILEEN, & JOHN OBERDIEK, EDS., ARGUING ABOUT LAW (Routledge 2008);

KRAMER, MATTHEW, OBJECTIVITY AND THE RULE OF LAW (Cambridge Univ. Press 2007);

LUBAN, DAVID, LAWYERS AND JUSTICE: AN ETHICAL STUDY (Princeton Univ. Press 1988);

MCDOWELL, GARY L., THE LANGUAGE OF LAW AND THE FOUNDATIONS OF CONSTITUTIONALISM (Cambridge Univ. Press 2010);

MELISSARIS, EMMANUEL, UBIQUITOUS LAW: LEGAL THEORY AND THE SPACE FOR LEGAL PLURALISM (Ashgate 2009);

MILLER, JOANN, & DONALD C. JOHNSON, PROBLEM SOLVING COURTS: A MEASURE OF JUSTICE (Rowman & Littlefield Pubs. 2011);

MYERS, VERNA A., MOVING DIVERSITY FORWARD: HOW TO GO FROM WELL-MEANING TO WELL-DOING (American Bar Association 2012);

PALOMBELLA, GIANLUIGI, & NEIL WALKER, EDS., RELOCATING THE RULE OF LAW (Hart Pub. 2009);

PEJOVICH, SVETOZAR, LAW, INFORMAL RULES AND ECONOMIC PERFORMANCE: THE CASE FOR COMMON LAW (Edward Elgar Pub. 2010);

POLANYI, MICHAEL, PERSONAL KNOWLEDGE: TOWARDS A POST-CRITICAL PHILOSOPHY (University of Chicago Press 1974);

POLANYI, MICHAEL, THE LOGIC OF LIBERTY (Liberty Fund 1998);

POLANYI, MICHAEL, THE TACIT DIMENSION (University of Chicago Press 2009);

PORTER, JEAN, MINISTERS OF THE LAW: A NATURAL LAW THEORY OF LEGAL AUTHORITY (Wm. B. Eerdmans Pub. Co. 2010);

SHAFFERN, ROBERT W., LAW AND JUSTICE FROM ANTIQUITY TO ENLIGHTENMENT (Rowman & Littlefield Pubs. 2009);

SHEARED, VANESSA, JUANITA JOHNSON-BAILEY, SCIPIO A.J. COLIN III, STEPHEN D. BROOKFIELD, & PHYLLIS M. CUNNINGHAM, EDS., THE HANDBOOK OF RACE AND ADULT EDUCATION: A RESOURCE FOR DIALOGUE ON RACISM (Jossey-Bass 2010);

STONE, HARLAN FISKE, LAW AND ITS ADMINISTRATION (Gale 2010);

TAMANAHA, BRIAN Z., LAW AS A MEANS TO AN END: THREAT TO THE RULE OF LAW (Cambridge Univ. Press 2006);

TAMANAHA, BRIAN Z., ON THE RULE OF LAW: HISTORY, POLITICS, THEORY (Cambridge Univ. Press 2004);

TAYLOR, CHARLES, SOURCES OF THE SELF: THE MAKING OF THE MODERN IDENTITY (Harvard Univ. Press 1992);

TAYLOR, CHARLES, THE ETHICS OF AUTHENTICITY (Harvard Univ. Press 1992);

URBINA, SEBASTIAN, LEGAL METHOD AND THE RULE OF LAW (Springer 2002);

VAGO, STEVEN, LAW AND SOCIETY (Prentice Hall 10th ed. 2011);

VON MEHREN, ARTHUR T., & PETER L. MURRAY, LAW IN THE UNITED STATES (Cambridge Univ. Press 2d ed. 2007);

WOLTERSTORFF, NICHOLAS, JUSTICE: RIGHTS AND WRONGS (Princeton Univ. Press 2010);

ZITRIN, RICHARD A., & CAROL M. LANGFORD, THE MORAL COMPASS OF THE AMERICAN LAWYER: TRUTH, JUSTICE, POWER, AND GREED (Ballantine Books 2000).

Appendices

Appendix A
Process Model

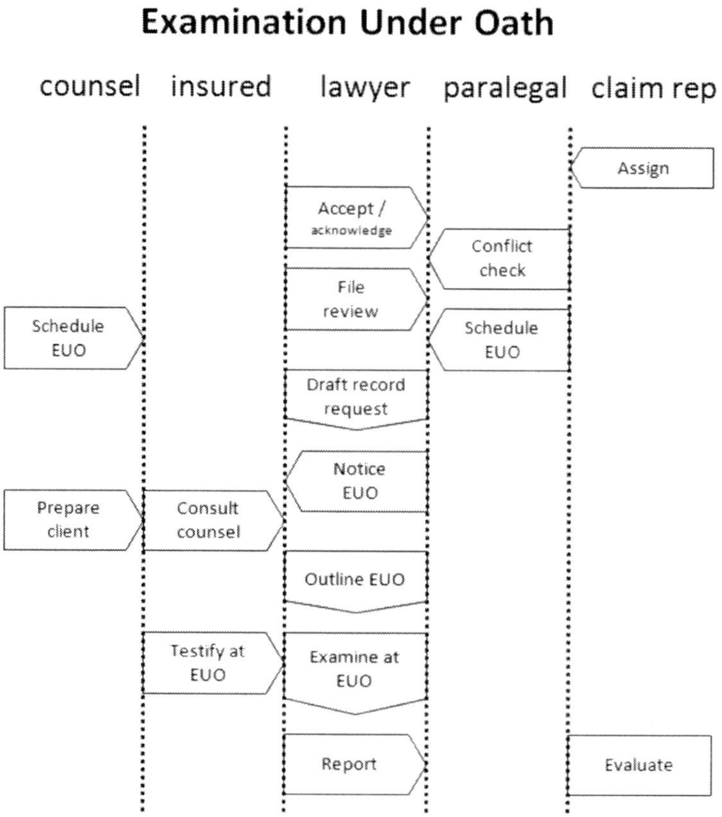

Appendix B
Activities Assessment

Date: ___/____/_______

Complete this section before the activity:

Activity: ______________________________

Contact: ______________________________

Location: ______________________________

Goal: ______________________________

____

____

Audience: ______________________________

____

____

Complete this section after the activity:

Information: ______________________________

____

____

Time spent: ____________ **Activity value:** _____/10

Continue?: YES / NO

Assess time frame: ___________________________

____

Trigger for Activity Change: ______________________

Complete this section if follow-up is appropriate:

Date: ______________________________

Result: ______________________________

____

____

Activities Assessment—Complete Sample

Date: 5/10/2012

Complete this section before the activity:

Activity: Working with local small business association for minority business owners to help them draft state paperwork.

Contact: Talk to Lynn Jones at (616) 555-1234 for the number of businesses I can stop at and the number of weeks I can commit to (they do this every other weekend).

Location: SBA remote offices on site throughout the day.

Goal: Complete formation paperwork for the businesses. Yet the businesses may have more than just their pressing legal needs. They may have an IP issue, may need to comply with new legislation, or may need a comprehensive assessment to evaluate legal risk.

Audience: The owners, but also support staff to see what they do.

Complete this section after the activity:

Information: The formation issues went as planned, but one of the businesses is using music in their store and in products without addressing the copyright issues. The owners also want to form a new small business as a retirement project to teach their children business skills. They also want to transition the company to the children and need a succession plan.

Time spent: 8 hours **Activity value:** 7/10

Continue?: YES / NO

Assess time frame: Do 8 more sessions of these business formations over the next 5 months. These individuals are not aware of unaddressed issues that can impact their businesses. Plus it is great to get out and meet more of the movers and shakers in the community.

Trigger for Activity Change: If the same businesses seek reassurance on the same issues we already addressed. The significant time investment warrants a return at least 4x. I will spend 64 hours over the next 5 months which is $6500+ of billable time. If after 5 months I do not recoup $13,000 of new business, I will not continue at this rate. If I hit my goal of $26,000 after 5 months I will continue the program while evaluating what has worked and not worked for me to become more strategic in my selection of businesses to help and questions to ask.

Complete this section if follow-up is appropriate:

Date: Business A: Meeting Next Tuesday at their office at 1 pm. Business B: They are coming into the office on Thursday at 10 am.

Result: Business A: Once I saw exactly how they were obtaining the music and how it was being redistributed it was clear the license they obtained allowed for commercialization of those pieces. I advised them on how to ensure no 3rd party rights were being infringed. I am meeting with them to develop an IP plan for their own products.

Business B: The couple had little experience with the legal system even while being very educated and business savvy. I developed a proposed business-succession plan for them and how they could pull money from the business to support their retirement. They are meeting with a financial advisor. I will follow up with them after their meeting to see exactly how they want to proceed.

Appendix C
Varying Process Models

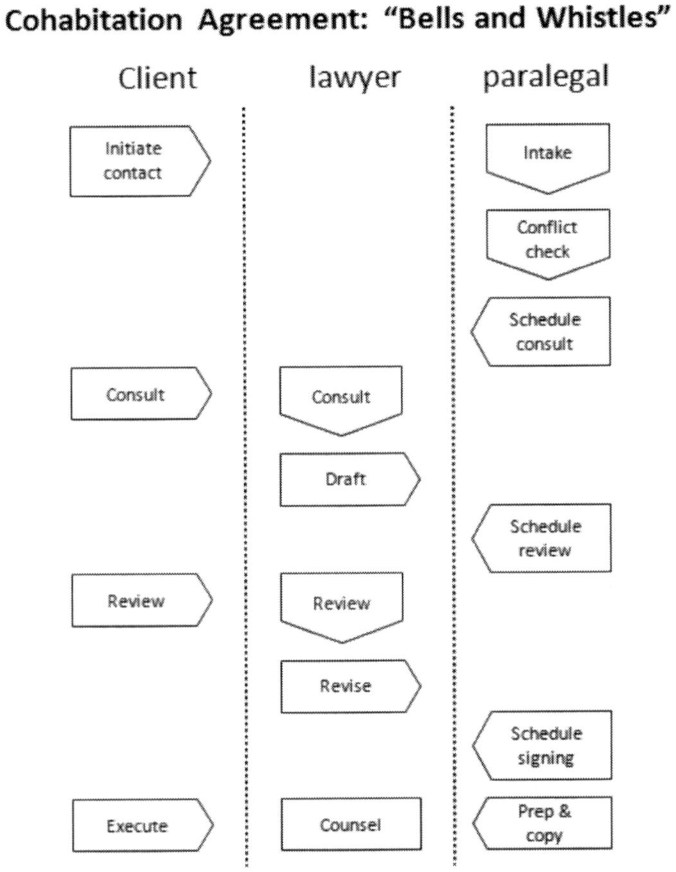

Cohabitation Agreement: Basic Process

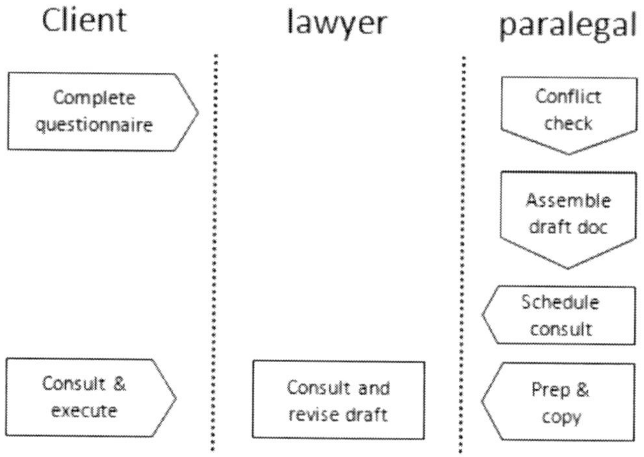

Cohabitation Agreement: Automated Process

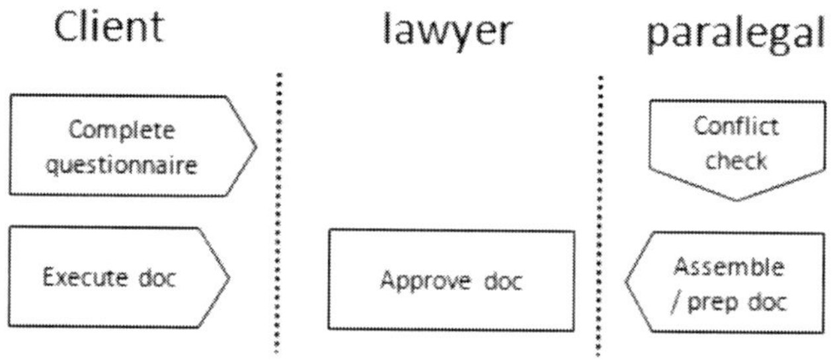

Appendix D
Client Satisfaction Survey

LAW OFFICE OF JANE M. SMITH, P.L.L.C.
123 MAIN DRIVE, GRAND RAPIDS, MICHIGAN 49505
(616) 555-9756 / FAX (616) 555-9876
E-mail: smithj@anymail.com / Website: www.SmithLaw.com

May 1, 2012

John M. Doe
23 Old Road
Grand Rapids, MI 49505

Mr. Doe:

Thank you for selecting us for your law-service needs. Enclosed as part of our ongoing commitment to serve you is a client-satisfaction survey. Please complete the survey, returning it to us in the enclosed postage-prepaid envelope. You can also access it on our website at
www.SmithLaw.com/Survey.

Please do not place any identifying information (name, case, address, telephone, etc.) anywhere on the survey. Please do not use this survey to convey urgent information concerning your case or pending problems with your lawyer. Address any such issue immediately and directly with your lawyer.

We will use your responses for in-house firm and performance reviews. If you have any questions please call us directly at (616) 555-9756.

Sincerely,

The Law Office of Jane M. Smith

Client Satisfaction Survey

How long have you worked with our firm on your **current** matter? ________________

Please check the column corresponding to your impression of the level of our service:

(Omit any item not applicable.)	**Exceeded Expected**	**Average**	**Below Expected**
Your treatment when first contacting us by telephone, email, in-person, or online.			
How easy we made it for you to work with us.			
Your overall comfort level during initial intake with our lawyer.			
How well we explained the legal concepts applying to your matter.			
How well we explained your fee agreement with us.			
How accessible your attorney was by:			
Telephone			
Email			
Online (videoconference) meeting			
In-person meeting at our office			
In-person meeting at your location			
The interest your attorney took in your matter.			
The overall quality of the service we provided.			
Our explanation of any associated expenses that you incurred.			
Your treatment by other attorneys in the firm and administrative staff.			
The location of our office.			
The outcome or current status of your matter.			

If you rated us **"Below Expectations"** as to any item, then please indicate the reason:

____

____

Could we improve in other areas not addressed above? If so, then please describe:

____

____

How likely is it that you would either return to our firm or refer others to us?

Very ___ **Somewhat** ___ **Not** ___ **Unknown** ___

Please contact your attorney to address any concern that may affect your legal rights.

Appendix E:
Process-Improvement Studies

Matter General	Client Intake			Role Counsel

	Task	Resource	Analysis	Improve	Control
1	Record contact.	Paralegal .1 hours	Ensure ability to contact.	Build market database.	
2	Obtain conflict information.	Paralegal .1 hours	Record all interested parties.	Automate into electronic conflict-check.	
3	Perform conflict check.	Lawyer .1 hours	Compare to client list.	Automate into electronic conflict-check.	Managing partner review.
4	Complete intake information.	Intake form Paralegal .5 hours	Record detailed information.	Ensure complete intake form. Develop client questionnaire.	Lawyer review to ensure complete.
5	Decide whether to consult.	Lawyer .1 hours	Make preliminary decision.	Check against market study.	
6	Communicate consultation decision.	Firm brochure Paralegal .1 hours	Contact client.	Confirm in writing to client. Give firm brochure.	Lawyer review.
	Total:	Lawyer .2 hours Paralegal .8 hours		Reduce paralegal time.	

Matter General	Initial Consultation			Role Counsel

	Task	Resource	Analysis	Improve	Control
1	Obtain completed client questionnaire.	Questionnaire Paralegal .1 hours Lawyer .1 hours	Supplies preliminary information.	Convey and receive as electronic file.	Lawyer review completed questionnaire.
2	Calculate and calendar limitations periods.	Paralegal .1 hours Lawyer .1 hours	Ensure timely handling of all matters.	Calendar with both lawyer and paralegal.	Lawyer review.
2	Schedule appointment.	Paralegal .1 hours	Confirm time and place of meeting lawyer.	Confirm in writing. Limit to 30 minutes?	Lawyer approve appointment after questionnaire review.
3	Conduct initial consultation.	Lawyer 1 hours	Determine achievable objectives.	Confirm consultation results in writing with client present.	Partner review.
4	Execute fee agreement.	Fee agreement Lawyer .2 hours	Confirm terms in writing using template.	Generate in client's presence.	Partner review
5	Assign follow-up tasks.	Lawyer .2 hours	Initiate tasks promptly.	Use process models.	Partner review.
	Total:	Lawyer 1.6 hours Paralegal .3 hours			

Matter Civil Litigation	Settlement				Role Defense Counsel
	Task	**Resource**	**Analysis**	**Improve**	**Control**
1	Secure preliminary confirmation.	Lawyer .5 hours	Memorialize terms for time to draft detailed agreement.	Query confidentiality and its enforcement, and indemnity.	Review every material term with client, confirming those terms in writing.
2	Give preliminary notice.	Paralegal .5 hours	Notify tribunal and witnesses, to ensure no further costs.	Prompt notice is critical to cost control.	Lawyer review paralegal actions to ensure all notice.
3	Order funds.	Correspondence Lawyer .5 hours	Notify insurer of amount and payees to initiate funds processing.	Confirm that all plaintiffs and plaintiff's counsel will be on check.	Compare amount to settlement agreement and payees to claimants.
4	Draft settlement agreement.	Agreement Lawyer .5 hours	Use template. Determine terms to include. Convey to counsel.	Should the cover letter explain the choice of disputable terms?	Work from a template that includes all possible clauses.
5	Draft dismissal order.	Order Lawyer .5 hours	Confirm with-prejudice dismissal and identity of dismissed parties.	Have paralegal assemble?	Every dismissal should be with prejudice unless otherwise approved.
6	Obtain client approval and signatures on settlement agreement.	Correspondence Lawyer .5 hours	Alert in cover letter to key terms and disputable provisions.	Justify debatable choices. Anticipate client issues and concerns.	Calendar client response. Contact within one week to ensure client satisfaction.
7	Obtain counsel's approval and plaintiffs' signatures.	Correspondence Lawyer .5 hours	Tender agreement and dismissal order under cover letter. Escrow signed agreement to convey funds.	Call plaintiff's counsel in advance to discuss disputable terms.	Confer with managing partner over disputable terms.
8	Convey funds on receipt of signed agreement and order.	Correspondence Lawyer .1 hours	Standard cover letter conveying funds and confirming release of escrow.	Have paralegal assemble?	No staff conveys any funds. Lawyer must convey.
9	Submit and obtain dismissal order.	Correspondence Lawyer .2 hours	Include extra copies to conform and return.	Have paralegal perform?	Lawyer must review and approve any paralegal action.
1 0	Convey signed agreement and dismissal order to client and counsel.	Lawyer .2 hours	Cover letter to client should indicate closing file.	Include client-satisfaction survey?	Review with managing partner to ensure appropriate closure.
	TOTALS:	Lawyer 4.0 hours Paralegal .5 hours			

Appendix F
Project-Management Plan

Project-Management Plan		
Matter Business Litigation	ABC Corp. v DEF Corp.	Role Plaintiff's Counsel

Stage	Time (Months)													
	1	**2**	**3**	**4**	**5**	**6**	**7**	**8**	**9**	**10**	**11**	**12**	**13**	**14**
Intake	*.2*	*Minimal risk of conflicts arising.*												
Consult	*1*	*.5*	*Minimal risk of termination of representation.*											
Investigate		*2*	*Some risk of discovering substantial defense.*											
Pleading		*2*	*Some risk of counterclaim.*											
Discovery									*Some risk of discovering substantial defense.*					
Documents			*1*	*1*	*1*	*Small risk of proprietary disclosures.*								
Interrogatories			*1*	*1*	*.5*	*.5*	*Small risk of proprietary disclosures.*							
Depositions					*2*	*2*	*2*	*2*	*Small risk of proprietary disclosures.*					
Experts							*2*	*2*	*Fair risk of additional experts.*					
Mediation		*Some risk of unwarranted disclosures.*							*5*					
Motions			*Some risk of summary judgment.*						*6*	*4*				
Pretrial				*Some risk of adverse rulings.*					*2*	*2*				
Trial					*Fair risk of adverse verdict.*						*24*	*8*		
Judgment							*Low risk of relief from judgment.*					*2*		
Post-judgment							*Fair risk of non-collection due to bankruptcy.*						*2*	*1*
Closing														*.5*
Totals	*1.2*	*4.5*	*2*	*2*	*3.5*	*2.5*	*4*	*4*	*13*	*6*	*24*	*10*	*2*	*1.5*
														80.2

Project-Management Plan

Matter		Role
Incorporating Charity	Well Families Ministry	Counsel

Stage	Time (Weeks)													
	1	2	3	4	5	6	7	8	9	10	11	12	13	14
Intake	*.2*													
Consult		*1*												
Articles			*.3*	*Small risk of state requiring change to articles causing 2-week delay.*										
EIN			*.1*											
Bylaws				*1*	*.5*	*May require meeting with directors.*								
Conflict-of-Interest Policy					*.2*									
Form 1023						*1*	*1*							
Narrative						*.5*								
Budget							*.5*							
Respond to IRS						*50% probability of response extending time by 2-4 weeks.*					*.5*			
Approval							*Some risk of 4-12 week delay; small risk of 12-30 week delay.*					*.3*		
Solicitation License												*.5*		
Compliance discussion													*1*	
Closing														*.2*
Totals	*.2*	*1*	*.4*	*1*	*.7*	*1*	*1*				*.5*	*.8*	*1*	*.2*
														8.8

CPSIA information can be obtained at www.ICGtesting.com
Printed in the USA
BVOW060424090812

297457BV00005B/1/P

9 781600 421730